HITLER'S GOLD

ARTHUR L. SMITH, JR.

Hitler's Gold

The Story of the Nazi War Loot

BERG

Oxford / New York / Munich

Distributed exclusively in the US and Canada
by St Martin's Press, New York

First published in 1989 by
Berg Publishers Limited
Editorial Offices:
77 Morrell Avenue, Oxford OX4 1NQ, UK
165 Taber Avenue, Providence RI 02906, USA
Westermühlstraße 26, 8000 München 5, FRG

British Library Cataloguing in Publication Data

Smith Jr., Arthur L.
    Hitler's gold: the story of the Nazi loot.
    1. West Germany. Bavaria. Gold reserves. Robbery,
    history
    I. Title
    364.1′552′09433
    ISBN 0–85496–601–3

Library of Congress Cataloging-in-Publication Data

Smith, Arthur Lee, 1927–
    Hitler's gold : the story of the Nazi war loot / Arthur L. Smith, Jr.
        p.   cm.
    Includes bibliographical references.
    ISBN 0–85496–601–3; $34.00 (U.S.: est.)
    1.   World War,   1939–1945—Destruction and pillage—Europe.
2.   World War,   1939–1945—Confiscations and contributions—Europe.
3.   Gold.   4.   World War,   1939–1946—Economic aspects—Germany.
5.   World War,   1939–1945—Reparations.   6.   United States—Foreign
relations—Soviet Union.   7.   Soviet Union—Foreign relations—United
States.   I.   Title.
D810.D6S55   1989
332.4′222′09409044—dc20   89–35878
                                                                                          CIP

Printed in Great Britain

To Nettie Evelyn Smith

Contents

Abbreviations

BA	Bundesarchiv, Koblenz
BIS	Bank for International Settlements, Basel
CIC	Counter Intelligence Corps
D.G.F.P.	Germany, *Documents on German Foreign Policy, 1918–1945*
FED	Foreign Exchange Depository, Frankfurt
F.R.U.S.	United States, *Foreign Relations of the United States*
IARA	Inter-Allied Reparation Agency
IfZg	Institut für Zeitgeschichte, Munich
I.M.T.	*Trial of the Major War Criminals before the International Military Tribunal*
NA, RG	National Archives, Washington, D.C., Record Group
N.C.A.	*Nazi Conspiracy and Aggression*
OMGUS	Office of Military Government United States
PRO	Public Record Office, London
SHAEF	Supreme Headquarters, Allied Expeditionary Forces
USFET	U.S. Forces European Theater

Preface

This book is about gold and war; how the monetary gold looted from Europe's central banks by the Nazi regime was used to bolster Hitler's war efforts, and later, how it became a pawn in the burgeoning Cold War struggle between the United States and the Soviet Union.

The story is an important economic dimension of the Second World War and its aftermath that, to date, has not been pieced together or related as part of a historical continuity. That is to say, the "gold war" did not end in 1945, for the looted gold that was recovered from a defeated Germany continued to be a controversial factor in international politics for years afterwards. Thus, the gold story really has two halves that fit together: the gold that the Nazis looted and used during their wartime occupation of Europe and the long and complicated restitution of some of this same gold by the Western Allies after the war had ended. In tracing the events of this gold war, care has been taken to deal as closely as possible with what the Allies defined as looted monetary gold, that is, all gold which, at the time of its looting or wrongful removal, was carried as a part of the claimant country's monetary reserve either in the account of the claimant government itself or in the accounts of the claimant country's central bank or other monetary authority at home or abroad.

The twentieth century has the distinction of having introduced the world to total war, and a vital ingredient in that process is the ability to pay for it. Given certain circumstances gold could have unusual importance for a participant in such a war provided that the nation in question had access to vast quantities of monetary gold and a means to turn it into the proper credits. From 1938 until 1945 Nazi Germany met these requirements admirably as Hitler looted the central banks of occupied Europe while several neutral states, but primarily Switzerland, supplied the necessary banking services.

In the beginning, in 1938 or 1939, Hitler experienced little problem in finding nations and banking systems willing to provide Nazi Germany with all the credit it needed. As the war continued and the possibility of a German defeat began to surface, however, things changed. They did not change fast enough to suit the Western Allies, especially the United States, but then certain of the neutrals such as Sweden and Switzerland had to live with the real threat of a Nazi invasion.

Using a pre-1939 monetary value, the Nazis seized approximately $625,000,000 in gold from the central banks of occupied nations.[1] Since Allied forces, primarily American, recovered about $330,000,000 in monetary gold that had been hidden by the German Reichsbank, it must be assumed that the other $295,000,000 had passed into the bank vaults of neutral Europe. Evidence clearly points to Switzerland as the recipient of the largest amount of looted monetary gold.

Knowledge of the amounts of gold held by Europe's central banks was not a secret before the war, although Nazi Germany had surreptitiously been building a reserve. Excepting Germany, it was a matter of record in banking circles just how much gold was held by various nations and when it was transferred from account to account. Therefore, it became only an arithmetical calculation to arrive at a fairly accurate estimate of just how much monetary gold fell to the Nazis as each occupation occurred. Of course, the trail was lost once the gold had disappeared into the Reichs-bank coffers.

According to the Allied definition of looted monetary gold the Nazi seizure of treasures from occupied central banks began with the *Anschluß* of Austria in 1938 and continued in that same year with the annexation of the Sudetenland. Swiss banking connections were already proving useful as the Bank for International Settlements (BIS) in Basel arranged for certain gold-account transfers.

When the war started in 1939 with the German attack upon Poland, the threatened central bank in Warsaw sought safety for its gold by shipping it to France. Unfortunately, this faith in the invulnerability of the Maginot Line was shared by other central banks as well, and gold flowed into the Bank of France one step ahead of the Nazi invaders. With the French collapse, the Reichsbank gained access to millions in gold, although taking actual possession was not quite as easy as anticipated for the French had moved large quantities to Africa and the logistics of recovery proved rather difficult for a time.

As Allied strength grew, their efforts to place increased pressure upon the neutrals to cut commercial ties with Nazi Germany met rather mixed

---

1. Not such an astronomical figure by today's standards, but an enormous sum of extremely fluid capital for that time.

results. The United States, less concerned about postwar trade recovery than Great Britain, took the initiative in the search for more punitive measures against certain neutrals who, from both fear and profit, continued to conduct financial transactions with the Nazis. The search was to prove rather useless, however, especially with Switzerland.

By the time the war ended in 1945, the fervor for instituting some restrictions of an international nature against Switzerland or any of the other neutrals (Sweden, Spain, Portugal, and Turkey) who had accepted looted monetary gold for trade was canceled out by the stronger sentiment to simply get on with reconstruction. For this purpose every resource was needed, and some Western statesmen felt that they could not afford to alienate the neutrals. An economically devastated Europe and a potentially menacing Soviet Union pushed many a wartime grievance into the background.

As the rift with the Soviet Union widened, Western leaders saw the recovered monetary gold as a weapon that could be used in the Cold War. They were agreed that restitution should be made as quickly as possible to those non-Communist nations in the West, but for those Communist nations in central and eastern Europe it would be a different story. The United States, Great Britain, and France established the Tripartite Commission for the Restitution of Monetary Gold, which soon completed its work of returning the looted gold to Western nations. Claims from central and eastern European nations have required years to resolve, and literally decades in certain cases, as negotiations continue to the present day.

Certainly historical interest in the subject of gold and the Second World War has not been absent, but many of the books about it focus upon the sensational, usually a tale of large quantities of gold either stolen from the Reichsbank during the final hectic days of the Third Reich or stolen after the war had ended, when Germany was still in a state of chaos. The documentation is fragile at best and rife with unsubstantiated rumor and hearsay. The aim of such works is to present an account of mystery and intrigue while preserving the impression of a documentated exposé.

Perhaps the earliest of such books, and maybe the best, is *Gold Is Where You Hide It: What Happened to the Reichsbank Treasures?* by Stanley Moss.[2] Henriette von Schirach, wife of the Hitlerjugend leader Baldur von Schirach, added the touch of the eyewitness with her account, *The Price of Glory*.[3] The latest, but probably not the last, is a book by two British

2. London: Andre Deutsch, 1956.
3. London: Frederick Muller, 1960. A later version with the title *Der Preis der Herrlichkeit* (Munich: F.A. Herbig Verlagsbuchhandlung, 1975) was reprinted as late as 1987. A chapter, "Der Schatz der Nibelungen," is devoted to a description of the intrigue surrounding the gold stolen from the Reichsbank.

journalists, Ian Sayer and Douglas Botting. Their work, *Nazi Gold*,[4] is the most ambitious, although much of the basic information was covered by Moss in his 1956 publication.

There are, of course, serious and scholarly works that treat gold as one of the important economic factors in the Second World War such as Alan S. Milward, *War, Economy, and Society*, 1939–1945;[5] Willi Boelcke, *Die deutsche Wirtschaft*, 1930–1945;[6] and David L. Gordon and Royden Dangerfield, *The Hidden Weapon*.[7] None of these works, however, examines the relationship between looted monetary gold, the Reichsbank, and Switzerland as a significant factor in Germany's wartime economy. A recent book by Werner Rings, *Raubgold aus Deutschland: Die "Golddreh-scheibe" Schweiz im Zweiten Weltkrieg*,[8] draws upon the new documentation from Swiss banking records and provides an excellent look at the Swiss-German banking relationship during the Second World War. To date there is no published work known to this author that contains a history of the Allied Tripartite Commission for the Restitution of Monetary Gold.

Before the gold war described here could be researched, it was essential to have access to the relevant Reichsbank records and the deliberations of the Tripartite Commission. It is only after these two sources are coordinated that a complete picture of the gold war emerges. The search for the Reichsbank files on the gold transferred from banks in occupied territories was a lengthy one. Both the Bundesarchiv in Koblenz and the Zentrales Staatsarchiv in Potsdam disclaim possession.[9] Complete copies of Reichsbank accounting books and financial files were finally located, however, in the voluminous records of the Office of Military Government United States (OMGUS). They had been taken intact with the gold from the Reichsbank in 1945. Later these records were turned over to the newly created Bank Deutscher Länder.

Admittedly, the search for the Reichsbank records had been time-consuming, but once located, access proved no problem. The situation was somewhat different for the records of the Tripartite Commission. The fact that it is still in existence, with active representation from the United States, Great Britain, and France, meant that inquiries about its past activities were met with polite but firm refusals to supply any documen-

4. New York: Congdon and Weed, 1984.
5. Berkeley and Los Angeles: University of California Press, 1977.
6. Düsseldorf: Droste Verlag, 1983.
7. New York: Da Capo Press, 1976.
8. Zurich: Artemis Verlag, 1985.
9. The West German Bundesarchiv suggested contacting the Zentrales Staatsarchiv in the DDR, but the Potsdam depository insisted that they did not have any materials relating to the gold policies of the "Fascist German state." Letters to the author from the Bundesarchiv, 3.10.83, and the Zentrales Staatsarchiv, 4.4.84.

tation. Beginning in the spring of 1982, this author spoke with the U.S. representative to the Tripartite Commission in Brussels, requesting information about the commission, but the representative, Mary McDonell, said that she knew very little about its history. She suggested contacting the U.S. State Department, but that was an equally frustrating experience. After a two-year period of letters and telephone calls failed to elicit any meaningful material on the Tripartite Commission, the author turned to his congressman for aid and submitted a Freedom of Information request. In rejecting these efforts, the State Department wrote, "After preliminary discussions with retrieval specialists . . . it appears that . . . almost all the documents retrieved would be found, upon review, to be classified and therefore withholdable from release and copying pursuant to FOIA [Freedom of Information Act] exemption (b) (1)."[10]

This did not end the quest, however, and continued searching eventually located some extensive Tripartite Commission records that detailed the work of the commission up to 1949 and had been deposited in the U.S. National Archives. This was a most fortunate discovery, since the chronological scope of this study is the decade between 1938 and 1948, and it permitted the original plan for the work to be carried out.[11]

10. Letter to author from U.S. State Dept., 29.5.84.

11. One cannot help but speculate on what the entire gold story might have been had the advancing Soviet forces instead of the American Third Army units recovered the gold hidden by the Reichsbank. It would not only have completely changed the Allied plan for gold restitution but would also have prevented any research into Reichsbank activities, except for whatever information the Soviets chose to share from the records that were with the gold.

Acknowledgments

I am indebted to a number of people who aided me in a variety of ways to complete this work. The assistance invariably came willingly and with a kindness for which I will always be grateful. I was provided with leads to important materials, given answers to questions, gently reminded of mistakes, and permitted to be a bore when too full of the subject.

All of the following people were involved in rendering me help in one or more of the above categories, and it is with profound pleasure that I acknowledge it: Charles Burdick, Richard Burns, Richard Gould, Josef Henke, Udo Heyn, Maria Keipert, Hans-Dieter Kreikamp, Carlos Moorhead, Kathy Numoto, Jean O'Hagan, Klaus Oldenhage, Earl Phillips, William Walsh, Leon Wazsak, Herman Weiss, and Claus Wolf. Thanks also to my editor, Deborah Del Gais Muller. A special debt is owed to my wife Jutta for possessing an enduring patience whenever I am involved in research and writing.

CHAPTER 1

Introduction

Adolf Hitler's primary interest in Europe's gold reserves was based upon the need to finance war. Between 1938 and 1945 the Germans spent not only their own gold but most of what had belonged to occupied Europe.[1] Throughout this seven-year period the Germans were able to turn their vast gold supplies into war supplies only with the help of the neutral nations of Spain, Portugal, Turkey, Sweden, and Switzerland.

The broad outline of the gold war was not determined entirely by the early German military conquests, for with the later growth of Allied strength policies were formulated that added to its complexity. The Allied principle of eventual restitution provided a challenge to the neutrals and was to make the tracing of gold movements far more difficult. It was an Allied decision to set the beginning date for Nazi gold looting with the *Anschluß* of Austria and to define stolen gold as all gold that had been legally in the possession of central banks taken over by German occupation forces and either looted or wrongfully removed.[2]

While the ultimate profitability to the Nazi war effort derived from occupied nations may well have some debatable aspects,[3] the value of seized monetary gold always represented a powerful asset. It was easily transferable to Reichsbank possession, and most importantly, given the proper connection, it was easily disposed of to friend and foe alike. Although some of the trading neutrals eagerly accepted any German subterfuge, no matter how flimsy, to conceal the gold's origin, they probably would have taken it without explanation. Gold nations do not have a history of refusing a gold influx, and everyone would agree that the precious yellow metal does not have a smell to it.[4]

1. NA, RG 84, OMGUS POLAD, D.R. Heath to R. Murphy, 29 July 1945.
2. *New York Times*, 14 March 1947, p. 6.
3. For a discussion of the economics of occupation see Milward, *War, Economy, and Society*.
4. Willi A. Boelcke, "Zur internationalen Goldpolitik des NS-Staats—Ein Beitrag zur deutschen Währungs- und Außenwirtschaftspolitik, 1933–1945," in *Hitler, Deutschland, und die Mächte*, ed. Manfred Funke (Düsseldorf: Droste Verlag, 1977), p. 309.

1

Although Austria would be included in the roster of nations that had lost gold to the Germans, this view only came with the advent of war. There was no prevailing sentiment in 1938 that Austrian properties were being "looted" by the Germans. In fact, there was considerable legal opinion that regarded the merging of the two nations as a palatable event, as illustrated by the decision handed down in a United States court case involving Austrian assets in America in 1940: "This change [the annexation] has occurred in a manner acceptable to our notions of international law; the *Anschluß* has in no way been disavowed by the [United States] Department of State."[5] After the *Anschluß* the Nazis moved quickly to formalize the act of incorporation and on 17 March 1938 the Austrian National Bank was liquidated and all assets transferred to the German Reichsbank against a Reichsmark equivalent. To comply with the new German exchange regulations all gold in private hands was confiscated, and by late April most individuals had complied.[6]

The total gold stock removed from the Austrian National Bank was placed in a Reich account with the Precious Metals Department of the Reichsbank. The department head, Albert Thoms, had the gold placed together with the regular Reichsbank reserves.[7] The amount of gold acquired by the Germans from the Austrian National Bank was 91,256.9156 kilograms broken down as follows: 78,267.1464 kilograms of gold bars and coins (22,341.1695 kilograms of this were in the Bank of England); an additional 12,989.7692 kilograms of gold were delivered between 17 March and 30 June as ordered by German exchange regulations. The dollar value at the time was $102,689,215.94.[8] Most of the gold bars were sent to Berlin in several shipments during 1938, some of them to be resmelted along with quantities of gold coinage. The Austrian gold on deposit with the Bank of England was transferred via the BIS in Basel to the German Reichsbank.[9]

The German annexation of Austria and the subsequent plebiscite

5. Martin Domke, *The Control of Alien Property* (New York: Central Books, 1947), p. 56. In October 1943 the United States, Great Britain, and Russia agreed in Moscow to a declaration on Austria, stating that they did not regard any changes made in the country since 15 March 1938 as binding. It should be noted that several nations, including Switzerland, in 1938–39 rejected German efforts to gain access to Austrian assets abroad. See Paul Einzig, *World Finance, 1939–40* (London: Kegan Paul, Trench, Trubner and Co., 1940), p. 61.

6. NA, RG 260, OMGUS FINAD, A. Thoms report, "Gold of Austrian National Bank," pp. 1–3. Prior to 25 April the Reichsbank paid RM 3,966.27 per 1,000 grains fine for gold coins. After that date the rate was reduced to RM 2,784 per 1,000 grains fine gold. Ibid., p. 3. Some of the gold collected by authorities in Austria after the *Anschluß* became the focus of Allied debate in 1946–47 as the Salzburg gold issue. See Chapter 6.

7. Ibid., p. 1.

8. Ibid., Brey, FED, to Dir. Finance Div. OMGUS 20 April 1947.

9. Ibid., Thoms report, "Gold of Austrian National Bank," pp. 4–7.

presented a thin façade of legality sufficient to allow the world of banking to continue to do business as usual. Thus, the absorption against payment of Austrian gold reserves by the Reichsbank raised no international outcry from financial institutions nor did it bring forth any hints of submerged outrage in the banking community. It is at this very juncture, however, in March of 1938, that the trail of looted monetary gold begins. It was absolutely vital to the economic success of the Hitler regime that the German dictator secure the cooperation of the banks in neutral lands in disposing of the gold. It was not until well after the entrance of the United States into the war in 1941 that the Allies attempted to persuade—even by force, if necessary—neutrals to stop accepting the looted gold from Germany. They were never completely successful.

Much of the credit for the success of the Nazi gold policy was due to the able apparatus of the Reichsbank and certain of its key personnel. The Reichsbank was originally Germany's central bank for over fifty years before the Nazis rose to power. During the first six years of the Hitler government the bank president was Hjalmar Schacht, widely hailed as the financial wizard who had brought the disastrous inflation crisis of 1923 under control. It was during Schacht's tenure that the Reichsbank embarked upon a hidden-gold-reserve program reminiscent of the German gold buildup before the First World War.[10]

Schacht was replaced by a faithful Nazi party functionary named Walther Funk, who had little banking experience but very strong political connections. He had the backing of a number of powerful party leaders like Hermann Göring, who wanted a bank president totally supportive of the Four-Year Plan. The functioning of the bank on a daily basis was in the hands of members of a directorate and a vice-president, all men with long years of banking experience and impressive reputations in the international banking world.[11]

In terms of gold policy, perhaps the most influential individual in the Reichsbank was the vice-president, Emil Puhl, who came to the position at the same time that Funk became president in January 1939. Puhl had been a bank director under Schacht and gained wide recognition as a knowledgeable financier as a result. At one time he had even been offered a leading position with New York's Chase National Bank. The importance of his role in directing the flow of looted gold into Germany's war economy cannot be overestimated. His connections to the banks of neutral nations during the war, especially those in Switzerland, were of inestima-

---

10. Ibid., OMGUS AG, 1945–46, Clay to Hilldring, 10 December 1945, enclosure, "Report on Hidden Gold Reserve Program."

11. In a careful study of the Hitler economy Willi Boelcke has noted, among Funk's other inadequacies, his fondness for alcohol and high living, *Die deutsche Wirtschaft*, pp. 187–89.

ble value. Although Funk had the title, Puhl was regarded as the man who really ran the Reichsbank.[12]

While Puhl made gold policy, he did have a number of talented career people who assisted him in its execution. One of these was a longtime employee named Albert Thoms, who had served the Reichsbank since 1910. He had been in the Precious Metals Department for over fifteen years and was in charge of it at the time of Schacht's departure. It was under Thoms's direction that all gold was received, acknowledged, weighed, stored, transferred or resmelted, and recorded. He described his position thus: "I was not replaceable in the bank."[13] The gold books maintained by Thoms and his staff contained precise information on the quality of gold received (three different grades), an exact record of all storage, and a disposition history on all gold deposits, including those that belonged in other accounts.[14] During the war gold bars were sent out to some twenty Reichsbank branches, both for storage and sometimes for payment (*Sonderlagerung*). Presumably all final gold disposition was decided by officials of the Four-Year Plan.[15]

Funk later confirmed that he had little or no bank gold dealings: "I never bothered about individual transactions, not even gold transaction, or even the slight variations in the individual gold reserves, *et cetera*. If large deliveries of gold were expected the Directorate reported to me."[16] The Reichsbank president estimated the German gold reserve at some 500 million Reichsmarks when he assumed office. This was about seven times the figure that monetary statisticians thought it to be in 1939,[17] obviously the result of Schacht's hidden-gold-reserve program.

With the gold increase the Reichsbank needed the services of the international banking community from time to time, and none proved more helpful than the Bank for International Settlements in Basel, Switzerland. The BIS was to play a pivotal role in the German acquisition of Czechoslovakia's monetary gold reserve. By this time Hitler had already taken control of part of Czechoslovakia as a result of the Munich Agreements in September of 1938, occupying those areas that were determined by Austrian census figures of 1910 to be predominantly German-speaking.

12. *I.M.T.*, vol. 13, pp. 161 and 559–60.

13. NA, RG 260, OMGUS FINAD, "Statement of Albert Thoms, Merkers, Germany, 12 April 1945," p. 1.

14. Some of these accounts were subsidiaries of the Reichsbank and had been established as "hidden" gold accounts when Schacht was president, while others belonged to various ministries and were stored for safekeeping only. The stored accounts belonged to Asservat Devisen Reserve (Der), Golddiskontobank (DEGO), Treuhandgesellschaft, Rearmaments Ministry, the Military, etc.

15. NA, RG 260, OMGUS FINAD, Thoms Interrogation, 18 April 1945.

16. *I.M.T.*, vol. 13, p. 168.

17. Ibid., and OMGUS AG, 1945–46.

All of the assets of Czechoslovakia in this ceded Sudetan territory were absorbed by Germany, and this included some fifty-seven banks, branches mostly of the Bohemian Discount Bank and the Bohemian Union Bank.[18] Within six months Bohemia and Moravia became a German protectorate, and the Nazis had access to the gold reserves of the Czechoslovakian National Bank in Prague. In anticipation of this threat to their reserves, bank officials had already arranged the transfer of a large portion to the Bank of England through their account with the BIS. However, Reichsbank representatives who had accompanied the Wehrmacht into Prague immediately instructed Czech bank officials to order the transfer of all assets to them. With the compliance of intimidated Czech personnel and a plan for reorganizing the bank, the Reichsbank now gained access to some $44 million worth of Czech gold.[19] Emil Puhl said that the Reichsbank had no problem in getting either the Czechs to comply or the BIS to agree to carry out the order to transfer the gold to German control.[20] However, about $26 million worth was deposited in the BIS account with the Bank of England, and this required a release from them as well. The ready acquiescence of the Bank of England brought down public wrath when the news leaked out, and some of it was directed at the BIS, too.

Johan W. Beyen, a distinguished Dutch banker and BIS director in 1939, recalled that on March 20th he had received a telegram from the Czechoslovakian National Bank with instructions to transfer their gold holdings into a Reichsbank account. Since the gold was held in the BIS account in London, the order entailed transferring it to the German account with the Bank of England. Since the Bank of England presumably did not know the identity of subaccounts, they had no reason not to do as instructed. Beyen also pointed out that all BIS assets were immune from seizure. His conclusion: "The execution of the order of the Czecho-Slovak National Bank was a matter, therefore, of the BIS, and in no way of the Bank of England."[21] After receipt of the transfer order Beyen's general manager, Roger Auboin, discussed it with the governor of the Bank of France, and a colleague in the Bank of England, "who did not want to interfere in the matter; the Governor of the Bank of France did not want to act alone. . . . I therefore executed the order."[22] Although not an impar-

---

18. Ibid., vol. 8, pp. 4–5.
19. NA, RG 260, OMGUS AG, 1945–46, OMGUS AG to CAD, 3 January 1946. There were smaller amounts of Czech gold deposited in various accounts in London, Washington, D.C., and Basel which the Germans did not get. See Vojtech Mastny, *The Czechs under Nazi Rule: The Failure of National Resistance, 1939–1942* (New York: Columbia University Press, 1971), p. 67, n. 10; and Rings, *Raubgold aus Deutschland*, p. 37.
20. NA, RG 332, ETO, SGS, 123/2, McNarney to Nixon, 30 November 1945, p. 2.
21. Johan W. Beyen, *Money in a Maelstrom* (New York: Macmillan Co., 1949), p. 137.
22. Ibid., p. 138. Paul Einzig does not dispute Beyen's account factually, but insisted that

tial observer of these events, Beyen leaves the impression that he would have followed a different course if the central banks had so desired.

Somewhat uncharacteristically, the British government did act rather quickly in requesting the Bank of England to hold the BIS request, for it was common knowledge that this was Czech gold even if the bank professed not to know who the subaccount belonged to. In addition, in making the request it was assumed that shortly the responsibility would not be the bank's anyway because a law was pending in Parliament that would permit the freezing of all Czech assets in England. As Sir John Simon, the chancellor of the Exchequer, assured House members, this "is a matter on which we ought all to be perfectly clear."[23] Suddenly, what had been a routine banking affair for the BIS became, as Beyen described it, "a first class political sensation," with the banks under fire for letting the Czech gold fall so easily into the Germans' hands. In Beyen's view the BIS and the Bank of England were unfairly made the villains of the piece; in his opinion the blame rested with the governments of England and France.[24] Such logic failed to halt the attacks, however.

The fact that the entire business had been transacted in secret did not do much for the banks' images, for it was some two months after the German occupation of Czechoslovakia began before the news became public. Considering the gloomy political outlook surrounding the events of that spring and summer, the rising tide of public anger against the appeasing policies of France and England is understandable. When the news story describing the London arrival of a Reichsbank delegation to formalize the gold transfer broke on May 18th, Prime Minister Neville Chamberlain labeled the whole affair a "Mare's nest." Confusing the issue further, the prime minister insisted that his government's treasury had not agreed to any release of gold.[25] This was, no doubt, true, for the British Treasury controlled neither the Bank of England nor the BIS.

As the furor grew it became clear that there really was not one party that carried all of the responsibility for what had occurred; it had been a joint effort and there were shares of blame. The British public had to be told that the government could not really prevent the transfer although some critics felt that more pressure could be put upon the Bank of

---

there were protests from Aubion and Fournier, governor of the Bank of France. *World Finance*, pp. 60–61.

23. Great Britain, *Parliamentary Debates*, House of Commons, vol. 345, pt. B, March 1939, p. 1482.

24. Beyen, *Money in a Maelstrom*, pp. 138–39.

25. *New York Times*, 20 May 1939, p. 5. The *Oxford University Dictionary* definition of a mare's nest is "to imagine that one had discovered something wonderful" (Oxford: Clarendon Press 3d ed., 1955, p. 1205). Just how Mr. Chamberlain intended this expression to apply to the situation must be judged within the context of the debate.

England. Mr. Montagu Norman, governor of the bank, was also one of the two British members of the BIS directorate. He had no responsibility to notify the treasury of transactions with BIS, and the opinion was that he had not informed them of the request to transfer the gold in the BIS subaccount to the Reichsbank (assuming, of course, that Norman knew to whom the subaccount belonged).[26] Stung by the mounting wave of criticism of the treasury's nonaction, Simon promised to try to stop the gold from leaving the country since it was still in the bank's vaults. The plan was to ask the courts to rule on the legality of the transfer since many critics said the gold was "stolen" and therefore the Bank of England was not legally bound to obey the BIS order under such circumstances.[27] However, this was a short-lived hope and Simon had to admit that in the final analysis the government was helpless to prevent the gold transfer. Speaking before the House of Lords, the chancellor told of his desperate search for some legal precedent that would enable him to stop the gold transfer, but his legal experts had informed him that "His Majesty's Government are precluded by the terms of the Protocols of 1930 and 1936 from taking any steps, by way of legislation or otherwise, to prevent the Bank of England from obeying the instructions given to it by its customer the Bank for International Settlements to transfer gold as it may be instructed."[28]

In a sharp departure from its traditional reticence on its banking affairs, the BIS had announced at the end of May that there had been no alternative but to obey the Czech bank order to transfer the gold to the Germans. The BIS spokesman explained that an official order was given from the new administration of the Czech bank with signatures that proved authentic, and no course remained open but to process it.[29] Of course, the Germans, desirous of preserving the appearance of legality, had not liquidated the Czechoslovakian National Bank or merged it into the Reichsbank as they had in Austria. Instead, it was reorganized into the National Bank of Bohemia and Moravia, retaining collaborative personnel and giving the outward impression that it was autonomous as an institution in the new protectorate.[30]

---

26. Paul Einzig, a bank critic and well-known writer and journalist who specialized in economic affairs, reported that he was told by British officials in 1944 that Norman had "in fact consulted the Treasury" on BIS orders. *In the Centre of Things* (London: Hutchinson, 1960), p. 192.

27. *New York Times*, 31 May 1939, p. 1.

28. *Parliamentary Debates*, House of Commons, vol. 348, pt. B, 5 June 1939, pp. 35–36.

29. *New York Times*, 31 May 1939, p. 9.

30. NA, RG 332, ETO, SGS 123/2, "Report on the Gold of the National Bank of Bohemia and Moravia," 1 November 1945, p. 2. The foreign general manager of the Czechoslovakian National Bank, M.J. Malik, escaped from his homeland, later visiting the BIS in its Basel

Despite the numerous government explanations in Great Britain, the public mood remained bitter and the episode refused to disappear. As Lord Strabolgi discussed the matter with his peers in mid-July, he described it having "created a great surprise and indeed resentment in the minds of the British public." He scoffed at the notion that Britain was legally bound by the Hague agreement to obey the BIS requests, insisting that the Czech invasion was "a gross illegality."[31] On 5 May 1939, a sum equivalent to that held in the Bank of England as the BIS subaccount (for Czechoslovakia) was established in the Reichsbank in Berlin in the name of the National Bank of Bohemia and Moravia.[32]

Both Puhl and Thoms later stated that while the BIS made the gold transfer to the Reichsbank account in London, the Germans did not actually transport any gold from England at the time; the transaction was completed through the BIS in Basel.[33] In June 1939 the National Bank of Bohemia and Moravia was notified by the Reichsbank that "in Berlin we have taken care of the gold put at our disposal from your account by the Bank for International Settlements," and within months some $13,500,000 worth of Czech gold had been "purchased" by the Reichsbank.[34] Together with Austrian gold reserves, the Czech gold totaled over $146 million, a sum now at Germany's disposal to help replenish their own gold supply.

Chronologically, Poland was Hitler's next victim and by rights should have yielded up some more gold, but the German occupiers found the Bank of Poland almost empty. As the German military forces threatened Warsaw, the chief personnel of the Bank of Poland (Bank Polski) had abandoned the city taking with them some $64 million worth of the Polish gold reserve. Traveling by train and truck south and east through Rumania, Turkey, and Lebanon, the Polish bank staff finally arrived in France in late October 1939, where they were granted office space and storage vaults in the Bank of France in Paris and here continued to conduct business, such as it was.[35]

---

headquarters to protest the surrender of Czech gold. He insisted that if the national bank ever regained its independence it would never again do business with the BIS. Einzig, *World Finance*, p. 67.

31. *Parliamentary Debates*, House of Lords, vol. 114, no. 84, 11 July 1939, pp. 50–54.

32. NA, RG 332, ETO, SGS, 123/2, "Report of Gold of National Bank of Bohemia and Moravia," 1 November 1945, p. 3.

33. Ibid., RG 260, OMGUS FINAD, Nixon to Bernstein, 11 August 1945.

34. Ibid., RG 332, ETO, SGS, 123/2, "Report of Gold National Bank Bohemia and Moravia," 1 November 1945, p. 4. Three separate accounts for the Czech gold were established in the Reichsbank; one of them remained intact until war's end and contained over two thousand bags of gold coins.

35. Count Edward Raczynski, foreign minister for the Polish exile government until 1943, estimated the Polish gold reserve at eighty tons, *In Allied London* (London: Weidenfeld and

After the German invasion of the Low Countries and France began in May of 1940, however, the Polish government in exile informed the French government that it intended to transport their gold reserve to Canada and the United States. The Polish note, dated May 22d, resulted in a verbal agreement between the Bank of Poland and the Bank of France whereby the French Admiralty was to be entrusted to convey the gold on a French warship to the United States.[36] One of the Polish Bank directors, Stefan Michalski, accompanied the gold when it was put aboard the French cruiser *Victor Schoelcher* in the harbor of Lorient. The ship's destination was Martinique, but with the French collapse imminent the orders were changed at the last minute to the French West African port of Dakar. Michalski was now instructed by the Polish government in London to utilize the services of a Polish ship at anchor in Dakar to transport the gold to America.[37] When this plan proved impractical General Wladyslaw Sikorski, head of the Polish London government, appealed to the British government for aid in rescuing the gold. It was an intriguing proposal and of a nature that attracted Prime Minister Churchill's interest, but in passing it on to the Foreign Office for further consideration he had to ask: "But how are we to get hold of the Polish . . . gold for them? What is proposed?"[38]

Given the state of British relations with France following the abortive 4th of July attempt by the British Navy to seize the French fleet, it was obvious that any approach to Vichy was impossible. On the other hand, the British were not anxious to see Michalski somehow succeed in finding another ship for the gold, probably a French ship that would take it to Martinique. If this was attempted the British Admiralty was prepared to try to intercept the vessel and direct it to Canada.[39] Although the British Naval staff was doubtful that a successful bombardment of Dakar could be carried out at the moment, Winston Churchill decided to authorize the attack. Codenamed "Menace," the operation consisted of combined Anglo-French (free) forces that arrived off the coast of Dakar on September 23d. General Charles de Gaulle, who was on the mission, attempted to persuade the Vichy authorities there to come over to the Allied side, but they refused. With little or no alternative but an attempted landing, the French and British forces encountered such fierce resistance from Vichy

---

Nicolson, 1962), p. 77, n. 1; however, the sixty-four-ton figure appeared in both the German and American war documents; BA, Bestand R2, Aktienband 25175, Schöne letter, Paris, 29 October 1941, p. 3; and *F.R.U.S.*, vol. 3, 1943, p. 444.

36. PRO, Premier, 4/19/1, p. 283, F.O. to Consul, Dakar, 6 July 1940.
37. Ibid., F.O. to Consul, Dakar, 7 July 1940.
38. Ibid., Troutbeck to Martin, 7 July 1940.
39. Ibid.

naval units out of Toulon that the operation was finally canceled, and on the 25th the Allies withdrew.[40]

In the meantime, the Germans found that while the Polish gold still appeared elusive—in fact, they were not even sure yet where it was—they had secured the gold reserves of the Bank of Danzig. In August 1939 the Bank of Danzig had about $4,000,000 worth of gold which Poland considered to be theirs, for the return of which Poland would make a postwar claim.[41] And, while neither Denmark nor Norway provided the Germans with much in the way of gold reserves, having wisely sent most of it off to America and England before surrender, there were huge gold reserves awaiting them in the Low Countries.[42]

The Dutch surrender to Germany in May of 1940 opened the way to the large gold supply in the Bank of Amsterdam. Continuing their practice of "purchasing" gold, the Reichsbank directors opened a new account in their Berlin bank for the Dutch. Under entries marked "occupation costs," "prize gold," "Devisen laws," and later the "eastern campaign," the Reichsbank obligingly made room for the arrival of Holland's gold reserves. Of the total $163,000,000 in looted gold that the Germans removed from the Netherlands over the duration of the occupation, the largest portion disappeared into the "eastern campaign" entry.[43] According to Arthur Seyss-Inquart, Reichskommissar for the occupied Netherlands, the Dutch "declared themselves ready" to aid Germany in the war against bolshevism after the attack upon the Soviet Union by subscribing to a monthly payment of 50 million Reichsmarks, 10 million of which were to be paid in gold. This was to include credit given by the Reichsbank toward the support of a Dutch Legion, a unit of volunteers fighting with

40. See Winston S. Churchill, *Their Finest Hour* (Boston: Houghton Mifflin Co., 1949), p. 467. Later, in the summer of 1941, German foreign minister Ribbentrop asked the chief of the German High Command, Field Marshal Keitel, to station an air squadron at Dakar to aid the French in the event of an English attack, but Keitel refused, explaining that this was not possible until Russia had been defeated. *D.G.F.P.*, ser. D, vol. 13, pp. 33–35 and 70–71.

41. NA, RG 43, Records of International Conferences, Commissions and Expositions, World War II Conference Files, Fletcher to Reinstein, 19 April 1948, p. 1, "Polish Claim for Restitution of Gold Looted by Germany." Hereafter NA, RG 43, WWII Conf. Files.

42. As of 20 March 1940, Norway had gold accounts amounting to $88 million in the United States and Denmark had $51 million. *Morgenthau Diary*, vol. 1 (Washington, D.C.: U.S.G.P.O., 1967), p. 95. One of the Reichsbank directors, Karl Jahnke, reported that no gold transactions were made with either Norway or Denmark between 1938 and 1945. NA, RG 260, OMGUS FINAD, Jahnke report, "Special Gold Transactions 1938–1945," 17 November 1946. Much of the credit for rescuing Norwegian gold went to Oscar Torp, minister of finance. He personally supervised the transport of the gold from Oslo to the west coast, and under heavy German bombardment, the gold was loaded aboard ships for England.

43. BA, R2, 14552, correspondence, "Kriegskostenbeitrag der Niederlande zum Kampf gegen den Bolschewismus; hier: Zahlungen in Gold," 28 March 1942, 27 January 1943 and 21 April 1943.

the German Wehrmacht on the eastern front against the Russians.[44]

Unlike the Netherlands, both the Luxembourg and the Belgium national banks had delivered their gold reserves to the Bank of France in a
futile effort to avoid German capture. Unfortunately for the Luxembour-
gers, the gold from their Sparkasse, some $4,857,823 worth, was still in
France when that nation surrendered to Germany in June 1940. There, at
the Bank of France branch in Marseilles, presumably awaiting momen-
tary shipment out of the country, was the gold of Luxembourg. It was
turned over to representatives of the Reichsbank, who insisted that it was
a perfectly legal transaction "because officials of the Sparkasse Luxembourg did accept payment in Reichsmarks offered them."[45]

At first it appeared as if Belgium might escape the fate of Luxembourg.
As soon as the German attack on Belgium began, the leading personnel of
the National Bank of Belgium followed the example of Poland and fled
along with their gold reserves to France. Again like the Poles, the Belgian
bank staff left for England before France collapsed, but they too had to
leave their gold behind, hopeful that France would ship it to safety abroad
before it was too late.[46] France did indeed send the Belgian gold abroad to
their West African colony just as they had some of their own gold and the
Polish gold. When France surrendered, however, the inescapable conclusion was that by virtue of the Nazi occupation of these states all of the gold
would soon be returned to the Germans as war booty.

For a brief time after the French surrender the Germans were not
certain about just what happened to the gold in question and no one
appeared eager to enlighten them. The conspiracy of silence began to
unravel after the Belgian king, Leopold III, requested his German captors
to return Belgium's gold from France, for he thought it to be still located
there.[47] It was almost three weeks after the French–German armistice had
been signed before the chief of the German economic delegation, Johannes
Hemmen, conferred with General Charles Huntzinger, chairman of the
French armistice commission, about the gold. Hemmen, an aggressive
personality who commanded considerable authority not only in his position as economic head but also as the director of the Ministry of Foreign
Affairs in Berlin, was acting under the direct orders of Ribbentrop.[48]
Hemmen wanted to know exactly how much gold bullion and coin the
Bank of France possessed, where it was located and in what amounts, and

44. Ibid., report of 28 May 1942.
45. NA, RG 332, ETO, SGS, 123/2, Bernstein to Clay, "Report on the Gold of Sparkasse
Luxembourg," 21 October 1945, p. 1.
46. See *N.C.A.*, vol. 7, pp. 643–44; and Rings, *Raubgold aus Deutschland*, pp. 20–21.
47. Rings, *Raubgold*, p. 11.
48. NA, German Records microfilmed at Alexandria, VA, microcopy T–501, roll 121,
frames 616–17. Hereafter NA, T–501, roll and frame.

how much belonged to those states now under German occupation. Citing chapter and verse from the newly signed armistice agreement (article 10), Hemmen let the French general understand his displeasure at what was an obvious maneuver to confuse the Germans.[49] Huntzinger's answer, almost four weeks later, briefly outlined the facts. Hemmen was informed that most of the gold, French and otherwise, had been sent abroad and could now be found in London, New York, Dakar, Martinique, and Casablanca.[50] It was, no doubt, a disappointing bit of news for Hemmen. Whether Huntzinger, soon to become Vichy's minister for war, was ignorant of some of the details, such as the fact that both Belgian and Polish gold was under French control in West Africa, is not entirely clear. It is likely that he did have some knowledge of these matters and simply decided that it was not necessary to tell Hemmen everything; however, this cannot be determined from his answer.

The apparent reluctance of the Germans to simply dispatch a force quickly to French West Africa and return the gold was related to the nature of the armistice settlement. As a war participant, Italy's Armistice Commission had agreed with their German counterparts on areas of control, and although no discussion of Africa was included, the general assumption was that this would be left to Italy as a responsibility. The German navy patrolled the approaches to the Atlantic ports of Africa, but rarely sent any vessels into the ports: "The [German] Armistice Commission has the impression," wrote one of the members, "that it is in accordance with the wishes of the Führer to avoid anything which might lead to conflicts of authority with the Italians concerning Africa."[51] The friendship of the dictators was still much in evidence.

The Germans did have reason to worry about the safety of the gold, and they were well aware of this fact. In anticipation of a British attack, Hemmen notified French authorities that they would be held accountable for any gold loss and advised that the treasure be moved away from the coast immediately. In an emergency he promised to aid the French with some German aircraft.[52] A few days later—it was mid-September—Yves Breart de Boisanger, the French head of the economic delegation to the Armistice Commission and also governor of the Bank of France, assured Hemmen that he was equally concerned about the gold's safety and that every precaution was being taken to protect it. In fact, he wrote, the gold was already being moved some distance inland and Vichy had assigned

49. Ibid., T–501, 363, 86–87.
50. Ibid., T–501, 121, 624–25.
51. *D.G.F.P.*, ser. D, vol. 11, p. 7 and n. 4.
52. Ibid., p. 59.

additional guard units for more security.[53] On September 20th Hemmen received a second message informing him that the gold had been secreted at Kayes, some four hundred kilometers east of Dakar, and there was every confidence that it was out of reach of the British.[54] This turned out to be not a minute too soon for three days later a combined Anglo-French force arrived off Dakar prepared to invade the city.

As a reward for having demonstrated their loyalties, Vichy now suggested to Hemmen that if the Belgian gold was returned as planned, then France should receive that amount on credit for what they had already advanced Belgium: "As for the Polish gold, the Bank of France took the position that since its advances to the Polish government in exile exceeded the amount of Polish gold, the Bank of France must regard this gold as their own."[55] Appreciative though they were for the Vichy stand at Dakar, the Germans were not quite ready to write off vast quantities of gold for it. Tactfully, Hemmen suggested that the matter of the claim for credit for the Belgian gold might better be discussed between the respective Belgian and French bank heads. As for the Polish gold, Hemmen was more blunt and rejected outright any claim as having no basis whatsoever for "the Polish Government in exile was no longer entitled, after the collapse of the Polish state, to dispose of the gold."[56]

In their continuing efforts to cloak their gold looting with some semblance of legality, the Germans arranged for the signing of a formal agreement in October 1940. This document was written by de Boisanger, head of the French economic delegation, a German named von Becker, commissioner for the National Bank of Belgium, another German, Dr. Schaefer, commissioner for the Bank of France, and finally, Hemmen. Thus, three Germans and a Frenchman concluded a lengthy (ten pages) and detailed contract specifying the return of the Belgium gold from Africa at the expense of the Belgian bank. The Bank of France assumed full responsibility.[57] In the agreement it was noted that the Bank of France (in this case, Schaefer) promised to return the Belgian gold, but it was understood that French bank officials had never looked into the 4,944 sealed boxes they had received from the National Bank of Belgium. Therefore it was further agreed that the boxes were to be delivered to the Reichsbank representatives at Marseilles in the exact same condition. The dollar value of the Belgian gold was estimated at approximately

53. NA, T–501, 363, 71.
54. *D.G.F.P.*, ser. D, vol. 11, p. 59, n. 4.
55. Ibid., p. 197.
56. NA, T–501, 121, 639–53.
57. Ibid.; and RG 260, OMGUS AG 1945–46, "Gold of the Banque Nationale de Belgique acquired by the Reichsbank, Berlin from the Banque de France," 23 August 1945.

$223,200,000.[58]

As the arrangements went forward Ribbentrop impressed upon Hemmen the importance of relocating the Belgian gold in Berlin, and a plan emerged to establish a National Bank of Belgium account in the Reichsbank. Ribbentrop's motivation was to secure a portion of the gold for the Foreign Office before it all disappeared into the coffers of Göring's Four-Year Plan.[59] Göring agreed to Ribbentrop's request, and the Foreign Ministry began collecting on the first plane load that landed in Marseilles in November 1940. The foreign minister's goal was to create a fund of some $2,500,000 in gold from the Belgian reserves.[60] Arnold Barsch, chief accountant for the Foreign Office, confirmed that the foreign minister planned to build a special account from Belgian gold just for ministry use. This account was later to be dubbed "Ribbentrop gold" by Allied investigators.[61]

After the first Belgian gold shipment from West Africa had arrived, Hemmen announced that the remainder would quickly follow, a statement that he later no doubt wished he had not made. Even though there were over two hundred tons still to come, he thought it not overly optimistic at the time to inform his superiors that he planned to have all the gold back in Europe by Christmas.[62] His message had hardly reached Berlin before the troubles began. First of all, the German insistence on following a certain protocol involved what they obviously deemed the legal steps in acquiring possession of the gold but really meant needless complications. For instance, the Belgian–French gold agreement they had so carefully orchestrated in the previous October (with no Belgian signatory) was not acceptable to Vichy Minister President Pierre Laval, who was insistent that no gold could be released at Marseilles without approval of the governor of the National Bank of Belgium. Laval had decided that there was too much risk of a future claim otherwise and demanded some Belgian participation. The problem was that no Belgian

58. Ibid., T–501, 363, 20–21.

59. Ibid., 24–25.

60. Ibid., RG 260, OMGUS FINAD, Roberts to Wolfram, 3 July 1950, and enclosure, "Data re German Foreign Office Gold Reflected by Records of Foreign Exchange Depository," 3 May 1949. The FED estimated the Foreign Office gold that was captured in 1945 at something over four tons (over $4 million). Robert M.W. Kempner, a deputy chief counsel at the Nuremburg trials, thought the Ribbentrop fund was as high as fifteen tons of gold. Ibid., Kempner to Laukhuff, 28 December 1948.

61. NA, T–105, 363, 24–25.

62. Ibid., 14–17. Rings, in his recent study of wartime banking, wrote that Janssen was deliberately kept away from the October 1940 conference where the French–Belgian gold agreement was worked out. This permitted Hemmen, knowing that Janssen opposed it, to announce the Belgian's support for returning the gold from Africa. To insure there were no problems, Hemmen monitored all communication between Belgium and France during the meetings.

would sign the necessary documents. The bank governor said that he had not signed the October agreement and would not approve any gold release. Hemmen deftly sidestepped this problem, however, by promising Laval a letter absolving the French government of any responsibility in the event of later claims. As for the needed signatures, de Boisanger agreed to sign in his capacity as French bank governor and simply to ignore the nonparticipating Belgians. It was understood that the transaction did not relieve the Bank of France from its original obligation to the National Bank of Belgium, however.[63]

It was still early December, and although a little behind schedule, it appeared that Hemmen would soon have the operation back on the track. Actually, the problems that he soon had to confront were unavoidable. Not only was it a world at war where anything might happen no matter how good the planning, but weather and logistics were sometimes overwhelming. The transport route decided upon entailed moving about 240 tons of gold through thousands of miles of West African interior, the Sahara Desert, to Oran and Algiers. This circuitous trail, thought necessary for security, was to present many difficulties. Each shipment was loaded onto a train at Kayes and transported to Bamako on the banks of the Niger River. Depending upon the availability of additional transport, the gold was put aboard light trucks or riverboats for the trip to Timbuktu and, finally, Gao. Both modes of transportation meant problems, for the trucks lacked spare parts and needed tires while the riverboats were often stalled due to heavy rains.[64] At Gao the gold was loaded onto heavy-duty vehicles if they were available; if not, camels were used. The caravan then began the long and dreary journey north through the Sahara to Colomb-Béchar on the Moroccan border; here the gold was reloaded into a train for the final leg in Africa to Algiers. Hemmen had counted on a thirty-day timetable to this point with each shipment fifteen days apart. The one-thousand-kilometer air trip from Algiers to Marseilles took about five hours with each plane carrying two tons of gold.[65]

Throughout the first months of 1941 attempts to bring the Belgian gold out of West Africa met with one frustration after another. Most of the trouble was related to the spreading war that had now engulfed the Balkans and North Africa with an intensity that made convoys of any nature extremely dangerous. The demands on all forms of transport were critical and schedules simply could not be met. This was very evident in the many reports Hemmen sent off to the Foreign Office, for dates on gold

63. Ibid., RG 260, OMGUS AG 1945–46, Bernstein to Clay, 23 August 1945, "Gold of the Banque Nationale de Belgique."
64. Ibid., T–501, 363, 186.
65. Ibid., 187–88.

shipments were being constantly revised to later times.[66] During the months of summer movement often came to a standstill because of the lack of transport and fuel. When shipments did get through the size was smaller than planned, usually no more than a few tons. The fall months were better and schedules seemed easier to maintain. By December Hemmen was impatient on the shipment size and wanted to increase each one to at least ten tons on a weekly basis. The French reply through de Boisanger was always the same—not enough aircraft or trucks. The working arrangement was that the Germans would provide the aircraft and fuel at French expense and fly the gold from North Africa to Marseilles. However, according to de Boisanger, too many of the planes were unable to make safe flights due to lack of spare parts and proper maintenance. The only solution, he advised Hemmen, was for the German to persuade his government that this project was of top priority.[67] By this time Hemmen was more than a year behind schedule and there was no end in sight. Not only had the operation suffered from bad weather, lack of adequate transport, and enemy attacks but, Hemmen complained, he had to deal with unimportant issues as well. One of these distractions was brief but rather interesting; it concerned the gold from Latvia and Lithuania.

The gold from these two Baltic states was stored with the Belgian and Polish gold in French West Africa, and soon after the German attack on the Soviet Union in 1941, de Boisanger had some news for Hemmen. He told the German diplomat that before the attack Vichy had been secretly negotiating with the Russians on the possibility of opening some trade relations. The Russian interest was in securing the Baltic gold which they knew to be in French possession. Of course, de Boisanger assured Hemmen, since the attack all communications had been broken, and he did not think any of the early discussions had been very serious anyway.[68]

Equally interesting and more prolonged was Hemmen's worry that the United States would attempt to seize the $245 million worth of French gold stored at Fort-de-France in Martinique. Germany had not given up the hope that somehow Vichy could be persuaded to return this gold to metropolitan France. They pressed the argument that the gold was at risk, for even if the Americans did not attempt to seize it, they would blockade the island and render it useless. The governor of the French islands was an admiral named Robert, a staunch supporter of Pétain, and it was his contention that the gold was perfectly safe where it was. He did not

---

66. Ibid., 126–28.

67. Ibid., 95–98. Additional correspondence noted that only three of the eight planes available were in flying condition, ibid., 105.

68. BA, R2, 30113, Coenen to de Boisanger, 26 June 1941; and Hemmen to de Boisanger, 7 July 1941.

believe that the United States would try to get it for he had promised the Americans that the gold would not be moved without their knowledge. This promise had been made with Vichy's consent soon after the Franco-German armistice, when there was fear that there would be an American invasion of the islands. Now, Robert felt that had passed and there was little need for worry.[69]

France had shipped the gold to Martinique in the spring of 1940, and its presence there was closely monitored by the United States, which had an additional concern for 106 American-made planes that had been destined for France as news of the armistice came. During 1941, the expanding but undeclared war between German submarines and American shipping in the Atlantic heightened the tensions surrounding these valuable resources on Martinique.[70] Throughout most of that year the situation did not change very much, but with the entry of the United States into the war in December, Vichy fears were instantly renewed. It was decided that at any indication of an American plan to invade the islands all French shipping and the gold would be sunk. De Boisanger and Hemmen agreed that sinking the gold would not prevent the Americans from recovering it with divers, but they also felt that it was too risky at the moment to try to move it elsewhere.[71]

The Americans had become a problem in another area of Hemmen's work, too. At the request of former Belgian premier Georges Theunis, a plenipotentiary had initiated a suit in the New York State Supreme Court claiming French gold deposited with the U.S. Federal Reserve Bank. The court had agreed to place a hold order on the $260 million worth of French gold stored in New York in order to "secure the claims of the National Bank of Belgium against the Bank of France."[72] When de Boisanger discussed the situation with Hemmen in February, he said his own government had not even been informed of the U.S. court's action, but had only read of it in the newspaper. The details were still lacking, he complained, and they had no idea how Theunis's representative had been able to persuade the court to do such a thing. As if this were not enough, de Boisanger stated, the Belgians were even demanding interest on their gold dating from 18 June 1940. He assured Hemmen that the Vichy govern-

69. NA, T–501, 363, 117–31.

70. See William Langer, *Our Vichy Gamble* (New York: Alfred A. Knopf, 1947), pp. 104ff.

71. NA, T–501, 363, 750.

72. *N.C.A.* vol. 7, p. 647. In *Banque de France* v. *The Supreme Court of the State of New York*, involving an attempt by representatives of the National Bank of Belgium to recover gold from the Bank of France, it was held: "The United States recognizes as the only legitimate Government of Belgium the group of exiles who are exercising in a country not subject to the domination of Belgium's conquerors, governmental power entrusted to them by the laws of Belgium," Domke, *The Control of Alien Property*, p. 218.

ment had sent a lawyer to America, and it would soon be demonstrated that Theunis had no case.[73] He had the fullest sympathies, Hemmen answered, but he was pessimistic that a Vichy lawyer could win a reversal of the New York court decision. Germany was a veteran of such American injustices, Hemmen wrote, and such actions were common in that country. In spite of all this, the German diplomat informed him, Germany was still very pleased that France had not allowed this affair to interfere with the return of Belgian gold.[74]

In circumstances not dissimilar to the Belgian claim against the French gold in New York, a representative of the Polish government in exile appeared and made a claim against the Bank of France for gold entrusted to it by Poland in 1939. However, in this instance the Bank of France mounted an intriguing defense. Their lawyer carefully pointed out that Poland, unlike Belgium, never actually officially transferred their gold to the care of the Bank of France. An exact itinerary covering the arrival of the Polish gold in France in October 1939 was developed, with French banking officials insisting that the Polish gold never left the possession of Polish bank personnel who were under the supervision of the director, Stefan Michalski. From October until June of 1940, the Polish gold occupied French bank space, but was never under French administration.[75] Much later, when Michalski did bring charges, it was against the government of France and not against the Bank of France. This was proof, the bank argued, that it could not possibly be a defendant.[76]

In December 1940 Hemmen informed de Boisanger that it was the German viewpoint that the Bank of Poland still existed as a legal entity. Since there was no successor bank he was requesting that France return the gold and other valuables that belonged to the Polish bank. He assured de Boisanger that at least two signatures from Polish bank officers on the directorate in 1939 would support the request.[77] De Boisanger did not deny the fact the Polish gold was in West Africa, nor that it belonged to the Bank of Poland, but he did ask consideration for the position that France was in after having guaranteed the payment of specific debts against the Polish state. De Boisanger pointed out that the gold was the

73. NA, T–501, 363, 201.

74. Ibid., 93–94 and 202–3.

75. Ibid., 108–9. See also Racizynski, *In Allied London*, p. 77, n. 1; and Rings, *Raubgold*, pp. 13–14.

76. NA, T–501, 363, 109 and 379.

77. BA, R2, 14552, Hemmen to de Boisanger, 20 December 1940. It was also the German contention that the Bank of France owed Germany any losses from the Polish bank gold account in New York. France had paid out some $1,000,000 to Polish exile government officials, ibid.

only tangible asset of that state that Vichy controlled. He also questioned Hemmen's assertion that the Bank of Poland still existed in Warsaw, pointing out the obvious fact that the directorate had fled with the gold in September 1939. He admitted that there was no successor bank, but referred to the creation of a Polish note bank in Krakow that was using Reichsmarks and not gold as backing for its issue.[78] As for the promised signatures of former Polish bank officers from 1939, de Boisanger was doubtful that this could be managed. He admitted that Hemmen might find one or two former bank employees who would provide signatures, but not members of the directorate, for they had long since departed Warsaw. He did not see how either Vichy or the Bank of France could accept such substitutes on a matter of this importance.[79]

De Boisanger refused to accept Hemmen's comparison of the Polish case with that of Belgium. First of all, he noted, Belgium was completely occupied by German forces, which was not true of Poland. It was a land divided into three areas with the western region integrated into Germany, the General Government in the middle, and the eastern provinces under the U.S.S.R. This arrangement had absolutely no relationship to the Franco–German armistice of 1940 and no connection to French responsibility for Polish gold. Certainly, de Boisanger reasoned, France had no obligation toward the Russo-German creation that had been Poland, and any future diplomatic recognition would have to await the establishment of proper borders and a peace treaty. Then, he concluded, the question of returning Polish gold would be considered.[80]

Such an explanation may have sufficed between two sovereign nations in peacetime, but circumstances were quite different now and the Germans were in no mood to be bluffed by officials of a state they had so recently defeated in war. Citing a gross violation of article 10 of the armistice agreement, the Germans reminded Vichy that they had promised to deny aid to Germany's enemies in every form. Now, to prevent German access to Polish gold while permitting enemies to draw on the Polish deposits in the Bank of France abroad was intolerable. Their further refusal to accept the signatures that Hemmen offered was nothing more than a stalling maneuver.[81]

It might be asked why the Germans simply did not demand the gold under threat of reprisal, but certain factors had to be considered. Despite

---

78. Ibid., 25175, de Boisanger to Hemmen, 26 February 1941, pp. 1–4.
79. Ibid., p. 5.
80. Ibid., pp. 6–8.
81. Ibid., Schelling letter, 20 March 1941, "Erste Stellungsnahme zur Note der französischen Abordnung bei der deutschen Waffenstillstandskommission von 26. Februar 1941."

foreign propaganda about Nazi tactics, the Germans were determined to pursue their own brand of legality even if it meant the loss of the Polish gold. Of even greater importance for the moment was to continue to receive the full cooperation of the Vichy government and prevent serious occupation problems. Thus the question of returning the Polish gold was still sought within the de Boisanger–Hemmen framework, at least for the time being. In a more gentle but still persistent vein Hemmen reminded de Boisanger that neither of them wanted the gold to fall into enemy hands, and it was becoming clear that to continue to defend it in Africa was a perilous course. It was obvious, he continued, that the logical course was to bring the gold back to Europe. Reluctantly de Boisanger agreed, but suggested that the Belgian operation be completed first.[82]

This occurred at the end of May 1941, when Germany was poised for an invasion of the Soviet Union. Hitler's Operation Barbarossa would soon send German armies deep into Russia, radically altering the Polish situation. Nazi occupation of the remainder of the former Polish state brought renewed pressures upon Vichy to recognize what was left of the Bank of Poland in Warsaw as the legal owner of the gold in Africa. By German direction the new Polish bank director in Warsaw, Wydzial Zagraniczny, wrote to the Bank of France and formally requested the return of the bank's property. But the Bank of France responded just as it had in the American court case that any claim for Polish gold had to be taken up with the French government since the French bank had never had legal possession of the Polish gold as a responsibility; it had been entrusted to the French government and left in control of Polish bank personnel.[83]

This explanation was totally unacceptable to Funk, who insisted that the Bank of France had accepted 1,208 cases of Polish gold and therefore carried the responsibility for it; however, he could not find any documentation attesting to this fact (presumably Hemmen had made a search). Therefore, after some consultation with his staff, Funk decided that it would be wiser to shift their pressures to Vichy: "This second possibility offers us some advantages," he thought, "for it would permit the French government the excuse to withdraw from this [situation] because of their position that [this] is a strictly private demand by the Bank of Poland which the Bank of France does not recognize and can only be decided by a court decision."[84] This would mean the defense the Bank of France had

82. NA, T–501, 363/189, Hemmen to de Boisanger, 20 March 1941; and 133, de Boisanger to Hemmen, 31 May 1941.

83. BA, R2, 25175, Zagraniczny to Banque de France, 5 August 1941; and Schöne letter, 29 October 1941.

84. Ibid., Reichsbankdirektorium to Reichsminister der Finanzen, 24 November 1941.

devised would be swept away and the Polish gold would be returned.

Funk's strategy did not produce any immediate change in the situation, however, as matters continued to drag along with an exchange of much correspondence and few results. Finally, in the summer of 1942, an exasperated Hemmen proposed that France move a commensurate quantity of their gold still in Africa to Clermont-Ferrand as a guarantee until the U.S. court case involving Polish gold was concluded. The Vichy government agreed but with the stipulation that the transfer did not constitute a recognition of Germany's demand for the Polish gold.[85] Confident that there was still time to make the transfer the Germans hastily made arrangements to provide the necessary planes from the Luftwaffe to fly sixty-five tons of gold out of Africa to France. Time had run out, however, for it was already October and the British Eighth Army was pressing Rommel's Afrika Korps at El Alamein on the eve of a massive Anglo-American landing in North Africa. Soon all French and German communications to Dakar and points east would be severed.

When the Allied armies landed in Africa, that indefatigable protector of Polish gold, Stefan Michalski, manager of the Bank of Poland, immediately contacted Robert Murphy, the personal representative of President Roosevelt, who was now in North Africa and requested that the Polish gold be shipped to America. He had already located it and had negotiated an agreement with the French Committee of Liberation to release it to him. Murphy's reaction was favorable and Michalski was informed that as soon as he decided on what basis the gold should be imported into the United States—either to sell or deposit—an American naval vessel would be provided at Polish expense. Ironically, as soon as the Polish gold was deposited with the U.S. Federal Reserve Bank, the Polish ambassador in Washington, Jan Ciechanowski, told the American State Department that the Bank of Poland suit against the Bank of France in New York had been halted.[86]

Although the Germans had failed to get the Polish gold before the Allied invasion of North Africa, they had succeeded in getting all of the Belgian gold out. By the end of May 1942, some 4,854 cases of Belgian gold were deposited in the Berlin Reichsbank vaults. And, as usual, the fiction was maintained that it was an account belonging to the National Bank of Belgium. The rather ridiculous paper work mounted as ways to transform the account into a German credit by what the Germans deemed legal means were pursued. As the major beneficiary, Göring's office

85. Ibid., Hemmen to For. Off., 9 May 1942; NA, T–501, 363, Hemmen to de Boisanger, 10 September 1942; BA, R2, 24175, de Boisanger to Hemmen, 19 September 1942; and ibid., For. Off. to German Armistice Delegation, 23 September 1942.
86. *F.R.U.S*, vol. 3, 1943, pp. 443–44, 495–96.

readily supplied a number of possible options. Speed was of the essence, but the problem did not appear too complicated as his staff outlined it: "Legally speaking, three ways can be taken for the confiscation of the gold, namely: 1) The sale of the gold through the Belgian National Bank to the Reichsbank; 2) The claiming of the gold from the Belgian Chief Secretaries, a group of relatively cooperative Belgian officials, under the title of 'external occupation costs' or as an anti-bolshevistic contributions; and 3) A requisition on the basis of paragraph 52 of the Hague Regulation concerning the land war."[87] The first way was ruled out on the advice of General von Falkenhausen, German military commander of Belgium and northern France. It was the general's considered opinion that all of the directors of the National Bank of Belgium would resign en masse if such a maneuver were attempted, and this would only reinforce their position that they had never been a party to the so-called Belgian–French gold agreement. Additionally, he advised against the second possibility because this would probably result in the resignation of all of the Belgian chief secretaries.[88]

It was finally decided that the "unpleasant character" of the gold transaction could only be avoided if the third way were chosen:

> In the case of requisition of the gold on the basis of paragraph 52 of the Hague Regulation concerning land war, the Chief Secretaries would not have to cooperate. They would simply have to acknowledge the requisition. For this reason a resignation could probably be avoided. The requisition of the gold is also permissible according to international law—that is the opinion of the legal division of the Ministry of Foreign Affairs.[89]

The charade called for General Falkenhausen to reject officially any claim of the National Bank of Belgium in favor of the Reichsbank and then inform the chief secretaries of his decision. The transfer of the gold to the Reichsbank was then confirmed by a certificate from the Belgian bank and a recompense paid. In early September 1942 Göring ordered the Belgian gold placed at the disposal of his office as commissioner of the Four-Year Plan with the terse explanation, "The bullion is needed for purposes of war."[90] The reaction of the National Bank of Belgium to the gold confisca-

87. *N.C.A.*, vol. 3, p. 439.
88. BA, R2, 14552, von Falkenhausen to Göring, 14 May 1942.
89. *N.C.A.*, vol. 3, p. 440. Under the terms of article 52 of the 1907 Regulations Respecting the Laws and Customs of War on Land, goods in kind and services could be requisitioned for the needs of an army of occupation. It also stated that the requisitions "shall only be demanded on the authority of the Commander," which accounts for the prominent role of von Falkenhausen in the transfer. See James Brown Scott, *The Hague Peace Conferences of 1899 and 1907*, vol. 2 (New York: Garland Publishers, 1972), p. 399.

tion was to declare itself, as it had before, a creditor of the Bank of France, and refuse to accept any Reichsmark compensation. The Belgian bank continued to carry the gold holdings on its balance sheet just as it had since May of 1940, in an act of nonrecognition of German action.[91]

The vital importance of the Belgian gold to Germany's war economy is seen in a message Göring sent to Funk soon after the transfer occurred. After expressing his astonishment at how quickly he had been deluged with requests from other government agencies, including the Foreign Office, for a share, Göring wrote: "I must make them aware that this Belgian venture will not be repeated and the gold we have confiscated represents our last reserve. I am determined that this reserve will be utilized in the most sparing manner."[92] His comments drew an angry response from Ribbentrop, who was just as determined that his ministry get a share of the Belgian gold. He protested Göring's arbitrary stance on the issue directly to the Reichsmarschall: "I must call attention to the fact, not entirely unknown to you, that it was entirely through my initiative and the quick and energetic intervention of my office that the total gold reserve of the National Bank of Belgium . . . was conveyed to us."[93] He also reminded Göring that the extensive negotiations carried on over the past two years had been conducted through the Foreign Office (Hemmen). All arrangements for transport and security had been carefully worked out by his people, Ribbentrop wrote, and it should not be forgotten that the Führer himself had entrusted the foreign minister with the responsibility for conducting affairs with foreign nations, which obviously included the subject of Belgian gold. Since there was apparently some confusion on this point, Ribbentrop suggested to Göring that they take the issue to Hitler for settlement.[94]

This may not have been the wisest suggestion, for Göring certainly knew that Ribbentrop did not have much influence over foreign policy and war needs had a far greater priority. In 1943 the Reichsbank informed the National Bank of Belgium that 4,854 cases of their gold had been turned over to the commissioner of the Four-Year Plan the previous year.

---

90. *N.C.A.*, vol. 7, p. 618. The Germans offered RM 2,784 per kg. fine gold minus testing and refining costs.

91. Ibid., vol. 3, p. 707. The Germans decided that an evaluation procedure could determine the worth in Reichsmarks of the gold, which could then be deposited with a designated law court as the Belgian account.

92. IfZg, MA 326, p. 9634.

93. Ibid., p. 9636.

94. Ibid., pp. 9637–38. The Göring–Ribbentrop correspondence was evidently monitored by the SS, for a note from Himmler's office expressed astonishment at the tone of Ribbentrop's message: "Unerklärlich ist mir, wie ein Reichsaußenminister an den Reichsmarschall einen solchen Brief schreiben kann." Ibid.

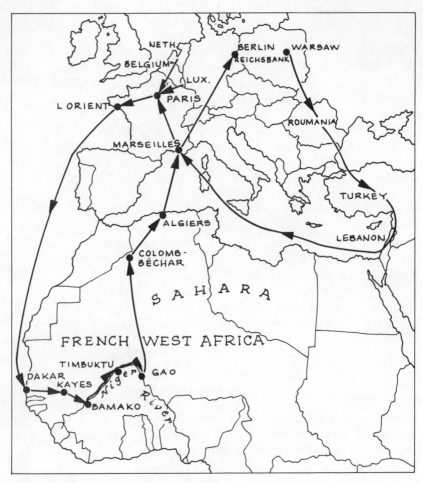

Map 1.1 The Looted Gold Route, 1939–1942

1939:   Polish gold ($64 million) went by train and truck through Romania, Turkey, and Lebanon; then by ship to France (Paris). Scheduled for transport to Canada and the U.S., orders were changed and the gold left Lorient harbor for Dakar.

1940:   Luxembourg gold ($4,857,823) was entrusted to the Bank of France, but before it could be moved to French West Africa, it was seized in Marseilles by the Germans.

1940–42:   Belgium gold ($223,200,000) was sent by France to Dakar before the French collapse, then moved inland to Kayes prior to British attack on the 23d of September 1940. The Vichy government agreed to meet the German demand that the gold, some 4,944 sealed boxes weighing over 240 tons, be returned to Europe and the German Reichsbank. The first shipment started in October 1940; at Kayes it was loaded on a train to Bamako on the Niger River, then light trucks and riverboats transported it to Timbuktu, and finally Gao. From there it was moved by truck and camel north through the Sahara to Colomb-Béchar, with the last stretch by train to Algiers. The one thousand kilometers by air to Marseilles was done with both French and German aircraft (two tons per trip); the last of the gold reached Berlin in May of 1942.

24

In turn, and despite the absence of Belgian bank cooperation, the Reichsbank credited the Belgian account with over 552 million Reichsmarks, the approximate value of the gold confiscated.[95]

The lengthy process had ended in Göring's favor, but his prediction that this represented the last of the gold that could be expected did not prove entirely true. As chance would have it, the Germans were presented with an opportunity to take over Italy's gold reserves. In September 1943, when Marshal Pietro Badoglio surrendered southern Italy to the Allies, German forces occupied Rome. They now ordered the Bank of Italy (Banca d'Italia) to move its $80,000,000 in gold northward. During the last week of September, assisted by German troops and transport, the gold was packed up and shipped to Milan, now within the new Fascist republic that had been proclaimed by Mussolini.[96]

By December, however, the military situation in Milan became critical and it was decided to move the gold to the stronghold of La Fortezza, an Italian site near the Brenner Pass. The governor of the Bank of Italy, V. Azzolini, described the arrangements:

> Fortezza was chosen by the German military authorities as offering greater security against eventual enemy air raids in view of the fact that the gold is stored between remarkably thick walls of underground rock tunnels. Although the gold is not stored in the vaults of one of our branches, the Banca d'Italia . . . is the sole owner thereof. . . . Until further notice, the security measures for the integrity of the tunnel will be entrusted to German military authorities.[97]

Azzolini left no doubt that he believed the gold was given over to the Germans for safekeeping only, but Emil Puhl recalled the circumstances differently. He clearly remembered, he said, that just before the gold was removed from Milan, Rahn, the German ambassador, had negotiated an agreement with the Italian minister of finance, Pellegrini, "whereby the German government was to take the gold of the Banca d'Italia as Italy's 'contribution' to the war on the eastern front."[98] Shortly thereafter the gold was moved to Berlin.

Ribbentrop may have lost out to Göring on the Belgian gold but he saw another chance with Italy's gold since his people had been involved in the negotiations. This time he was to have some success for, after two shipments of Italian gold to Berlin in March and October 1944, Reichs-

---

95. NA, T–501, 122, 24–25.

96. NA, RG 43, WW II Conf. Files, Stribravy to Reinstein, 1 June 1947, "Gold Uncovered at La Fortezza, Italy."

97. Ibid., Azzolini to Bernhuber, 28 December 1943.

98. BA, RG 260, OMGUS FINAD, R.A. Nixon to Gen. Clay, 14 December 1945.

bank records show a transfer of 197 bags of gold coin valued at 20 million Reichsmarks to the Foreign Office account.[99]

Undoubtedly the Germans felt fully justified in taking the Italian gold for they knew that some of it had probably been looted from Yugoslavia by Mussolini's forces in 1941 when it was decided that Italy should receive the Dalmatian coast as part of the spoils of Mussolini's Balkan campaign. In April of that year Axis forces had invaded and occupied Yugoslavia with Italian troops taking over Croatia.[100] In an attempt to avoid capture, the National Bank of Yugoslavia had trucked their gold reserve westward from Belgrade and, just one step ahead of the Italian forces, hid it in several places (Cetinje, Mostar, and Herceg Novi) on the Dalmatian coast. For a very brief interval a Montenegrin committee, acting in the capacity of local government, succeeded in keeping the locations secret, but as Italian occupation authorities took command the hiding places were soon revealed.[101]

On 29 May, on orders from the German commander, the National Bank of Yugoslavia was liquidated and its remaining property divided with Italy. Up to this point the Italians had said nothing about the Yugoslav gold which had come into their possession, but it was not too long before some Yugoslavian bank employees informed the Germans. One of the German Reichsbank directors, Alfred Zabel, conducted an investigation and soon confronted Italian authorities with the evidence of their gold find. Conceding nothing and refusing to admit they had dealt with an ally in an unethical manner, the Italians defended their action on the basis that they had seized legitimate war booty and were under no legal obligation to share it.[102]

What had been anticipated by the German Foreign Office as an affair to be resolved in their favor now that the gold was located instead lengthened into a long series of strenuous diplomatic efforts to actually secure it. It took months just to find the officials in the Italian government who would admit they knew anything about the gold. A state secretary who finally agreed to open correspondence on the subject insisted that the gold

99. Ibid., On 6 May 1945, units of the U.S. Fifth Army opened the Fortezza tunnels, where a quantity of Italian gold was still buried. Later it was returned to Rome and placed in custody of the Allied Financial Agency pending disposition by the Combined Chiefs of Staff, NA, RG 43, WW II Conf. Files, Stribravy to Reinstein, 1 June 1947.

100. See Hans-Adolf Jacobsen and Arthur L. Smith, Jr., *World War II Policy and Strategy: Selected Documents with Commentary* (Santa Barbara, CA, and Oxford, England: ABC Clio, 1979), pp. 110ff.

101. BA, R2, 30651, Georgiev to Zabel, 23 January 1942.

102. Ibid., Fabricius to Foreign Office, 5 June 1942; Fabricius to Foreign Office, 18 June 1942. In May 1941, a message from the German ambassador in Ankara said that there was reliable information that some of the Yugoslavian gold had slipped out to Egypt before that nation had been occupied, Sonderauftrag Fabricius, 7 May 1943.

in question had not come from the National Bank of Yugoslavia, but had been the property of the Yugoslavian government. His reasoning was that since it was former government property found in an area now occupied by Italian forces, it properly belonged to Italy. After presenting their evidence proving that the gold had indeed belonged to the National Bank of Yugoslavia and the government, the Germans insisted that the gold be shared. With Allied forces advancing northward and threatening the German position, the Italians finally agreed to permit the movement of the gold into Germany.

With the end of the war in sight the question may well be asked; Just how much looted monetary gold did Germany actually get from Europe? Taking the statistics from the documentation utilized here and calculating the gold value at $35 to the troy ounce, the following picture emerges: Austria, $102,689,215; Czechoslovakia, $44,000,000; Danzig, $4,100,000; Holland, $163,000,000; Luxembourg, $4,857,823; Belgium, $223,200,000; and Italy, over $80,000,000. This comes to a grand total of $621,847,038 in gold.

CHAPTER 2

The Gold Bank of Europe

There were any number of reasons why bankers and businessmen in neutral states were reluctant to engage in trade with Germany, but there was no confusion about Hitler's desire to secure goods for his war machine or the fact that he had a compelling inducement to do business with gold. It is ironic that at one time several Nazi leaders had ridiculed the use of gold as a standard irrelevant to an autarchy, and yet gold was to become Germany's most important medium of exchange during the war.[1]

Walter Funk knew the importance of gold to Germany's war economy, but recognized some of its problems as well: "It was very difficult to pay in gold . . . [b]ecause the countries with which we still had business relations introduced gold embargoes. Sweden refused to accept gold at all. Only in Switzerland could we still do business through changing gold into foreign currency."[2] It should be noted that these observations only apply after 1942, when the Allies had begun to apply pressure on neutrals.

Soon after Funk became Reichsbank president but before the war had started, he bragged to Hitler that the bank was becoming so strong that even the wildest fluctuations in the international money market would have little effect. His vice-president, Puhl, was already directing a plan to convert all German assets abroad into gold so they would not face any risk in changing currency values. It was Puhl's opinion that Funk's gold policy was quite standard and modest in most respects, but he felt the president's actions were definitely linked to an anticipation of war with Poland. Little consideration was devoted to a possible war in the West when "gold politics" were discussed at the bank. Unfortunately, Puhl concluded, they

1. Robert Ley, leader of the Labor Front, had labeled gold as the weapon of Jews, and Walter Funk, minister of economics and Reichsbank president, vowed that Germany would never return to the gold standard, Thomas Reville, *The Spoil of Europe: The Nazi Technique in Political and Economic Conquest* (New York: W.W. Norton and Co., 1941), p. 137.
2. *I.M.T.*, vol. 13, p. 162.

had not developed policy sufficiently before the war came.[3]

As noted, the hidden-gold-reserve program had started during Schacht's presidency and many of the practices were simply continued by Funk. Despite Puhl's description of Funk's gold policy as "standard," a later and more objective analysis based upon Reichsbank records concluded that both Schacht's and Funk's gold policies were unusual in their intensity during the 1930s.[4] The gold that Germany acquired as part of the hidden reserve was deposited in five confidential accounts whose activity remained a bank secret known only to a handful of staff members. The balances were concealed in the annual statement in "suspense" or "miscellaneous" categories. A published gold statement indicating the bank balance (*Bankbestand*) was still maintained as usual. Thus, an interested observer of German gold activity before the war would have had to assume from the printed report that it represented the total quantity of gold reserves in the Reichsbank on that date. By the time Schacht departed the presidency, however, "the balances of the hidden gold accounts totaled no less than six times the published figure on that date."[5]

A history of Reichsbank gold acquisitions after Hitler assumed power reveals a sharp increase in the last half of 1933. The first hidden reserve was created in December with $17 million in gold, approximately 10 percent of the Reichsbank's total gold reserve. Determined not only to preserve the hidden account but to increase it vastly, Schacht raised it steadily throughout 1934 to 1938. The regular published gold account dropped to an unprecedented low of $55.5 million worth while the hidden account soared to $27 million in gold by June of 1934. The Reichsbank's regular gold account was to drop even lower before 1939.[6]

The first two hidden gold accounts created by Schacht, the Konversionskasse and the Asservaten Sonderkonto, were used only in the beginning, serving as a starting point, and were not maintained over the entire period leading to the war. The third hidden gold account, the Goldankauf, had actually existed as a legitimate purchasing account established after the First World War to buy gold for government use in connection with reparation payment. Later it served as the Reichsbank's suspense account for gold transactions with the public. In this capacity it was a legitimate suspense account and its activity was included in the regular published bank balances. In November 1934 it was transformed into a hidden gold

3. Ibid., vol. 40, pp. 332–36.
4. NA, RG 260, OMGUS AG, 1945–46, Clay to Hildring, 10 December 1945, enclosure, "Report on Hidden Gold Reserve Program," 14 November 1945, p. 1.
5. Ibid.
6. Ibid., p. 2.

account, however, and was no longer posted with the bank balance. As a hidden account, Goldankauf was extremely active and during the next several years spawned two other hidden gold accounts.[7]

As the size of the Goldankauf grew rapidly from a beginning balance of $7,000,000 worth in 1934 to $43,000,000 in barely a year, a fourth new account was created. Called the Treuhandgesellschaft, this account also grew quickly at first, reaching $68,000,000 by the spring of 1937. After its establishment as a new account, Treuhand absorbed the gold balances of both the Konversionskasse and the Asservaten Sonderkonto as well as more than 90 percent of the Goldankauf.[8] Puhl stated that the Treuhand-gesellschaft had existed prior to 1935, but "had lost its original functions and had been completely inactive prior to this transfer [of Reichsbank gold]." It was Schacht's idea, Puhl said, to take this "empty shell which had two old Reichsbank officials for its directors, as a device for concealing a part of the Reichsbank's gold reserves." He noted that when the war started it had a balance of about $75,000,000 in gold, but by the time the Reichsbank moved the gold out of Berlin in February 1945, this balance had been reduced to about $43,000,000.[9]

The largest and most active account at times was the Asservat Devisen Reserve, or Der, which had been established during Schacht's tenure. This had happened in March 1937, with a modest $4 million in gold, and the account grew to over $50 million worth by the time Schacht left. Der records reflected the expenditures for war and war preparation more clearly than the other hidden accounts because huge sums were regularly withdrawn to buy foreign currencies. Most of the gold looted from occupied states went into the Der account; when the Belgian gold began to arrive the account swelled to $143 million and it still contained $59 million worth as a closing balance in February 1945.[10] When the Der account did fluctuate extensively it was a reflection of the demands of Göring's Four-Year Plan, which indicated the influence his office exerted over it. There was no formal agreement giving him exclusive use of the account, but his demands had first priority.[11] The Der account had a kind of subactivity called the *Sonderlagerung*, or special storage, which involved placing quantities of gold in various Reichsbank branches for later use. It

---

7. Ibid., p. 3.
8. Ibid., pp. 4–5. The Asservaten Sonderkonto is defined as a suspense account earmarked for a special purpose. See C.A. Gunston and C.M. Corner, *Deutsch-Englisches Glossarium, finanziellers und wirtschaftlicher Fachausdrücke*, 4th ed. (Frankfurt a.M.: Fritz Knapp Verlag, 1962), p. 87.
9. NA, RG 260, OMGUS AG, 1945–46, "Report on Hidden Gold Reserve Program," p. 4.
10. Ibid., pp. 5–6.
11. Ibid., p. 5.

was a relatively unimportant part of the German hidden-reserve picture, but assumed some significance at war's close when the Allies, mostly American, made a frantic rush to close all gold exits for Nazis trying to slip away.

In addition to the hidden-gold-reserve accounts the Reichsbank kept a gold account labeled the Konto "GR" for a company that was owned by the Deutschen Golddiskontobank (DEGO), which in turn was controlled by the Reichsbank. A similar arrangement existed between the DEGO and the Reichsbank, wherein a gold deposit was held on account for DEGO. Neither of these accounts was very large and there is no evidence that they were ever transferred into the Reichsbank's own gold reserves.[12] After the creation of this elaborate subterfuge the Goldankauf was continued as a suspense account that processed most of the newly acquired gold, and records showed a gold balance of $70 million worth in mid-1941.[13]

It is difficult to ascertain just how well defined Nazi aims were, in terms of a long-range plan, in the beginning of the Hitler government. Most of the older Reichsbank personnel, including Schacht himself, were veterans of the German experience in the First World War and the catastrophic aftermath. They had been witness to Germany's impressive industrial rise before the war, the great war effort on the battlefield and the home front, and finally, the inability to provide enough war supplies. It is highly unlikely that Schacht or any of his Reichsbank directors were autarchy advocates, or even fanatic National Socialists for that matter, but they did understand the vital importance of economic self-sufficiency when their nation pursued an expansionist foreign policy.

Older Reichsbank people remembered the large gold reserve that before 1914 had been built up secretly and stored in a structure located in the Spandau district of Berlin. It had been called the "Julius Tower," a term that came into use again after Schacht initiated the Treuhandgesellschaft account in 1935. Puhl said, "This expression was first used at an occasion [in 1935] when we spoke about the gold reserve (Schacht . . . and I). I heard the word *Juliusturm* in this conversation, but it was used in a joking manner."[14]

The Reichsbank vice-president denied that the hidden-gold-reserve program was undertaken in the beginning with the idea of serving a war purpose. However, he made this statement after the Second World War, when his desire was obviously to minimize his participation in what the Allies called the "common conspiracy" of Nazi leaders to plan and

12. Ibid., p. 4.
13. Ibid.
14. Ibid., p. 6.

execute aggressive warfare. Puhl did admit that "more and more it became evident that in the case of war these gold reserves of the Reichsbank would play a similar part as the *Juliusturm* had played in the First World War."[15] Puhl said that he had the distinct impression that Schacht did not discuss the details of the hidden gold reserve with many of the top Nazi figures in government and doubted that he had ever supplied Göring with the details of the program, although Puhl felt that the Reichsmarschall knew about it from other sources. Puhl believed that the program was part of Hitler's plan of war, but he never heard Schacht speak of it as such. It was a different situation with Funk, however, who immediately upon taking over had detailed reports on the hidden-gold-reserve accounts regularly prepared for both Göring and Hitler.[16]

When Schacht was dismissed from the Reichsbank in 1938, the hidden-gold-reserve program had been in existence for over four years, and he had built a structure and staff now experienced in the amassing of gold on a confidential basis. Funk would continue the work, depending on banking talent from Puhl on down who had become experts in the purchase, transfer, storage, bookkeeping, smelting, and hiding of gold. Their contacts with the banking brotherhood of neutral Europe after 1939 were to prove invaluable as it became imperative that huge quantities of looted gold be exchanged for foreign currencies and credits. These contacts, plus human greed and fear of Nazi reprisal, were the most powerful forces that insured Reichsbank success in carrying out its mission.

Hjalmar Schacht was still Reichsbank president when the gold stock of the Austrian National Bank was taken over in March 1938 against a Reichsbank payment. He instructed Albert Thoms of the Precious Metals Department to place the Austrian gold into the Reichsbank's reserves. The acquisition of the Austrian gold started the German policy of paying a Reichsmark compensation for gold removed from central banks of conquered states, a practice that was to continue throughout the war years.[17] In at least one instance, with Czechoslovakia, the Reichsbank offered freely negotiable foreign exchange for their gold stock. After the Czech gold reserve came under Reichsbank control, the Czechs were permitted the option of receiving the negotiable currency or a limited amount of gold that was purchased by the German bank, according to Karl Jahnke, one of the Reichsbank directors at the time. He termed the Reichsbank offer not a standing one, but one made only "when necessary."[18] Some of the

---

15. Ibid., p. 7.

16. Ibid., pp. 7 and 2.

17. The Reichsstelle für Edelmetalle was one of some thirty Überwachungsstellen created in 1934 to oversee all phases of the Nazi economy, such as textiles, iron, etc. In 1939 they were named Reichsstellen, BA, R8X, *Reichsstelle für Edelmetalle 1934–46*, p. 93.

gold from the Czechoslovakian National Bank was still in Reichsbank accounts at the end of the war, and some was in the Swiss National Bank in Bern. There is no evidence that there was any attempt by the Germans to ever disguise the origin of the Czech gold before delivery, and the gold bars remained in their original state.[19]

After the Czechoslovakian National Bank had been reorganized by the Germans and was replaced by a central bank for Slovakia, the personnel and all major assets stayed in Prague as the National Bank of Bohemia and Moravia. A secret American military report described this transformation and the new relationship to the Reichsbank:

> The origin, the nature, even the disposition of several accounts in which the Reichsbank held gold for this National Bank of Bohemia and Moravia, all reflect the Reichsbank's efforts to preserve the fiction of its autonomy by superficial observance of the formalities of legitimate dealings with a truly independent bank.[20]

The degree of independence enjoyed by the Czech bank is illustrated by the nature of the account created in the Reichsbank for the Czech gold. The gold was not absorbed directly into the Reichsbank's own reserves, as would later happen with Belgian and Luxembourg gold, nor was any of it resmelted. Instead, it was all placed into several separate accounts as Czech deposits, and when quantities were withdrawn the transaction was always recorded with payment for countervalue received by the Czechs. This was all carefully monitored by Dr. Friedrich Müller, the Reichsbank director appointed to a position of special bank representative in Prague at the beginning of the German occupation.[21]

It was clear that the Germans exercised total control over the Czech gold stock from the outset when the $26 million in gold on deposit with the BIS was transferred to the Czech account in the Reichsbank a few days after the German occupation. The transfer order came in the form of an official communique from the Czech bank to the BIS. Emil Puhl later reluctantly admitted that "pressures" had been applied to certain key Czech banking officers in order to "make the necessary arrangements." There was no hint in the BIS reply that they regarded the transfer as more than a routine matter: "According to the directions you gave us . . . we

---

18. NA, RG 260, OMGUS FINAD, Karl Jahnke report, "Special Gold Transactions 1938–1945," 17 November 1946, p. 1.
19. Ibid., RG 332, ETO, SGS, 123/2, Nixon to Clay, 1 November 1945, "Report on the Gold of the National Bank of Bohemia and Moravia," p. 7.
20. Ibid., p. 2.
21. Ibid., pp. 2–3.

drew from the gold we are holding in our name, but for your account, at the Bank of England, London, *1845 gold bars* . . . which we placed into the account of the Reichsbank, Berlin, at the Bank of England."[22]

On 5 May 1939, the Reichsbank deposited the first of the Czech gold into a special account, the Sonderlagerung wegen National Bank für Böhmen und Mähren. It did not consist of the 1,845 gold bars mentioned by the BIS, but an obvious substitute of 1,880 gold bars from the Bank of England.[23] In June a second Czech account was established with the inventory from the original Depot der National Bank für Böhmen und Mähren in the Reichsbank, which now called it a regular deposit, or *depositum regulare*. Reichsbank files show no withdrawals from this account, and its contents were evacuated from Berlin along with the other Reichsbank holdings in February 1945. The account contained a wide variety of foreign gold coins and was valued at over $7,000,000. When discovered by American forces in the mine where it had been placed, the coinage was still in the original bank bags from Prague.[24] The third Czech account in the Reichsbank was created in October 1940, and its history shows a steady influx of gold during that and the following year. The account was labeled the Separat-Depot der National Bank für Böhmen und Mähren, and the gold was transferred to it from the Der account. It consisted of 800 gold bars and a small amount of coinage with a total dollar value of $10,843,219. In September 1942 the Reichsbank delivered 59 bars from this account to the Swiss National Bank in Bern; the remaining 741 gold bars were eventually included in the Berlin evacuation in 1945.[25] An American investigator of Reichsbank gold practices characterized the delivery of the 59 gold bars to Switzerland as a "washing" that made them negotiable.[26]

In this manner the Czech gold was acquired by the Reichsbank at different intervals and under varied circumstances reflected in the accounts established. The special account (Sonderlagerung) was opened by a transfer of gold formerly held in the BIS Bank of London account; the regular deposit came from the actual transfer of gold coinage from Prague to Berlin; and the Separat-Depot received Czech gold via the Der account in the Reichsbank, presumably after purchase or credit was extended. Of the total amount of Czech gold which the Germans controlled, some $29 million worth remained untouched throughout the war while $15 million worth was used by the Reichsbank.[27]

22. Ibid., p. 3, and A–3.
23. Ibid., A–1.
24. Ibid., B–1 to B–5.
25. Ibid., C–1 to C–2, and G–1.
26. Ibid., RG 260, OMGUS FINAD, Bernstein to Clay, 1 November 1945, p. 3.

In some ways Poland was more fortunate than Czechoslovakia since its gold succeeded in eluding the long arm of the Reichsbank. But the Germans did not give up easily, and while they failed to get the Polish gold, they could still hold the French responsible for what had been drawn on the Polish account through the Bank of France in the United States. They continued to pursue the matter during the entire period of their occupation of France, and the French just as persistently defended their position on the grounds that the 1940 armistice agreement did not hold them responsible.[28] There were obviously moments of frustration and vexation on both sides during this time. At one point de Boisanger sent Hemmen an angry note to the effect that France had presented sound reasons for refusing them and it was completely unfair to continue the constant harassment.[29] It was also clear on both sides that the Germans would take no drastic measures to secure the gold at the expense of destroying the spirit of collaboration that existed with Vichy.

The sum involved was small compared to the earlier lootings, only $776,318, but by 1944, the date of the last correspondence on the matter, Germany was becoming desperate. As late as May of that year Hemmen rejected all of de Boisanger's pleas for fairness and ordered compliance.[30] Considering the lateness of the date, it is doubtful if even Hemmen expected much response, although he probably did not know that this would be the last time he broached the question of Polish gold either. Of course, the Reichsbank never did get the Polish gold out of Africa nor did they get the indemnity demanded of the Bank of France. The last Reichsbank entry on Poland was made by Director Jahnke, who closed the subject in one brief sentence, "No gold transactions . . . made."[31]

While Nazi officialdom continued the farcical pretense that their gold acquisitions from the central banks of occupied Europe were perfectly legal, they also used a number of means to try to make the looted gold more acceptable to the trading neutrals. In addition to providing letters of assurance that the bullion in question had been legitimately acquired, which many bankers were quite willing to accept at face value, the Germans did have methods of changing the identity of the gold. Official documents, such as inventory sheets, closing balances, and bank and case

---

27. Ibid., OMGUS AG, 1945–46, AG to CAD, 3 January 1964.

28. BA, R2, 25175, Hemmen to de Boisanger, 8 September 1943.

29. Ibid., de Boisanger to Hemmen, 18 April 1944.

30. Ibid., de Boisanger to Hemmen, 13 May 1944. On 26 May 1944, in a lengthy and detailed letter, the German Foreign Office informed Göring's office and the Reichsbank (among others) of the state of negotiations to that date, ibid., Dumont of AA to Göring, et al., 26 May 1944.

31. NA, RG 260, OMGUS FINAD, Jahnke report, p. 1.

numbers, could all be altered to accompany a specific gold shipment. The most convincing items of identification, the smelt number and date, required resmelting. This made the bookkeeping more complicated too, because the original smelt number was used to trace a gold bar through banks (accounts) and was pasted in the bar books along with a cross-reference number that was assigned by the originating bank. Although the numbers continued to be used in each transaction, it was not uncommon for banks to dispose of old ledgers when they became a storage nuisance. Thus, short of resmelting, the only really reliable identification was the original smelt number. There were no serial numbers on the gold coins, only on the bags, and once removed from the bags the coins were not traceable unless they belonged to a special collection.

Evidently Germany did not feel any deception was necessary with gold bullion acquired against a Reichsmark equivalent for they regarded this as a legal transaction. There was no attempt made to disguise the gold from either the Netherlands or Luxembourg, and they found no difficulty in getting the cooperation of banking officials from both of these nations when making the gold transfers.

It was quite a different story with Belgium, the nation that ultimately provided the Reichsbank with the largest gold reserve of them all. Try as they would, the Reichsbank and Foreign Office negotiators could never make the Belgians accept payment for their gold. The stubborn Belgians held fast to their contention that their gold had been entrusted to the Bank of France and that it remained a French responsibility. No amount of German cajolery or threat could make the Belgian bankers change their position as they continued to ignore the German-established Belgian account in the Reichsbank. In the face of resistance the Germans decided it might be more prudent to disguise the Belgian gold before offering it abroad. It is not clear just who made this decision, probably a collaborative effort between the Reichsbank and the Foreign Office, but the rationale was obvious. "Proof" of ownership, as in the Dutch and Luxembourg cases, could not be presented, so the only alternative was to resmelt the gold and give it new numbers and dates: "In Berlin wurde das Gold ausgepackt, eingeschmolzen, umgegossen und umdatiert, so daß seine Herkunft nicht mehr ohne weiteres erkennbar war. Schließlich gelangte es—nun als 'deutsches' Gold getarnt—von Berlin nach Bern."[32]

The predating of resmelted gold bars began in February 1943 when, under the direction of Thoms's Precious Metals Department, the Prussian mint resmelted all of the Belgian gold bars. They were stamped with dates arbitrarily selected from the years before 1939. From the time this work

32. Rings, *Raubgold*, p. 10.

started until early the following year large amounts of resmelted Belgian gold, together with significant quantities of gold coinage, were disposed of in transactions with banks outside Germany. Reichsbank records reveal that the largest amount went to Switzerland ($122.9 million worth); Romania ($33.7 million worth); Turkey ($3.4 million worth); and, Italy ($0.1 million worth).[33]

It was not a Reichsbank practice to resmelt gold coinage since its origin was not generally detectable, but its value could not be determined as precisely as that of gold bars. The usual method was to calculate face value from existing records (if any), multiply this by mint weight, and subtract 2.5 percent for wear. The job of evaluating the enormous quantities of gold coinage was a formidable one and was overwhelming at times. Evidence for this was the huge amounts of gold coinage that remained uncounted when the Reichsbank tabulated its closing balances in 1945.[34]

Unlike the Belgian gold, the gold from the Sparkasse Luxembourg was left untouched. After it had been turned over to the Germans at Marseilles by the Bank of France, the 357 gold bars, valued at $4,857,823, were packed in ninety cases and transported to Berlin in a series of shipments between December 1940 and January 1942. There the gold was entered in Reichsbank account Goldankauf Sonderlagerung II almost immediately, and in early April 1942 the entire amount was transferred to Der for use by the Four-Year Plan.[35] Although Emil Puhl alleged that the Luxembourg gold had been obtained legally since Sparkasse officials had accepted a Reichsmark payment, there was a delay of over a year before any of the gold surfaced in the Reichsbank books, that is, between the first shipment in 1940 and the last in 1942. Bank records give no indication of the reason for the delay although it may have been due to transport problems since the Luxembourg gold always arrived with Belgian gold shipments. Another explanation for the delay was the lengthy negotiations with Sparkasse officials. Shortly after the gold was transferred into the Der account, 272 bars were shipped to the Swiss National Bank in Bern, and the remaining 35 bars went to the Precious Metals Department in the Reichsbank; however, none were resmelted.[36]

As for the Dutch gold, the Reichsbank files show that it began to pass

33. NA, RG 260, OMGUS AG 1945–46, Bernstein to Clay, 23 August 1945, "Gold of the Banque Nationale de Belgique Acquired by the Reichsbank, Berlin from the Banque de France, Marseilles," p. 1.

34. Ibid., RG 332, ETO, SGS, 123/2 Nixon, "Report on Recovery of Reichsbank Precious Metals," 6 September 1945, p. 3.

35. Ibid., Bernstein to Clay, 21 October 1945, "Report on Gold of the Sparkasse Luxembourg," pp. 1, A–1, and B–1.

36. Ibid., pp. 2 and B–1.

into German possession in the fall of 1940. The next year, tagged with Reichsbank numbers but not resmelted, it was sent to the Swiss National Bank in Bern. This was the first of more than 5,000 bars of Dutch gold sent to Switzerland by the Germans, all still carrying the smelt numbers from the Bank of Amsterdam.[37] After the war the Dutch government reported that some of their gold had been resmelted by the Prussian State Mint and given prewar dates. A careful examination of the records of Thoms's Precious Metals Department failed to support the Dutch claim, however, and it was noted that "the first time this procedure [predating] was employed was on the occasion of the smelting transactions with the Belgian gold which began in early 1943."[38]

German gold policy, and thus Reichsbank policy, differed somewhat with each occupied nation, but some of the practices were similar. In the Dutch instance the "contributions" to the fight against communism consumed much more of their gold reserves than in either the Luxembourg or Belgian cases. In neither of these states had the willingness to contribute to the German war in Russia been declared in their names the same as in the Netherlands, where Reichskommissar Seyss-Inquart exerted such presence. The recruiting of volunteer "legions" for the eastern front had not been as successful either.

In carrying out the schedule of payments of 10 million Reichsmarks monthly in gold, the Bank of Amsterdam transferred nearly 200 million Reichsmarks to the Reichsbank. This was done in 1942 and early 1943 and consisted of payment in gold bars and Dutch gulden. By April 1943 German authorities concluded, "Further transfers from the Netherlands cannot be expected; the . . . gold depot . . . is exhausted."[39] It was the Dutch misfortune to have had a large quantity of gold in their bank vaults when the Germans arrived. It was estimated by Dutch banking officials who had fled into exile in May 1940, that approximately $200 million of their gold reserve still remained behind (from a total of $650 million in gold).[40]

To insure maximum coordination between the Reichsbank and the Four-Year Plan in securing full use of the Dutch gold, Dr. Wohlthat, a Reichsbank director and official in the Ministry of Economics, was appointed the German commissioner of the Netherlands Bank. Wohlthat already had a close working relationship with Göring and other Four-

37. NA, RG 260, OMGUS FINAD, "Gold, Netherlands, General Correspondence," 22 July 1947, p. 7.

38. Ibid., "Report of Netherlands Bank, Amsterdam, re. Looted Dutch Gold," 22 July 1947, p. 3.

39. BA, R2, 14552, correspondence "Kriegskostenbeitrag der Niederlande zum Kampf gegen den Bolschewismus; hier: Zahlungen in Gold," 21 April 1943.

40. Reville, *Spoil of Europe*, p. 134.

Year Plan officials and had a reputation as a skilled negotiator on economic matters. The situation was made somewhat easier by the fact that the president of the Netherlands Bank, Dr. Trip, and his successor Rost van Tonningen, offered every cooperation to the occupiers.[41]

France represented a far different situation. Most French gold had been shipped abroad although the Bank of France still controlled the large Belgian and Polish reserves in West Africa. The Germans immediately saw this gold within their grasp as the apparent tractability of the Vichy government seemed to eliminate the most important obstacle. They had judged correctly, for Vichy's cooperation proved absolutely vital in getting access to the Belgian gold. The most difficult leg of the journey was transporting the gold overland to the Mediterranean coast, and this was organized entirely by Vichy officials. Even if the Bank of France directorate had been willing to do this at the German request, it still could not have completed it without Vichy support. There is some opinion that the Vichy government, in ignoring the Bank of France when ordering the return of the Belgian gold, violated international law on this matter before the Germans did. The Vichy decision was followed up by a law giving the government control over the assets of the Bank of France, including the Belgian gold.[42]

The reasons behind Vichy's cooperation—or collaboration—on the Belgian gold can only be viewed in a larger context and against the background of a relationship that was continually subject to innumerable pressures. To remain a "viable" partner with the Germans, the Vichy government had to prove its usefulness in making the cost of unoccupied France worth the price. Both sides were acutely aware of the importance of maintaining that precarious balance at all times. The Germans were so encouraged by the degree of French cooperation that, by mid-April of 1941, there was strong consideration given to the idea that France should be permitted to keep some of their own gold. As one German official put it: "Such a demand [for all the French gold] could perhaps have been justified toward a France that was to be treated only as a vanquished foe, but France is now to be treated as an incipient ally. Such demands should not be maintained toward a prospective ally."[43]

The gold of the Bank of France was worth $2,000 million on the eve of the German invasion, but about two-thirds of this was moved quickly to the United States, Canada, and Great Britain. Most of the remainder went to French colonial possessions and only a limited amount was kept in metropolitan France. By even modest calculations this left Vichy in

41. Ibid., pp. 127–28.
42. Rings, *Raubgold*, pp. 23–25.
43. *D.G.F.P.*, ser. D, vol. 13, p. 27.

control of several hundred million dollars in gold in Martinique, Casablanca, and Dakar. Despite their relatively close working relationship, de Boisanger never supplied Hemmen with any exact figures on these various gold supplies. By providing the Germans with Belgian gold and the possibility of Polish gold, the French succeeded in saving most of their own. When interrogated on this point after the war one of the Reichsbank directors, Karl Friedrich Wilhelm, stated bluntly, "No gold owned by France was seized because the French had transported their own gold."[44]

No matter how desperately the war machine at home needed refueling, the Germans found it absolutely necessary to channel some of the precious gold into occupied areas at times. Despite every effort to make occupation currency effective in the purchase of desired goods in the local market, it rarely succeeded in bringing forth those goods that could be sold illegally. Depending on the particular situation, quantities of gold had to be pumped into the black market by the German occupiers in order to bring the wanted items to the surface.[45]

Such fiscal maneuvers only reflected the chronic failure of most military occupations, namely, the reluctance of a people to accept occupation money when barter was more advantageous. A currency especially created for an occupied state, without the support of a gold reserve and with a restricted circulation, is doomed from the beginning. At first Germany introduced an exchange control that prohibited the export of foreign currency, securities, or precious metals in all occupied states; this was relaxed somewhat in certain areas. In each state an issuing bank was established which handled the clearing process. It was generally responsible to the existing national or central bank and was granted authority to issue notes with cover coming from credit, loans, foreign currency (including the Reichsmark), and the Reichskreditkasse. The absence of gold was still the problem, however:

> The fact that the gold foreign exchange reserves were removed from occupied Europe, in part by the governments-in-exile and in part through confiscation by Germany, as well as the fact that claims against Germany in the form of frozen clearing assets or *Reichskreditkassenscheine* were introduced as cover for the new issues of local currencies, makes it obvious that the new currencies have no financial foundation whatsoever.[46]

44. NA, RG 260, OMGUS FINAD, "Wilhelm Memorandum for the Files," n.d., p. 1.
45. Ibid., Jahnke report, p. 2; and Boelcke, "Zur internationalen Goldpolitik des NS-Staates," p. 307. Gold was not the only thing that would lure goods out of hiding; sometimes precious stones, especially diamonds, were needed, ibid.
46. Raphael Lemkin, *Axis Rule in Occupied Europe* (New York: Howard Fertig, 1973), p. 56. See also *I.M.T.*, vol. 5, pp. 564ff.

Clearing, a vital institution in banking, is the adjustment of mutual claims by exchanging them and thereby settling the balances.[47] In the existing relationship between Germany and the controlled banking systems in the occupied states, it was obvious that "mutual claims" was not an accurate description of the clearing activity. Characterizing the steps of clearing in German foreign-trade transactions as inducive, oppressive, and spoilative, Raphael Lemkin, an early student of German economic behavior in occupied Europe, wrote:

> In this latter stage, which has now been reached [1942], Germany has frozen the clearing assets of the occupied countries for the so-called "duration." In the present situation, German trade is backed in the occupied countries by political power, and therefore economic and financial considerations count only to the extent that they are useful to Germany.[48]

Through clearings from Berlin, trade was conducted that involved transactions between two German-occupied states, or an occupied state and a neutral one, or an occupied state and a German ally. Most of these accounts were processed through the German Clearing Institute (Verrechnungskasse). By 1941 Germany had actually become Europe's banker, with over twenty-five banks around Europe.[49] Only early freezing measures taken by the United States and Great Britain prevented the Germans from gaining even larger quantities of wealth. By the beginning of 1941 the American and British freezing orders had shut Germany out from the wealth deposited abroad by every state under German occupation.[50] The two Western allies also brought strong economic pressure against neutrals and their citizens who continued to do business with Germany, applying the British Statutory List and the American Proclaimed List, which made the properties of such neutrals subject to seizure.

As the German economic situation worsened, the more important a continued gold supply became. By 1942, however, the Germans had "purchased," requisitioned, and seized all of the monetary gold that was available to them from Europe's central banks. It was at this juncture that

47. "The principle of the clearing system is as follows: The importer makes a deposit of the purchase in his own currency at the national clearing agency of his own country, which places the same amount to the credit of the clearing agency of the exporting country. The latter institution then pays the exporter in his own currency. Thus, if trade between the two countries is unequal the clearing agency of one acquires a claim against the agency of the other which, however, is satisfied only when a shift in the balance of trade gives rise to an offsetting claim," *N.C.A.*, vol. 1, p. 1068.

48. Lemkin, *Axis Rule*, p. 59.

49. Reville, *Spoil of Europe*, p. 147.

50. NA, T–501, 363, 9, "Wert der ausländischen Guthaben," 11 February 1941.

another source appeared, not as large, but still welcome. This was the gold taken from concentration-camp victims and stolen by the SS from other sources. Later the victorious Allies would decide that SS loot found in Reichsbank holdings should be excluded from their program of restitution, for it was not monetary nor usually identifiable. This had not minimized the value it represented to the Reichsbank, the Four-Year Plan or the SS during war, however.

Since the Reichsbank was such a vital institution to the success of Hitler's programs and was run by Nazis, it is difficult to regard it as very much different from any other bureau or ministry that served National Socialism. The Reichsbank had developed the hidden-gold-reserve program essential to war preparation and had readily filled the role of the master institution that absorbed, processed, and dispensed looted monetary gold from Europe's other banks. In so doing, the Reichsbank had engaged in extremely unethical banking practices, not to mention illegal ones such as falsifying the origins of looted gold. The Reichsbank was not able to dispose of its treasures without help, and the responsibility for a substantial share of its success must be borne by certain neutral nations and their banks. If there had been a unanimous refusal to deal in questionable or looted gold, as the Allies urged, important portions of the German armaments industry would have been badly crippled or even halted entirely. Therefore, it is really impossible to point the finger of blame at the Reichsbank without casting the net wider. The same is not true when dealing with loot received from the SS. Here the Reichsbank and its leaders incriminated themselves in conduct that definitely separated them from the rest of the banking world.

When the SS decided in 1942 that it needed the Reichsbank's services there was no hesitation on Funk's part to commit the bank to functions that he knew were criminal. There had been, of course, previous contact with the SS on a purely business level involving equipment loans, etc., but to accept, store, and dispose of SS loot was a considerably different matter. While the question may be asked whether or not Funk and his people really had any choice as to which services they offered and which they withheld, there is no evidence that even in casual conversation with his staff the Reichsbank president ever expressed any reservations. Puhl said that in principle neither he nor Funk had any objections to doing business with the SS; that it was looked upon as any other state organization with the same rights to services of the Reichsbank. He only thought, he explained, that there might be "difficulties" in agreeing to accept everything the SS wanted them to because there could be problems in storage and disposal that the bank was not equipped to handle. This possibility was once broached at a directors' meeting, Puhl recalled, but there was no real discussion of it, and it was not mentioned again. He did remember remarking on it to Funk, but Funk only said that by assisting the SS they were aiding their country. Puhl said Funk never did provide him with any details of the operation, nor did he give Puhl any exact idea of just what the SS would be bringing into the bank.[51]

The attitude reflected by the lower echelon bank personnel appears to have been simply an acceptance of the policy that came down to them from Funk or Puhl, and no question of individual responsibility seems to have been raised. Albert Thoms, head of the Precious Metals Department, probably spoke for most of his colleagues when he said that longtime employees just took orders without question. The bank directors were irreproachable, and the employees were not disturbed by the nature of the business with the SS: "I have already said that the term 'booty' was not unknown to us officials in the Reichsbank," Thoms stated, "because there was the order that all booty goods which came from the Army were to be delivered directly to the . . . Treasury of the Reich Government; and we in the Bank thought, of course, that the booty from the SS troops was to go through the Reichsbank."[52] When asked if he ever considered the association with the SS one that involved the Reichsbank in criminal activity, Thoms answered:

We assumed that these goods which the SS—after they had partly burned down towns in the East, particularly in the battle for Warsaw—we thought that afterward they captured this booty in the houses and then delivered this booty to our Bank. . . . It does not follow that an official who is entrusted with the handling of these things would have to consider these deliveries as being criminal.[53]

When asked much the same thing, Funk pleaded complete ignorance of the nature of business with the SS and their loot. He tried to shift the fault to others in the bank including Puhl, whom he blamed specifically for not informing him about what was going on. Under intensive questioning at Nuremberg, Funk said he could only vaguely recall that at one time a Reichsbank director, Herr Wilhelm, had cautioned him that the SS affair had presented the bank with a "serious responsibility . . . a heavy burden. . . . How could I," Funk pleaded, "have inferred from this that it was a moral burden?"[54]

A secret American military report in 1945 on "SS Loot and the

51. *I.M.T.*, vol. 13, pp. 566–68.
52. Ibid., p. 607.
53. Ibid.
54. Ibid., vol. 21, p. 241.

Reichsbank" noted: "The Reichsbank's awareness of wrong is attested to by the fact that all of the instructions and agreements were oral and all people participating in it were enjoined to utmost secrecy. The only writings that exist are the bookkeeping records and the correspondence resulting from the execution of the agreement [with the SS]."[55] Albert Thoms agreed that extreme secrecy surrounded the whole thing: "I would say that it went beyond the limits of top secrecy. For even I had been strictly forbidden to talk to anybody about it." On the other hand, Thoms estimated that there were probably twenty-five to thirty people in the bank who at one time or another were engaged in receiving and sorting SS deliveries arriving in the strong room. In addition, there was a constant stream of employees who routinely visited the strong room in the course of their daily work. It was true that the SS loot came in sealed boxes, but Thoms said it all had to be unpacked and sorted for inventory, which was done by spreading it over the room on tables.[56] It was Puhl's opinion that the business with the SS was a topic of general gossip in the Reichsbank, and while the details may have been missing, he was certain it was no secret. It was really unavoidable for employees had to be used to do the work and they had eyes to see what the SS shipments contained, he said.[57]

It was Funk's claim, when testifying at Nuremberg, that the affair with the SS began in the summer of 1942, when Reichsführer Himmler told him that they had ". . . confiscated a large amount of valuables [including gold] in the East, and we would like to deposit them in the Reichsbank." The Reichsbank president said that the conversation was very brief and he asked Himmler no questions. Later, when SS deposits began arriving at the bank, "Puhl and, as I recall, Wilhelm were present at a discussion, and they said that I should ask Himmler whether these things which had been sent by the SS as their deposit . . . whether they could be used by the Reichsbank. I did ask him and he said yes."[58] It was Funk's impression that this conversation marked the first time any business of this sort with the SS was ever discussed and that he did not ask what kind of deposits would be forthcoming nor their source; he assumed that they would be primarily gold and foreign money: "Thereupon I asked him [Himmler] to appoint someone to discuss the matter with Vice President Puhl."[59]

It was then arranged that Obergruppenführer Oswald Pohl, head of the SS fiscal affairs (Wirtschafts- und Verwaltungshauptamt), which included

55. NA, RG 260, OMGUS AG, 1945–46, Bernstein to Clay, 30 October 1945, report, "SS Loot and the Reichsbank," pt. 1, p. 2.

56. *I.M.T.*, vol. 13, pp. 603–4, 607, 611.

57. Ibid., pp. 584–85.

58. Ibid., p. 245.

59. Ibid., vol. 21, p. 238.

the administration of the concentration camps, would visit Puhl's office to work out the details. Puhl said he learned of all this when he, together with Reichsbank directors Wilhelm and Max Kretzschmann, met with Funk soon after his conversation with Himmler. Funk told them that he had agreed to accept SS deposits of gold and currency and other items for safekeeping. He mentioned that "other items" meant jewelry confiscated from occupied states. The proceeds from anything that was sold would be credited to a Reichsbank account. Puhl remembered that when he and Wilhelm remarked on the unusual nature of the deposits, they were advised not to inquire into the source of the loot. Funk said that the SS felt that they no longer had adequate storage space or security for the increasing volume of loot in their own cellars.[60]

The Reichsbank vice-president had known Oswald Pohl previously when bank credit had been extended to the SS; however, this had been largely conducted by telephone and Pohl had never been in Puhl's office. Puhl related that shortly after the Funk–Himmler talk, Pohl "telephoned me and asked if I had been advised of the matter. I said I would not discuss it by telephone. He then came to see me and reported that the SS had some jewelry for delivery to the Reichsbank for safekeeping. I arranged with him for delivery and from then on deliveries were made from time to time, from August 1942 throughout the following years."[61]

After it was established at the Nuremberg trial that Oswald Pohl had occupied such a central position of power in administering the concentration-camp system, many of the defendants attempted to distance themselves from him, which may account for Funk's denial that he had ever discussed anything with Pohl. Funk said that "before this trial I did not even know that the concentration camps were under Pohl's jurisdiction. I had no idea of the connection between the economic department of the SS and the concentration camps." In spite of Pohl's own testimony that he had discussed SS affairs with Funk in several instances, even telling him on one occasion that the deliveries were goods taken from dead Jews, Funk swore that he had only seen Pohl one time. "I saw him once at the bank, when he was having lunch with Mr. Puhl. . . . I passed through the room and I saw him sitting there. I myself . . . never discussed these matters with Herr Pohl." Funk later amended this testimony, admitting that he had seen Pohl perhaps three times.[62]

The arrangement between the Reichsbank and the SS was not based upon a written agreement since, given the nature of the business, everyone

60. NA, RG 260, OMGUS AG, 1945–46, Bernstein to Clay, 30 October 1945, "SS Loot and the Reichsbank," pt. 2, p. 7; and *I.M.T.*, vol. 13, p. 565.
61. *I.M.T.*, vol. 13, p. 171.
62. Ibid., pp. 233–34, 241.

seemed to be in accord that the less committed to paper the better. The bank machinery was put in motion to accept and process the SS deliveries "in accordance with an oral directive from Reichsbank President Dr. Walter Funk to Emil Puhl, the Vice-President of the Reichsbank. Schwerin von Krosigk, the Minister of Finance, also knew of the arrangements."[63] It was from Puhl that the rest of the bank staff received their instructions, and as Albert Thoms later said:

> The matter was treated as a verbal arrangement. . . . In matters concerning gold particularly instructions had to be given and approved respectively by the Board of Directors. I could therefore never act independently. Generally the instructions were given in writing and they were signed by at least two officials and one member of the Board of Directors. So that it was quite unique that in this case instructions were given in verbal form.[64]

After Funk informed him that bank services were now at the disposal of the SS, Puhl called in Reichsbank director Fromknecht, Thoms, and the director of the Hauptkasse, and told them that the bank would soon be receiving gold, silver, currency, and other valuables from the SS for deposit. He explained that the deliveries would also contain other properties, primarily jewelry, and that the Reichsbank had agreed to dispose of them. They were instructed to work out the necessary procedures for dealing with the assignment and, above all, keep it secret. If anyone inquired, they were to say they had the strictest orders to maintain secrecy and could not discuss it.[65] Puhl said that once he had put matters in motion he did not concern himself with day-to-day operations anymore, he rarely spoke with the staff about the shipments ("Herr Thoms himself admits that he did not see me at all for months"), and nothing more on the subject was discussed at bank conferences.[66]

In keeping with the policy of absolute secrecy, Puhl said, the Reichsbank decided to avoid using the words "SS Economic Department" in their records and substituted the general designation "head of a Berlin public office" for all references to Pohl. All SS deliveries to the Reichsbank were entered in the books under the code name of "Melmer."[67] Entrusted with servicing the SS account, Thoms contacted Pohl's office for details on deliveries and was told that they would arrive by truck and each trans-

63. NA, RG 260, OMGUS AG, 1945–46, Bernstein to Clay, 30 October 1945, "SS Loot," pt. 1, p. 2.

64. *I.M.T.*, vol. 13, p. 604.

65. NA, RG 260, OMGUS AG, 1945–46, Bernstein to Clay, 30 October 1945, "SS Loot," pt. 1, pp. 1–2.

66. *I.M.T.*, vol. 13, p. 585.

67. Ibid., pp. 583 and 602.

action would be monitored by an SS man named Melmer, who was to receive a receipt and tell Thoms which account was to be credited. Although Melmer was to wear civilian clothes, Thoms said that sometimes SS men came in uniform to help with the unloading.[68]

The SS deliveries contained jewelry of all kinds, eyeglass frames, dental gold, gold objects, bank notes, gold and silver coins, securities, platinum, precious stones, and valuable stamp collections. There was no schedule or size for the deliveries, although Thoms said there was never more than one truck load at a time and often smaller deliveries came in a regular passenger car.[69] In this manner, starting in August 1942, the SS made a total of seventy-six deliveries to the Reichsbank in Berlin. The value of the loot was estimated at approximately $14,500,000; of that sum, the largest amount came from foreign bank notes and gold.[70] Some months after the deliveries started Thoms said Puhl once asked him how things were going with the "Melmer affair," whereupon Thoms "explained to him that, contrary to the expectation that there would really be few deliveries, deliveries were increasing and that apart from the gold and silver coins they contained a great deal of jewelry, gold rings, wedding rings, gold and silver fragments, dental gold, and all sorts of gold and silver articles."[71] Thoms remembered that sometime in April 1943 slips of identification paper began appearing in the shipments with the names "Lublin" and "Auschwitz." He recalled an earlier delivery of gold teeth in November 1942 that had the stamp "Auschwitz" on it. At one point, Thoms said, "I called Vice President Puhl's attention to the composition of these deliveries. . . . He knew the contents of the deliveries."[72]

When the Reichsbank evacuated its holdings from Berlin in early 1945, the remaining SS deposits went to the Kaiseroda Mine at Merkers along with everything else. After the American forces found the Reichsbank gold horde there in April, the SS properties were not immediately evaluated with the rest but stored separately pending a later decision on their disposition. Throughout the war the Reichsbank had maintained about $30,500,000 in gold as a stationary backup for the paper currency in circulation in the Reich, but much of this was later transported to Merkers, too. When the Russians captured Berlin they found only about $4,300,000 in gold remaining in the Reichsbank, without a doubt a major disappointment.

68. NA, RG 260, OMGUS AG, 1945–46, Bernstein to Clay, 30 October 1945, "SS Loot," pt. 2, p. 2.
69. *I.M.T.*, vol. 13, pp. 615–16.
70. NA, RG 260, OMGUS AG, 1945–46, Bernstein to Clay, 30 October 1945, "SS Loot," pt. 1, Summary, p. 1. See also *New York Times*, 29 October 1945, p. 6.
71. *I.M.T.*, vol. 13, p. 602.
72. Ibid., pp. 608–10.

CHAPTER 3

The Swiss Connection

The manpower and wealth of occupied Europe were vital supports in the German war economy, but the unoccupied nations of Europe provided equally important services. These nations—Portugal, Spain, Turkey, Sweden, and Switzerland—varied widely in their forms of government, social structure, and political attitudes toward Hitler's National Socialist state. The ideological sentiments of Sweden and Switzerland reflected strong democratic institutions, quite different from the dictatorial and semi-Fascist states of Spain, Portugal, and Turkey, which found far less difficulty in engaging in financial and trade relations with the Germans. Each of the neutrals shared the fear that refusal to cooperate with Germany would lead to dire consequences. In terms of the importance of a gold outlet Switzerland eventually became the single indispensable state of the five neutrals, the only one Germany could not afford to occupy.

In the early years of the war each German success increased their control over the resources of the neutrals but later, as Allied military strength grew, the neutrals found themselves in the unenviable position of being pressed from both sides, although the Allies never succeeded in matching the German influence. Great Britain and the United States were never in complete agreement on the methods to be employed in applying pressures on certain neutrals. It was the British fear that tough U.S. economic measures against Spain would drive that nation into an alliance with Hitler and endanger Gibraltar. A frustrated American assistant secretary of state wrote, "the British thwarted all our efforts to use to the utmost our considerable powers to limit Franco's help to Germany."[1]

While Dr. Antonio Salazar's Portuguese regime was not that much different from Franco's, it had stronger ties to Great Britain and later granted the Allies the use of bases in the Azores. Trade with Germany

1. Dean Acheson, *Present at the Creation* (New York: W.W. Norton and Co., 1946), p. 53.

was not neglected, however, and after the war Allied investigators were able to identify over 950 bars of gold held in the Bank of Portugal as resmelted Belgian gold. Portuguese bank records were not made available, but the assumption was that these gold bars only represented a small portion of the looted gold that Germany had sent to Portugal during the war. A confidential Allied report noted:

> We also learned that much of the gold purchased by the Bank of Portugal from the Reichsbank depot in Switzerland was dated 1942 and accordingly does not consist of resmelted Belgian gold. However, . . . the bulk of the gold resmelted by the Prussian mint in 1942 consisted of . . . Netherlands bars. Accordingly we feel there is a strong presumption that the 1942 gold consists of gold taken by Germany from Holland.[2]

The importance of this complex banking subterfuge to the German economy is illustrated in a note from Johannes Hemmen when he wrote in May 1941 that a quantity of the Belgian gold in transit from West Africa had been diverted directly to Lisbon from Casablanca for credit by the Anglo-American Bank; it was then used for purchases from the United States![3]

Of the five neutrals, perhaps Turkey played the least important role in Germany's war economy although its geography was of importance. Like the Portuguese, the Turks were beneficiaries first of British and later of American aid as well, but this was no preventive to trading with Germans when the price was right.

As the neutral in the north, Sweden fully recognized that its independence was a precarious condition valid only as long as it served the German purpose. Compromise and cooperation were the roads to neutral survival and despite the most persistent of Allied efforts to force Sweden to reduce trade and concessions to Germany, only Allied victory could change the situation, although there were indications that even gold was beginning to lose its allure for the Swedes by the summer of 1944.[4] The relationship did not end though, for Puhl made a very successful visit to Stockholm in July, reporting that Germany would be able to sell gold to the Swedish Notenbank; this meant that they could now go outside the commercial clearing for the purchase of desired materials, an avenue that

2. NA, RG 260, OMGUS AG, 1945–46, "Gold Looted by Germany and Sold to the Bank of Portugal," 10 October 1946, and attached secret telegrams, 3 October 1946. Rings denies that any quantity of Dutch gold was resmelted; he wrote that it went into Swiss bank vaults untouched, *Raubgold*, p. 41.

3. NA, T–501, 363, 146.

4. Boelcke, "Zur internationalen Goldpolitik des NS-Staates," p. 309.

had heretofore been blocked.[5] Swedish commercial relations with Nazi Germany did not cease until December.

To Germany, Switzerland was without question the most important of the neutrals and proved the most difficult for the Allies to deal with. In the words of one American closely involved, "If the Swedes were stubborn, the Swiss were the cube of stubbornness."[6] Completely surrounded in a world at war, overpopulated, totally dependent on imports, Switzerland's options were nonexistent, and yet the Germans presented no ultimatums. It may be argued that no ultimatums were necessary given the Swiss vulnerability, but no doubt the nature of Allied pressures at the time reinforced the Swiss "stubbornness." Switzerland produced many useful items for the German war machine, but the heart of their commercial relationship rested upon the German gold transfers that provided credit and currencies.[7] It was the opinion of the German Foreign Office that the Swiss saw a certain stability in their situation by providing Germany with this service and that the feeling increased with Hitler's attack on the Soviet Union in June 1941. Not only did it move the war front far away, but "the major factor contributing to this sense of security of the Swiss evidently is the conviction that Germany, more than ever before, now had a direct interest in preserving Switzerland's position of neutrality and dependence for the duration of the war."[8] No matter how naive some of the Swiss bankers pretended to be, they could not turn a deaf ear to the warnings from foreign banks and governments that the gold flowing from Germany was looted from occupied Europe. The Swiss refusal to alter their policy of accepting gold from Germany until nearly the end of the war was to leave a deep and lingering bitterness. Writing more than twenty years after the event, former Secretary of State Dean Acheson noted, "Finally, in April 1945, the Swiss surrendered—only a month before General Jodl did."[9]

Germany's ability to dispose of large quantities of looted gold in Switzerland was greatly aided by the Swiss–German clearing agreements signed during the war years. In fact, the German opinion was that these agreements definitely placed the Swiss financial community in a compromised position. A secret German Foreign Office report stated:

The trade agreement recently concluded [18 July 1941] with Germany was just the outer frame of this development from which Switzerland simply could not

5. BA, NS6, Akt. 506, Funk to Führerhauptquartier, 5 July 1944.
6. Acheson, *Present at the Creation*, p. 52.
7. Ring, *Goldraub*, pp. 121–29.
8. *D.G.F.P.*, vol. 13, p. 332.
9. Acheson, *Present at the Creation*, p. 59.

escape whether or not she wished to do so. . . . Switzerland has . . . now committed herself to making continuing deliveries to the Reich on credit only, the value of which . . . will perhaps run from 800 millions to 1 billion a year.[10]

Each agreement was generally for a short duration, usually six months, and by 1944 the Germans were experiencing increasing problems as the Allies concentrated on Swiss gold and currency transactions that came from German sources. Karl Schnurre, a political trade expert in the German Foreign Office, complained that the pressures on the Swiss were growing daily and hinted that after the current clearing-agreement extension (29 July 1944) permitting the Reichsbank to sell gold and purchase needed currencies, the end was in sight.[11]

One of the Reichsbank directors, Karl Friedrich Wilhelm, who was in charge of the bank's Foreign Exchange Department, said that the Swiss government had requested that any direct gold transactions be conducted with the Swiss National Bank. "We lived up to that agreement," Wilhelm stated, "we have been doing business in gold in Switzerland for the past five or six years. . . . Switzerland was used as a clearing house for all our foreign transactions during the war. When the gold was transported to Switzerland, we usually had a couple of armed guards from the bank accompany it on the train."[12] The amount of gold that Germany sent to Switzerland from March 1940 until the end of hostilities was over $378 million. Together with the $252 million the Americans found at Merkers, the total approximates very closely the $625 million in gold carried on the Reichsbank books as the amount secured from occupation sources during the war.[13]

The Swiss bankers were only too aware that as the rest of neutral Europe became increasingly reluctant to accept gold directly from Germany, the neutrals had no problems accepting gold, or at least Swiss gold francs, from Switzerland. With a virtual monopoly over European gold trading, the Swiss accepted the Reichsbank gold bars—24,460 of them—for their depot in the Swiss National Bank of Bern, and the desired gold and currencies then passed into the banks of Sweden, Portugal,

10. *D.G.F.P.*, vol 13, p. 333; and BA, R2, 391, Bericht des Bundesrates usw., Drittes Zusatzabkommen zum Abkommen von 9. August 1940 über den deutsch–schweizerischen Verrechnungsverkehr, pp. 12–15. See also Robert Urs Vogler, *Die Wirtschaftsverhandlungen zwischen der Schweiz und Deutschland, 1940 und 1941* (Zurich: Schweizerische National Bank, 1983), pp. 150ff. and 213ff; Horst Zimmermann, *Die Schweiz und Grossdeutschland* (Munich: Wilhelm Fink Verlag, 1980), pp. 415ff; and Heinrich Homberger, *Schweizerische Handelspolitik im Zweiten Weltkrieg* (Erlenbach-Zurich: Eugen Rentsch Verlag, 1970), pp. 23ff.

11. Germany, *Akten zur deutschen auswärtigen Politik, 1918–1945*, ser. E, 1941–45, vol. 8 (Göttingen: Vandenhoeck and Rupricht, 1979), pp. 614–15.

12. NA, RG 260, OMGUS FINAD, Wilhelm Memorandum, 1 May 1946, p. 1.

13. Ibid., "Overall Gold Report," 20 November 1946, p. 2.

Turkey, Romania, and others.[14]

A key figure in all of this, perhaps indispensable, was Reichsbank vice-president Emil Puhl. The close personal contact that Puhl enjoyed with Ernst Weber, president of the Swiss National Bank, insured a smooth working relationship. It permitted the conduct of much business on the basis of an oral commitment, a practice only possible because of Puhl's status and reputation. When, from time to time, his Swiss friends expressed any misgivings about the origin of so much gold from the Reichsbank, Puhl reassured them that they were not dealing in looted gold. In fact, he told them that the gold stock from the occupied nations was stored separately from Reichsbank gold. These assurances were given at the very time that large quantities of looted gold began arriving in Switzerland with counterfeit papers, falsified stamps, and prewar bar dates.[15]

The Reichsbank gold program was ably assisted by the Bank for International Settlements, located in Basel, Switzerland. It was really a world bank and because of this enjoyed unique financial powers, one of which was keeping gold for central banks. The fact that the BIS[16] was headquartered in Basel did not make it a Swiss bank exactly, although it was granted extraordinary privileges by that nation. It was established under international charter in 1930 to further the cooperation among central banks searching for financial settlements and adjustments in the maze of First World War payments. By virtue of a convention signed by Germany, Belgium, France, Great Britain, Northern Ireland, Italy, Japan, and Switzerland, and with a subscribed charter from the central banks of those countries plus the United States, the BIS was guaranteed an absolutely untouchable status. Switzerland granted virtual exemption from their laws: "The Charter provides that the Bank, its property and assets, and all deposits and other funds entrusted to it shall be immune in time of peace and in time of war from any measure such as appropriation."[17]

Some observers felt that the idea for the bank came from Germany's Hjalmar Schacht[18] and certainly both he and Emil Puhl exerted much

14. Rings, *Goldraub*, pp. 63–68 and 195. Rings noted that there were four hundred banks in Switzerland—both Swiss and foreign—and just how much looted gold went into their vaults and how much they sold would be impossible to determine, ibid., p. 57.

15. Ibid., p. 48. Rings wrote that Weber even asked Puhl as late as 1944, "Sie schicken uns doch kein gestohlenes Gold?" ibid., p. 49.

16. While commonly referred to as "BIS" in English, the French is "BRI" (Banque de Reglements Internationaux) and the German is "BIZ" (Bank für internationalen Zahlungsausgleich).

17. Henry H. Schloss, *The Bank for International Settlements* (Amsterdam: North Holland Publishing Co., 1958), p. 38.

18. James S. Martin, *All Honorable Men* (Boston: Little, Brown, and Co., 1950), p. 281; and Charles Higham, *Trading with the Enemy* (New York: Delacorte Press, 1983), p. 1.

influence on BIS behavior at times. The first managing director of the BIS was, however, an American banker, Gates W. McGarrah, who had been with the Chase National Bank and the Federal Reserve Bank in New York. From the very outset the BIS placed high priority on secrecy in dealings, which meant avoidance of publicity as much as possible. Public relations were nonexistent, all actions remained strictly private, and meetings were closed to outsiders. It simply was not a bank in the conventional sense for its Basel headquarters was not open to the public and did not have any counters with windows and clerks, only conference rooms. Gold under BIS deposit remained in the vaults and strong rooms of the central-bank subscribers, which included, of course, the nearby Swiss National Bank in Bern.[19]

Soon after the BIS began business one of the primary reasons for its creation, helping with the administration of reparation payments, ceased to exist, although it still had the responsibility and function to facilitate closer working relations among the central-bank subscribers. It soon found its mission in attempting to save the gold standard and, working from an earlier proposal to establish an international system of gold clearing, the BIS aimed to make most gold transactions an act of book-keeping. This would end the practice of shipping gold provided that a large part of the world's monetary gold was on deposit with the BIS. It was a plan that found willing clients among the central banks, and there was a steady rise in the earmarked gold accounts with the BIS during the decade before the war.[20]

The BIS certainly did not care for the glare of publicity received as a result of its role in the Czech gold affair, but that did not deter the bank from continuing its profitable policies. A secret 1945 American government study on the wartime activities of the BIS and the gold question opened with the following paragraphs:

A significant by-product of the Gold Studies . . . was the repeatedly encountered evidence of the Reichmark's remarkably close and solicitous relationship with the Bank for International Settlements throughout the war, which raised strong suspicion of still unrevealed war-time advantages accruing to the Reichsbank, and to the German Reich in general from their relationship with the BIS.

Preliminary investigations in Germany have revealed some of the war-time activities of the B.I.S. which were of obvious advantage to the Germans and probably explain their concern for its continuance and welfare. This evidence

19. Roger Aubion, *The Bank for International Settlements, 1930–1955* (Princeton, NJ: Princeton University Essays in International Finance, 1955), p. 6.
20. Schloss, *The Bank for International Settlements*, pp. 86–87.

from German sources is sufficient to raise serious questions as to the legitimacy of much of the war-time business of the B.I.S.[21]

There have been any number of descriptions of the BIS and its directing personnel, some defensive, others offensive, depending on the particular source.[22] The international character of the bank's directorate during the war—composed as it was of American, German, Japanese, Italian, British, and Swiss members—made its activities controversial. Accusations that the top Swiss BIS people were more pro-German than the situation demanded began to surface before the war when the BIS president was a Dutchman named Johan Beyen. When British Lord Strabolgi was taking the BIS to task for transfering the Czech gold to the Reichsbank, he told his assembled peers that Beyen, at that point about to depart for a new position with Unilever, was a man with "well-known Nazi sympathies."[23]

Beyen's successor was an American named Thomas H. McKittrick, a New York banker who would soon become as controversial as Mr. Beyen. The growing body of American critics[24] was reluctant to accept the fact that an American now headed an institution that aided in carrying out the gold policies of the German Reichsbank. The situation was further aggravated in 1942, when McKittrick was endorsed by both Italy and Germany for another term. This event was described in the secret American gold report in rather precise and unmistakable terms: "It is clear from correspondence and from testimony that the management of the B.I.S. during the war was in the hands of the Administrative Council, in which Axis representatives have an authoritative influence, and that in 1942 the Germans favored the reelection of President McKittrick, whose 'Personal opinions' they characterized as 'safely known.'"[25]

There was no doubt that McKittrick occupied an extraordinary position and was accorded privileges that were nothing short of amazing considering that most of Europe was occupied by Germany. In late 1942 and into 1943, the American president of the BIS left his wartime domicile in Switzerland, a totally landlocked neutral surrounded by the Axis partners of Germany and Italy, and traveled to New York and back. Under the circumstances this was a journey that could only have been taken with complete Italian and German cooperation, for McKittrick had

21. NA, RG 260, OMGUS A, 1945–46, McNarney to Nixon, 30 November 1945, p. 1.

22. See, for example, Aubion, *The Bank for International Settlements*; Beyen, *Money in a Maelstrom*; Higham, *Trading with the Enemy*; Reville, *Spoil of Europe*; Schloss, *The Bank for International Settlements*; and Ray Vicker, *Those Swiss Money Men* (New York: Charles Scribner's Sons, 1973).

23. *Parliamentary Debates*, House of Lords, vol. 114, no. 84, 11 July 1939, pp. 505–53.

24. See *Morgenthau Diary*, vol. 1, pp. 1570ff; and Higham, *Trading with the Enemy*, pp. 7ff.

25. NA, RG 332, ETO, SGS, 123/2, McNarney to Nixon, 30 November 1945, p. 3.

to travel through Axis-held territory and war zones to reach his destination.[26] The cooperative spirit was not one-sided though, for McKittrick did enter and depart the United States as well and no doubt conducted business that was beneficial to the BIS. Puhl said later that after McKittrick had returned from his America trip, they had a long discussion, and the American gave him a "general picture of the current opinions and financial problems in the United States."[27] The pervasive influence of Nazi Germany in BIS affairs was not a new discovery with the beginning of the war but had been noticed some time before. In commentating on the annual meeting of the board of directors of the BIS in 1939, the *New York Times* made reference to the importance of Nazi racial policy in the bank management procedures: "Signor Nathan, who usually accompanies the Italian delegation, was excluded from his delegation because he had a Jewish grandmother."[28]

Since the BIS did not engage in conventional banking it did not require the usual banking quarters. There was no contact with the general public, and its gold, funds, and securities were (and are) kept at the central banks of the subscribers. This made it easy to relocate whenever the directorate deemed it necessary during the war. In September 1940 the BIS announced a temporary move from Basel to a hotel in the village of Château d'Oex in the Bernese Alps, reportedly because of the fear of a German invasion, but business went on as usual. "It offers the unique spectacle of a meeting ground of high ranking representatives of warring countries who collaborate daily without a single hitch in the name of their respective banks."[29]

When the war began in September 1939, the BIS formally announced its neutrality, promising to avoid any transaction that threatened to compromise the bank's standing, and declared "in a general way, to subject every operation to a searching scrutiny . . . especially from the standpoint of the rules of conduct which the Bank had laid down for itself."[30] By any standards these were admirable aims, but the Czechoslovakian episode was of too recent a vintage in the minds of many persons to dispel the doubt that the BIS would follow a hands-off policy regarding the gold that the Reichsbank had available. With business already sharply reduced due to the war, the BIS faced continuing losses unless it decided that Germany and the states occupied by that nation were viable markets

---

26. Higham, *Trading with the Enemy*, p. 11; and Schloss, *The Bank for International Settlements*, p. 116.

27. NA, RG 332, ETO, SGS, 123/2, McNarney to Nixon, 30 November 1945, p. 4.

28. *New York Times*, 8 May 1939, p. 30.

29. Ibid., 30 September 1939, p. 25.

30. Aubion, *The Bank for International Settlements*, p. 14.

for banking services.

The BIS staunchly defended its acceptance of German payments in gold (as interest on BIS-held investments) by insisting that to refuse only meant injury to the creditors. In the words of the BIS general manager, "After careful examination of the questions involved, the Bank decided: (1) to accept gold in respect of all transfers legally due to it; and, (2) to take steps to insure that at some future date an enquiry could be made into the origin of all gold bars which it had received."[31] Roger Aubion, the BIS general manager under McKittrick, said the dilemma was that "certain central banks had one managing body in the occupied territory and another on foreign soil, and to try to avoid problems it was decided . . . to offset in the Bank's books, whenever practicable, the claims and debts of the Bank in relation to each of the markets involved, so as to obviate the necessity for any actual transfers." He admitted that when this procedure was not successful, the BIS tried to postpone any actions involving the assets in question.[32]

The secret American study of the BIS indicated a far less objective role for the Swiss-based bank and a definite German bias:

> Within 3 days after the occupation of Prague the BIS is known to have acceded to the instructions of the German dominated Czech bank to transfer their gold deposited with the BIS to the account of the German Reichsbank; Puhl testifies that no significant objections to this transaction were made in the BIS.

> By contrast, in July 1940 when the central banks of Lithuania, Estonia, and Latvia in a similar fashion ordered delivery of the gold in their BIS accounts to the Russian State Bank whom they declared to have purchased it, the BIS refused to recognize these instructions. This action, based upon legal opinion, concluded that: "These orders apparently did not result from the free will of the 3 banks, but have presumably been influenced by the will of the Soviet Russian Government or of the political party controlling the latter."[33]

The BIS maintained that by accepting German gold for prewar debt, regardless of its origin, it was helping deplete the Nazi gold reserves. This argument was put forth in connection with Germany's obligations under the Young Plan of 1929, wherein the BIS was required by the creditor governments to make substantial investments in the German capital and money markets. The interest on these investments was paid by the German Reichsbank to the BIS in Swiss francs (purchased with gold) or gold. According to the BIS this arrangement continued without interrup-

31. Ibid., p. 16.
32. Ibid., pp. 15–16.
33. NA, RG 332, ETO, SGS, 123/2, McNarney to Nixon, 30 November 1945, pp. 4–5.

tion until 1942, but thereafter all payments by the Germans were made only in gold.[34]

The Allies, especially the Americans, strongly challenged the BIS assertion that it was draining off German gold by accepting it in payment. Instead, the acceptance of German gold actually increased the BIS annual dividends, a substantial portion of which went to various nations now occupied by the Germans: "This combination of transaction helped to keep up the presumption that the German investments of the B.I.S. were not frozen, but the actual sacrifice of the Reichsbank was less than would appear on the surface in so far as the gold given up to the B.I.S. was partly offset by the dividend indirectly acquired in Swiss francs."[35]

Even allowing that the BIS collections had some legitimacy, the secret American report could find no extenuating circumstances to excuse its receipt of the large quantities of gold from Berlin that were obviously looted. In one instance the BIS accepted gold that came directly fom the nation (Italy) from which it was looted. But "the most notorious case is that of the Belgian gold, a part of which, according to the testimony of former Reichsbank Vice President Puhl, was accepted by the BIS after McKittrick and other officials of that bank had been fully informed that it was Belgian gold for which payment by the Reichsbank had not been accepted."[36] Puhl also testified that BIS officials never made any effort to ascertain if the Germans had a gold equivalent. In every case the BIS accepted German assurances at face value long after McKittrick and Ernst Weber, director of the Swiss National Bank and chairman of the BIS administrative council, knew very well that the gold shipments "far exceeded the Reichsbank's published reserves of legitimately acquired gold; the records show that such shipments to the Swiss National Bank during the period from March 1940 to the end of the war alone totalled 378,000,000 dollars worth of gold, compared with the Reichsbank's published gold reserves of 29,000,000."[37] The BIS proved highly beneficial to the German Reichsbank in other ways too, Puhl testified. When various nations tried to block Reichsbank assets the services of the BIS could be extremely useful in making book transfers of balances, provided of course, there was sufficient warning. The Reichsbank was then able to dispose of the balances withdrawn directly with the BIS. In this manner, Puhl said, the Reichsbank salvaged many assets threatened by blocking.[38]

These activities certainly did not go unnoticed, but the BIS position

34. NA, RG 260, OMGUS FINAD, BIS President to L. Harrison, Bern, 2 May 1945, p. 1.
35. NA, RE 332, ETO, SGS, 123/2, McNarney to Nixon, 30 November 1945, pp. 4–5.
36. Ibid., pp. 1–2.
37. Ibid., p. 2.
38. Ibid., p. 3.

was virtually untouchable before the war and nothing could be done to restrict its actions. Not to be overlooked was the fact that the BIS had many powerful supporters in the international banking world, including Great Britain and the United States; nevertheless, the first serious attack upon the bank over the Czech affair in 1939 did come from the British. Frustrated at being unable to halt the Czech gold transfer to the Reichsbank, Britain's chancellor of the Exchequer, Sir John Simon, publicly advised a governmental review of his country's relationship to the BIS, implying the possibility of a withdrawal of British membership.[39] The opening of the war that summer swept away any further consideration of this issue, but the BIS was far from forgotten. When its 1942 annual report appeared and the data revealed a continued and close cooperation with the Reichsbank, it "aroused considerable indignation in England and the old cries of 1939 were resumed."[40] By this time the critics of the BIS had gained a powerful ally in American Treasury Secretary Henry Morgenthau.

An opportunity to strike a blow finally came with the convening of an Allied international monetary conference in July 1944. At Bretton Woods, New Hampshire, plans were drawn to create new financial institutions in anticipation of the economic problems that would come with peace: the International Monetary Fund and the International Bank for Reconstruction and Development.[41] Following directly upon a proposal by the Polish delegation at the Bretton Woods Monetary Conference that measures be adopted to prevent Nazi leaders from using gold to escape, the Norwegian delegation submitted a resolution to liquidate the BIS as soon as possible and meanwhile create an investigative body to examine the bank's wartime activities.[42]

It was clear when the conference opened that there were few neutral opinions where the BIS was concerned. Morgenthau introduced the question of looted property and the bank by commenting on Beyen, the former BIS president who was present at Bretton Woods as head of the Dutch delegation: "If anybody at anytime would like to know something more about him in the British Parliament, we have a very interesting document here." The American delegation then proceeded to draft a resolution calling upon all neutral states to halt the disposition or transfer

39. *New York Times*, 6 June, p. 6, and 21 June, p. 15.
40. Schloss, *The Bank for International Settlements*, pp. 116–17.
41. See *Proceedings and Documents of the United Nations Monetary and Financial Conference, Bretton Woods, New Hampshire, July 1–22, 1944* (Washington, D.C.: U.S.G.P.O., 1948); and *Bretton Woods Agreements Act: Hearings on Banking and Currency*, vol. 1, H.R., 79th Cong., 1st sess., 7–23 March 1945 (Washington, D.C.: U.S.G.P.O., 1945).
42. *Proceedings and Documents of the United Nations Monetary and Financial Conference*, p. 330.

of looted gold within their jurisdiction.[43]

There was a small but powerful body of resistance to any move that proposed immediate dissolution of the BIS, however. Dean Acheson, representing the U.S. State Department on the American delegation, thought any such action should be delayed until the war was over.[44] BIS General Manager Aubion suggested that any sentiment to dissolve the bank was based upon a lack of knowledge:

> Owing to the circumstances at the time, it is evident that little could be known concerning the precise nature of the Bank's activities during the war and its exact financial position, isolated as it was in a neutral country surrounded by belligerent countries and bound by the very rules of conduct which it had set itself to observe with the utmost discretion.[45]

Beyen and Aubion had the support of a number of influential American bankers who strongly opposed any action against the BIS and tried to block the Norwegian resolution entirely. One of these was Leon Fraser, head of the First National Bank of Manhattan and a former BIS president. He scoffed at the notion that the Germans exerted undue influence over the bank's actions and insisted that any hostility was politically motivated, fueled in part by President Roosevelt himself. In fact, Fraser contended that the BIS was really the logical institution around which postwar efforts for reconstruction should be centered.[46]

The resolution that finally passed did not include any provision to investigate the BIS, but did recommend liquidation "at the earliest possible moment."[47] Lord Keynes and the British delegation supported Acheson's position that the bank should be continued until the end of the war, although Keynes had agreed to Morgenthau's request for liquidation; the compromise was postponement.[48] Throughout the discussions centering on the BIS there appears to have been little or no consideration given to the question of authority, that is, did the Allies' meeting at Bretton Woods have the right to dissolve the BIS?

Of course, strictly speaking the BIS was not a Swiss bank, but the very

---

43. *Morgenthau Diary*, vol. 1, pp. 399–402. For an interesting description of some of the people attending the Bretton Woods Monetary Conference see Acheson, *Present at the Creation*, pp. 81ff.

44. *Proceedings*, pp. 404ff.

45. Aubion, *The Bank for International Settlements*, p. 17.

46. *Bretton Woods Agreement*, vol. 1, pp. 437–38.

47. *Proceedings*, p. 939. As soon as the war ended the Americans began conducting their own secret investigation of the BIS.

48. John Morton Blum, *From the Morgenthau Diaries*, vol. 2 (Boston: Houghton Mifflin Co., 1967), p. 268; and Armand van Dormael, *Bretton Woods: Birth of a Monetary System* (New York: Holmes and Meier Publishers, 1978), pp. 204–6.

privileged position that it occupied in that nation could not be overlooked. The close working relationship that the BIS enjoyed with Swiss banks, especially the Swiss National Bank headed by Ernst Weber, a member of the BIS directorate, virtually made Swiss banking policies at times indistinguishable from those of the BIS. The Swiss nation and its banking community had created an atmosphere of receptivity for Reichsbank transactions from the very outset of the war and had shared in the benefits. This provided a protection for the BIS that angered Allied leaders, who aimed their animosity at the entire Swiss banking system, although the BIS and Weber's Swiss National Bank remained special targets.

American frustration at being unable to document the dealings of the BIS and the Swiss National Bank in looted gold did not cease with the war's end. The American secret investigation of BIS wartime activities undertaken in November 1945 noted: "It is to be reiterated that tracing of the Belgian and other looted gold accepted by the BIS from the Reichsbank is dependent upon access to the Swiss National Bank's records concerning the Reichsbank's gold depot which was maintained there and through which nearly all these gold shipments were washed."[49] Despite the urgency to recover Reichsbank files after Germany's capitulation, the results were not entirely satisfactory. Record preservation had not been exactly a high priority in Germany during the last days of Hitler's empire, nor was it possible amidst the postwar chaos to locate people immediately who knew where materials were to be found.[50] Several months were to pass before the Americans were able to sift through what Reichsbank files they had found (mostly at the Merkers mine), and after doing so concluded that they needed to inspect the relevant files in the Swiss National Bank for a full picture. In August 1945, a secret U.S. Forces European Theater (USFET) report noted that "all investigations of the Reichsbank gold so far have shown the bulk of their gold shipments destined for Swiss National Bank in Bern. A part of these were certainly intended for the gold depot there in the name of the German Reichsbank."[51]

It was agreed that any further tracing of the dispositions of German looted gold, and especially the Belgian gold, required an inspection of the records in the Swiss National Bank. There was some reason to feel optimistic at this point, for the French were already in the process of arranging a visit to the Bern bank to try to trace the Belgian gold themselves (since the Bank of France was liable). The Americans decided that they could do the same. A USFET communique to Washington

49. NA, RG 332, ETO, SGS, 123/2, McNarney to Nixon, 25 November, p. 4.
50. See the Preface.
51. NA, RG 260 OMGUS FINAD, Nixon to Bernstein, 11 August 1945.

outlined the situation:

> Known German Reichsbank maintained gold depot Swiss National and some seven zero percent all gold sent abroad during war was destined for that bank. Absolutely no German records on depot with Swiss National available.

> Final report Belgian gold shows one two six million dollars or more than half going Swiss National despite Swiss assurances they not buying such gold from Germans.

> Access to Swiss records most essential both for discovering final destination and use of German wartime gold shipments in general and particularly for fixing present location more than half Belgian gold.

> Also believed Swiss books may throw light BIS withdrawal for German Czech gold London among other issues and on transaction interesting investigation German external assets.

> Important investigation made before Swiss have any excuse for destroying records as obsolete. Also French believed aware some Belgian gold in Switzerland and currently arranging investigation there; appears most important American investigation precede or accompany them.[52]

Although the Americans were far too optimistic about their chances of being permitted to see Swiss national records or any of the BIS files, they were not entirely without some evidence to support their charges against the Swiss. They had sufficient Reichsbank records that could, with careful study and reconstruction, provide them with enough data to make quite well educated guesses as to the disposition of some of the gold in question. In the material at hand all trails led to the Swiss National Bank.[53] Perhaps even more important, the Americans had key former Reichsbank personnel at their disposal whom they could interrogate at length. Albert Thoms, who had headed the Precious Metals Department, had already informed his American captors several weeks before the war's end that "the Reichsbank gold held in Switzerland is at the Swiss National Bank. . . . Each month in the last 5 to 6 years perhaps around 3,000 to 4,000 kilos of gold were sent to Switzerland. All shipments to Switzerland were sent first to the depot at the Swiss National Bank and later maybe sold."[54]

---

52. Ibid., Nixon to Schmidt, 28 August 1945.
53. Ibid., Bernstein to Clay, "Report on National Bank of Bohemia and Moravia Gold Acquired by the Reichsbank, Berlin," 1 November 1945, p. 3.
54. Ibid., "Secret Interrogation of Albert Thoms, 18 April to 19 April, 1945," p. 3.

By all available evidence the high point of gold transactions between the Swiss and the German Reichsbank occurred in 1943 when, as one writer put it, Switzerland imported more gold than goods from their largest trade partner. It was also the year that the Swiss National Bank began to accept the first "gefälschten" or disguised gold bars of Belgian origin, taking well over half (62.5 percent) of all arriving gold from Germany. The Reichsbank received payment in Swiss francs.[55] An American report tracing the course of seized gold belonging to the Bank of Amsterdam deduced from captured Reichsbank records that the Swiss National Bank had purchased 2,383 gold bars worth $31,381,684 from the German bank during 1942. The gold came primarily from looted Dutch guilders that had gone to the Prussian mint for resmelting. By a comparison of the new smelt numbers from the Reichsbank control ledgers with those on the bars sent to the Swiss National Bank, the investigators found that several shipments matched exactly.[56]

Long before the Americans and their allies gained access to the Reichsbank documentation that detailed some of the Swiss connection, they despaired of really exerting any influence on the actions of either the BIS or the Swiss National. However, they did regard it as absolutely vital to postwar decisions that a record of warnings be established, whether in the form of a declaration, a diplomatic note, or a radio broadcast, and they all conveyed the same message: Don't engage in transactions that could possibly involve the exchange of gold looted by the Germans.

It was evident by the end of 1944, as the German–Swiss trade agreement continued in force, that Allied pressures had not succeeded in altering Swiss banking practices. The Allies had already calculated that the German monetary gold reserve of some $70,000,000 had long since been exhausted and yet they had sent over $120,000,000 into Switzerland during 1943 alone.[57] It was also evident that the United States had long since taken the leading role among the Allies in the gold war with the Nazis.

During the first two years of the war in Europe, the neutrality of the United States provided the Americans with a unique position. Having been regarded as a nation with unparalleled security by other nations, it was entirely logical that substantial amounts of the world's gold found their way to America as political and military uncertainties mounted in the late thirties. Between the outbreak of war in 1939 and the end of 1941, the foreign gold holdings in the United States climbed from $770 million to

55. Rings, *Raubgold*, pp. 8–9 and 145.
56. NA, RG 260, OMGUS, FINAD, General papers on Gold Study, November 1946, "Looted Netherlands Guilders Resmelted by the Prussian Mint during 1942," p. 1.
57. Ibid., OMGUS AG, 1945–46, Heath to Robinson, 1 February 1946.

$20 billion![58] At the time of the German attack upon Denmark and Norway in 1940, a U.S. Treasury Department memorandum reflected the concern that now accompanied the expected acceleration of gold into America. Estimating that the neutrals had already stockpiled some $2 billion in gold in the United States, Treasury officials saw this as only the beginning.[59] In January 1941, at the urgent request of Treasury Secretary Henry Morgenthau, President Franklin Roosevelt extended his earlier freezing order over the total assets in the United States of all those nations that had fallen to the German invaders, and this included almost $2 billion in earmarked gold.[60]

America now occupied the rather anomalous position of having blocked the assets of those nations under Nazi rule while maintaining diplomatic relations with Germany itself. This situation was to continue despite a growing and open hostility manifested by the Germans, especially after the passage of the American Lend-Lease Act in March 1941. Relations then deteriorated rapidly, resulting soon after in undeclared war in the Atlantic. By June, with the two nations on the brink of a full-scale declared war, Roosevelt extended the freezing order to all German assets in the United States, a move strongly criticized by many Americans who desired a stricter neutrality. Others warned that the Germans would now retaliate with severe economic measures against U.S. holdings in Europe. At the time a Treasury report set the amount of gold still available to the Germans from other sources at $0.75 billion, coming primarily from looting the Polish, Belgian, Dutch, and French holdings.[61]

It was no secret that the Germans were stripping Europe of whatever resources they found helpful to their own economy at war but, beyond general condemnations against plundering, the Allies did not really focus any unified effort upon gold as such until well into 1942. There was no doubt that the Germans were utilizing neutral banking facilities in gold transactions, but many Allied statesmen felt that the freezing and block-ading programs that were already in place were the best that could be done. The fact that large quantities of Belgian and French looted gold had not yet begun to turn up in the international gold market was probably a consideration, too.

Early in 1942, English radio broadcasts occasionally contained warn-

58. *New York Times*, 29 May 1939, p. 14, and 12 September 1941, p. 33.
59. *Morgenthau Diary*, vol. 1, pp. 95–96.
60. *New York Times*, 19 January 1941, p. 9. While the United States had blocked the funds of those nations invaded after April 1940, this did not apply to Austria, Czechoslovakia, or Poland. It should be noted that the application of U.S. restrictions did not apply uniformly to all European nations for it was felt that greater flexibility toward Switzerland, Sweden, and Spain worked in Allied favor at times.
61. *Morgenthau Diary*, vol. 1, p. 131.

ings directed at Switzerland, usually pointing out the important services they were rendering the Nazi cause when permitting currency exchanges for gold. By midyear the British broadcasts were specifically referring to transactions in Switzerland and other neutral states involving looted gold.[62] The first declaration supported by the United Nations that made direct reference to the looted gold problem was issued in January of 1943. A British introduction to the "Inter-Allied Declaration against the Acts of Dispossession Committed in Territories under Enemy Occupation or Control," signed in London on 5 January 1943 by seventeen Allied nations, carefully pointed out the Nazi efforts currently underway to conceal plundered goods abroad. The message pointed the finger at neutral states that cooperated with the Germans, making such concealment possible. The language of the declaration was equally unmistakable:

> [We] hereby issue a formal warning to all concerned, and in particular to persons in neutral countries, that [we] intend to do [our] utmost to defeat the methods of dispossession practiced by the Governments with which they are at war against the countries and peoples who have been so wantonly assaulted and despoiled. . . . This warning applies whether such transfers or dealings have taken the form of open looting or plunder, or of transactions apparently legal in form, even when they purport to be voluntarily effected.[63]

In order that the precise meaning of the Inter-Allied Declaration was not lost upon those states for whom it was intended, a "Note on the Meaning" was appended stating that the declaration was communicated to all concerned neutrals as well as serving as an open invitation to other members of the United Nations to join in support.[64] In retrospect it would have to be concluded that the Inter-Allied Declaration was not ambiguous and served the warning in the strongest diplomatic terms, but it was still only January 1943 and for the neutrals the Nazi presence over Europe outweighed all other considerations. For the moment the Allies would have to be satisfied that they had stated their case as clearly as they could and it was now a matter of record.

Ironically, it was in the immediate months following the January declaration that huge quantities of looted Belgium gold began showing up in the German gold deposit in Bern. The value transmitted that year to the Reichsbank amounted to almost 589 million Swiss francs.[65] When full knowledge of this was received by the Allies, it brought home the fact that

62. Rings, *Raubgold*, p. 72.
63. NA, RG, WW II Conf. Files, "Inter-Allied Declaration against Acts of Dispossession Committed in Territories under Enemy Occupation or Control," 5 January 1943.
64. Ibid.
65. Rings, *Raubgold*, p. 196. Rings's figures were secured from statistics maintained by

they were not making much progress in the gold war. Since it was not yet possible to carry out any method of enforcement, the best that could be mustered was another warning with the hope that it would finally be heeded, especially by Switzerland. The initiative for the renewed warning was taken by the United States. American Treasury Secretary Morgenthau, securing the assent of leading United Nations members, including the Soviet Union, drafted a new and even more strongly worded "Gold Declaration." Released to the press on 22 February 1944, the message was brief. Wasting little time on preliminaries, the Morgenthau note came to the point: "The United States Government formally declares that it does not and will not recognize the transference of title to the looted gold which the Axis . . . has disposed of in world markets."[66]

An air of urgency accompanied Morgenthau's message, for the United States and Great Britain had decided, on the basis of the large flow of German-controlled assets abroad, that the Nazis were preparing themselves a postwar haven. The two Allies were in agreement that this had to be prevented by all means in their power or the world would again face the specter of a German military revival. Parallel with this growing new concern was the fact that, although the neutrals had not been exactly responsive to the Gold Declaration, they would soon have to face the loss of German-dominated trade markets.[67] Inevitably, this would mean neutral imports would soon be subject to Allied control as the German military machine ground to a halt, and neutrals would have to begin seeking accommodations with the Allies. Anticipating this, American planners felt that they could tie some neutral compliance to the gold issue and start drying up German sources of credit abroad. It would also enable the Allies to focus effectively on any transactions the Germans were engaged in, but the key to a workable plan lay with securing neutral cooperation.

The fear that the Germans would try to build a reserve to use in the postwar period by storing assets in neutral countries was widely held in the Allied camp, and concern about this issue had been expressed many times in official correspondence.[68] Generally, the German plan to create

---

Swiss customs on the amount of gold that entered and left Switzerland between 1940 and 1945.

66. United States, *Elimination of German Resources for War: Hearings before a Sub-Committee of the Committee on Military Affairs*, U.S. Senate: pt. 2: Testimony of State Department, 25 June 1945 (Washington, D.C.: U.S.G.P.O., 1945), pp. 134–35. The investigating committee was generally referred to as the "Kilgore committee," after the name of the chairman, Harley Kilgore, a West Virginia Democrat.

67. Allied warnings directed at neutrals dealing in Nazi spoils did not all suffer the same fate as the Gold Declaration did, for some of the efforts to frustrate sales in art objects, paintings, furs, etc., were successful.

68. Documented accounts of the successful evasions by the Germans of Versailles Treaty

for themselves a place of safety for secreted wealth abroad was referred to as "safehaven," and this later became the code word for Allied planning to halt it. A kind of precedent already existed with the record of Allied programs aimed at preventing Nazi economic penetration in Latin America, although the circumstances were quite different. In April 1944, the American secretary of state Cordell Hull sought the cooperation of his British colleagues in systematically gathering all available data on German efforts in secreting assets from the British missions in Bern, Stockholm, Lisbon, Madrid, Tangier, and Ankara.[69] As the diplomatic machinery moved forward it was buttressed by the Allied adoption of resolution VI of the Bretton Woods Monetary Conference (July 1944), which committed the full weight of the United Nations "to do their utmost to defeat the methods of dispossession" and made specific reference to the role of neutral countries and looted gold.[70] It was now time to draft a proposal for the neutrals.

At the outset there appeared to be little disagreement between the Americans and the British about the primary objective of "Safehaven" and offering the neutrals a trade proposal for the transition period.[71] Nor did there seem to be much disagreement about the content of the proposal to request the neutrals to aid the Allies in gaining control over German assets, help fulfill Allied procurement needs, and agree to contribute to the rehabilitation of liberated areas. The two Western Allies reasoned that "the bargaining power of the Allies will probably be at its height and the relatively strong position . . . in relation to the neutrals should be used to attain our economic objective."[72]

Anglo-American disagreement arose over the means of securing neutral agreement to the proposal. The American view was that neutral cooperation could be obtained without waiting for the transition period, that is, Germany's beginning military collapse, and was in favor of introducing some restrictive trade measures against them. The British position was to avoid any trade penalties in hopes that the neutrals, upon examining the Allied proposal, would see the wisdom of cooperating.[73] The differences were not so easily resolved and consumed the final months of the year

provisions meant to restrict their rearmament abound. Secret activities in a number of "neutral" states were important to their undertaking.

69. *F.R.U.S.*, vol. 2, 1944, pp. 215–16.
70. *Proceedings*, p. 939.
71. *F.R.U.S.*, vol. 2, 1944, p. 137.
72. Ibid., p. 150.
73. Ibid., pp. 217–18. A British historian has suggested that the difference arose over the American concentration on achieving their objective while ignoring vital British interests, citing the example of Britain's need for trade with Spain. William Medlicott, *The Economic Blockade*, vol. 2 (London: H.M.S.O., 1959), p. 625.

before an agreement was reached.[74]

Yet the period was not one of inactivity, for the United States continued to apply pressures to Switzerland to start implementing their gold proposal.[75] The Americans had actually introduced the subject to Swiss authorities through the U.S. mission in Bern as early as April 1944, but the Swiss response had always been negative. Finally, as U.S. efforts became more insistent, Switzerland directly refused all demands to initiate restrictions against Germany, arguing "that only by continuing trade with Germany . . . can they [the Swiss] obtain supplies essential to the Swiss economy."[76] U.S. negotiators were well aware that they could not force the Swiss to act against their own interests, and the assessment of the situation in December of that year was less than optimistic: "The Swiss expect to continue their assistance to the bitter end . . . [and] their collaboration with Germany on financial matters—cloaking of enemy funds, the purchase of Axis gold, the Swiss banks' assistance to the enemy, etc.—is also continuing, a fact which does not promise extensive voluntary cooperation in our financial objectives, especially on the problem of enemy assets."[77] The difference was that the Americans were now in a position to actually enforce measures against the Swiss for they controlled supply routes across France, but as part of "Safehaven" it was decided that an Allied mission should be sent into Switzerland to try direct negotiations first. The American delegation, soon to be joined by the British and French, was headed by a Roosevelt assistant named Lauchlin Currie; later correspondence would refer to this undertaking as the "Currie mission."

74. The United States wanted to ask the Soviet Union to join in issuing a gold-policy statement based on Bretton Woods resolution VI, but since the USSR did not have diplomatic missions in Madrid, Bern, Lisbon, or Tangier, they had to be satisfied with notes to the Swedish and Turkish governments. *F.R.U.S.*, vol. 2, 1944, p. 242.

75. The list of implementation measures numbered nine demands, including freezing all Axis assets regardless of ownership. *Elimination of German Resources for War*, pt. 2, pp. 136–37.

76. *F.R.U.S.*, vol. 5, 1945, p. 765. In October 1944 the Swiss had agreed to stop the export of arms, as well as other military supplies, to Germany and to close off one of the transit routes.

77. Ibid., p. 766.

CHAPTER 4

Safehaven

The closer victory came the greater the pressure exerted by the Americans on those neutrals still dealing with Germany. The United Nations declaration of January 1943 had warned that those who profited from looted gold would ultimately have to answer for it. By early 1944 the United States decided that the time had arrived to develop a plan that would not only pinpoint the areas where specific measures could be taken against those neutrals who continued to provide goods and services to the Germans, but would also insure that there would not be a buildup of hidden German assets abroad. The American program, codenamed "Safehaven," promised to be a cooperative effort with Great Britain to halt Germany's increasingly desperate gold operations successfully and close off all other avenues of economic flight as the war entered its final phase. Acting unilaterally, the United States instructed its missions in Lisbon, Stockholm, Madrid, Tangier, Ankara, and Bern to remind the appropriate officials in those neutral capitals that there had been a 1943 UN declaration and to suggest that they refresh their memories regarding its contents. The British soon agreed to support Safehaven, but with the reservation that no punitive measures against the recalcitrant neutrals be instituted that would conflict with planned postwar policies.[1] By late that summer the Americans had basic agreement on a brief but specific statement for endorsement. It forbade the acquisition or storage of Axis gold and set forth the principles in resolution VI of Bretton Woods. In general, the statement was meant to be endorsed by all nations outside the Nazi sphere, but by year's end those neutrals at whom it was primarily directed had failed to sign.[2]

With the approach of 1945, and little evident progress at bringing the

1. *F.R.U.S.*, vol. 2, 1944, pp. 213–20.
2. Ibid., pp. 225–26 and p. 236.

neutrals around to the support of the Allied gold policy, the Americans were becoming increasingly irascible. Convinced that Switzerland, the most important of the neutrals, had sufficient essentials stockpiled to last until the war was over, they had no patience with the Swiss argument that the Germans were just as desperate—or more so—to get full value out of their looted gold and were absolutely determined to keep Switzerland in their service. As one frustrated U.S. negotiator put it,

the Swiss expect to continue their assistance to the enemy's war economy to the bitter end, making any reductions only very haltingly and under the strongest Allied pressure. Their collaboration with Germany on financial matters—the cloaking of enemy funds, the purchase of Axis gold, the Swiss banks' assistance to the enemy, etc.—is also continuing, a fact which does not promise extensive voluntary cooperation on our financial objectives, especially on the problem of enemy assets. . . . [T]herefore the time has come when, for the sake of both present and future objectives, we must take immediate measures to convince the Swiss not only that we mean business, but also that to continue their present economic policy vis-à-vis the Germans would be disastrous to their own interests.[3]

Concerned that future economic relations with Switzerland would be irreparably damaged if too much force was applied, both France and Britain were for continued diplomatic negotiations with the Swiss. The Americans, advocates of a harder line, were prepared to take the first step and enlist wider support from UN nations in an application of pressure not only on the Swiss but on other neutrals as well. "The success of the [Gold] Declaration depends to a large extent upon the isolation from the world's gold markets of those countries which have been purchasing gold from the Axis," American Secretary of State Stettinius said. "This isolation can be made clear to them only if all of the United Nations announce their adherence to the Gold Declaration."[4] The message to the Swiss was not entirely negative, however, for Bern was informed that cooperation would have its rewards too. Fully cognizant of the precarious balancing act the Swiss were trying to maintain, the Americans suggested that any current trade negotiations with the Germans contain an "escape clause."[5]

When the United States first presented its demands in September 1944, the Americans had insisted that no concessions would be offered if Switzerland did not accept the terms within five days; nevertheless, they were still negotiating three months later. But a lot had happened in those

3. Ibid., vol. 5, 1945, p. 766.
4. Ibid., vol. 2, 1944, pp. 250–51.
5. Ibid., vol. 5, 1945, pp. 767–68.

three months, and the rapidly changing military situation meant that immediate answers were needed. They could no longer afford to indulge the Swiss in their waiting game. Sides had to be taken no matter how painful the decision, and the Americans felt this could only be accomplished favorably when negotiators met face to face. As one American policymaker observed, "it appears unlikely that a reorientation of their policy can be obtained simply by presenting another note to the Swiss government."[6]

The Swiss also wanted to find out precisely what the Allies had to offer, although they were determined to continue their financial and trade relations with the Germans as long as humanly possible. Therefore, they saw some validity in a meeting and invited the United States and Great Britain to send delegations to Bern for that purpose. The Americans wasted no time in responding and had a delegation ready to depart for Europe by the end of January 1945. Headed by a Roosevelt assistant and former official in the Foreign Economic Administration named Lauchlin Currie, the mission made its first stop in London. Strategy was discussed with the British delegation, led by Parliamentary Secretary Dingle Foot, and it was decided that France, as an interested party, should be included. With these matters settled the "Currie mission" proceeded to Bern.

The Swiss negotiating team, led by a professor of economics named William Rappard, waited somewhat apprehensively for Currie's arrival. According to one Swiss parliamentary member, the whole atmosphere was one of nervous tension and there was fear that Currie and his Allied colleagues were going to demand far more than Switzerland was prepared to give.[7] Currie did not disappoint them; in his opening statement he remarked on the fact that young Allied lives were being lost while they talked. He asked for immediate compliance with resolution VI of the Bretton Woods agreement and a cessation of all major contacts with the Germans. Thus began three weeks of intensive negotiation, climaxing with Currie's triumphant message to Washington on March 5th informing his superiors that "the Swiss delegation capitulated today."[8]

Rappard's delegation had agreed to recommend to the Swiss Federal Council the following: block all assets of Axis and Axis-controlled nations; tighten controls over all assets already transferred into Switzerland by those nations; complete a census of all assets held in Switzerland by blocked nations; strengthen measures to prevent any imports that might result from dispossession by Germany; refuse the purchase of any more gold from Germany except what was needed to provide funds for

6. Ibid., p. 766.
7. Homberger, *Schweizerische Handelspolitik*, pp. 117–18.
8. *F.R.U.S.*, vol. 5, 1945, p. 782.

prisoner-of-war pay, Red Cross, and German Legation expenses; and, consult with the United States, Britain, and France on all of the above when so requested. Currie was confident: "If this is approved by Council, bringing Sweden, Spain, and Portugal in line should prove easy and the second battle of Safehaven (Resolution VI being the first) will have been won."[9] In accepting the recommendations, however, the Swiss Federal Council would permit no mention of resolution VI or use of the word "enemy," presumably in reference to Germany. Currie especially noticed the resistance voiced by the Swiss Bankers' Association to the stipulation that no more gold be purchased from Germany.[10]

Throughout the negotiations the Swiss delegation clung stubbornly to their argument that certain demands, if acceded to, would compromise their neutrality and possibly their sovereignty. As one Swiss senator who followed the negotiations closely stated, Switzerland simply could not take the risk "as long as Germany remains in a position to bring suitable counterpressure to bear."[11] Among other points upon which specific agreement was not reached was the question of the gold Switzerland had acquired since 1939. The Swiss refusal to discuss this subject with the Currie mission hinted at the extreme secrecy that surrounded the issue.

In his final message from Bern, Currie's tone was one of confidence that his mission had accomplished its assigned task: "We have secured virtually everything we hoped for and Swiss appear well satisfied." On March 8th, the eve of Currie's departure, the three Allied delegations informed Rappard that they were ready to provide transit facilities across France for imports into Switzerland, to be limited only by the current military requirements.[12] Upon his return to America, Currie was received with high praise. "Dear Lauchlin," wrote Treasury Secretary Morgenthau, "I want to congratulate you on the fine job that you have just done in Switzerland. . . . I feel that you have not only thwarted the Nazis' plan for using Switzerland as a financial hideout, but also have laid the basis for the Allied Military Government in Germany to take control of German assets in Switzerland."[13]

Morgenthau told President Roosevelt that the Currie mission "has been conducted most ably and has yielded the largest wartime and postwar result. I know too, that the Swiss were impressed by the fact that an assistant to the President headed the American group." He suggested that Currie continue in this role in "following through on the Safehaven

9. Ibid., pp. 782–83.
10. Ibid., vol. 2, 1945, pp. 861–62.
11. Homberger, pp. 117–18.
12. *F.R.U.S.*, vol. 5, 1945, pp. 784–88.
13. *Morgenthau Diary*, vol. 2, p. 1164.

Program in the neutral countries."[14] Using the Swiss negotiations as the model, the objectives of Safehaven were pursued with the neutrals throughout 1945, even after the German collapse. The search for hidden German assets was pressed in Sweden, Portugal, Turkey, and Spain; although each of these nations presented problems that had to be dealt with individually, the final judgment on Safehaven was that it had been a success.[15]

The one critical area that had not been resolved by Safehaven was that of the looted gold that the German Reichsbank had delivered to Switzerland up to the time of Currie's arrival in Bern; this would have to await war's end for the resumption of discussions and the development of a specific Allied policy on restitution. Nor had the Currie mission succeeded in preventing the gold transactions that were underway almost simultaneously with the Bern talks. When the subject of looted gold was discussed the Swiss had expressed no opposition to the return of any identifiable gold, but the key word was "identifiable." Their position was and remained that Switzerland had not knowingly accepted any looted gold and the burden of proof rested with the Allies, a job that could prove impossible without Swiss cooperation. The attitude of the Allies toward the Swiss position was mixed. Churchill had confided to his foreign secretary that Switzerland had a better record than the other neutrals: "What does it matter whether she has been able to give us the commercial advantages we desire or has given too many to the Germans, to keep herself alive?" The British prime minister then quoted Stalin as referring to the Swiss as " 'swine,' and he does not use that sort of language without meaning it," he concluded.[16]

The engineer behind the final gold transactions between Germany and Switzerland was the Reichsbank's vice-president, Emil Puhl. Arriving in Zurich almost on the heels of Currie's departure, Puhl knew that he faced a battle, one that "is much worse than I even imagined in my most pessimistic expectations."[17] The press was hostile to Germany and the public mood was equally unpleasant, but more important to Puhl was the fact that he did not know what concessions had been made to the Allies. He was aware that as a result of the Currie mission Switzerland had issued a federal decree that regulated payments with Germany. It replaced all previous agreements and stipulated that all payments were to be made through the Swiss National Bank, in addition to placing exten-

14. Ibid., vol. 2, pp. 1164–65.

15. *F.R.U.S.*, vol. 2, 1945, pp. 862–932.

16. Winston S. Churchill, *Triumph and Tragedy* (Boston: Houghton Mifflin Co., 1953), p. 712.

17. NA, RG 260, OMGUS FINAD, Puhl to Funk, 19 March 1945, p. 1.

sive restrictions upon all German-held assets.[18]

Puhl's immediate concern was to determine just how damaging the Swiss–Allied arrangements would be to his current mission. He soon found that the Swiss National Bank did not have total control over the German payments but had to secure permission from the government clearing house, which charged 0.5 percent for this service. In Puhl's words this was "an exorbitant fee [and] makes business transactions even more difficult. It further even managed to stop the payment of money which was transferred from the Reichsbank for use of our Embassy."[19] He also discovered that important Reichsbank transactions were simply being left unprocessed and accounts were blocked. "This way Switzerland is trying to use our currency reserves for her own purposes," he commented. "I have found out from different conversations I held, that there is no doubt that it is the intention of Switzerland to take away from us the German accounts and to charge them against Swiss claims. . . . Unfortunately I have no illusions about the outcome of the negotiations after the highest authorities here have decided to carry on a policy of 'boot licking' to the British and Americans. The fear of the Russians is said to be probably the main factor responsible for this policy. They are looking toward the Anglo-Saxons for protection."[20]

Puhl decided that he would press for gold sales to the extent of filling the Reichsbank account at the Swiss National. He was told by the bank president, Weber, that those expenses agreed upon with Currie and his colleagues could be paid with gold, but Puhl wanted to enlarge on this and he was ready to use all the persuasion at his command, including the threat of halting all German obligations to Switzerland.[21] In Puhl's opinion the Swiss were not yet ready to sever relations but he felt that to secure what he wanted would require almost superhuman effort and wondered whether he was capable of it. He had already had a setback when the BIS decided to postpone Germany's annual dividend payment. "Today we really need every single franc and the dividends amount to a few hundred thousand francs," Puhl confided to Funk. "The management of the Bank for International Settlements has moreover received the approval of the American delegation . . . to accept from us in gold to cover

18. "Swiss Federal Decree regarding Provisional Measures for Regulation of Payments between Switzerland and Germany," United States, *Elimination of German Resources for War*, pt. 2, 25 June 1945, pp. 134–36.
19. NA, RG 260, OMGUS FINAD, Puhl to Funk, 19 March 1945, p. 1.
20. Ibid., pp. 1–2.
21. Ibid., p. 2. Puhl noted that the Americans had apparently left a good impression and remarked on the fact that Currie's second in command "had the good 'old American' name Schmidt," ibid. He was referring to Orvis A. Schmidt from Treasury, who was part of the Currie mission.

the interest due from us. Using the slogan of 'the stolen Belgium gold' the British and Americans have gone peddling in an unimaginable way and drove everybody crazy here."[22]

But Puhl was determined to remain in Switzerland until he had exhausted every possibility and exploited every contact. In wording curiously reminiscent of Currie's March 5th message to Washington, Puhl telegraphed Berlin on March 30th: "After great efforts the discussions have led to positive results in so far as the Swiss are now prepared to permit disposal of Reichsbank credits. . . . Furthermore the Swiss are prepared to purchase gold provided it is used for definite purposes such as payment of legations, military personnel, etc."[23] Puhl was quick to admit his surprise that he had been able to arrive at some decision with the Swiss so rapidly after anticipating long and difficult negotiations. One of the surprises was the significant number of bank directors and presidents who had contacted him personally, expressing interest in continuing their Reichsbank association. Especially eager had been the Kreditanstalt, the Bankgesellschaft, the Bankverein, the Eidgenössische Bank, and the Basel Handelsbank. "All realized that the blocking of German credits has a far reaching effect also upon Swiss interests at home," Puhl wrote.[24] Puhl attributed his success to the strong Swiss desire not to create a rupture with Germany. "Without going into technical details," he wrote Funk, "I may state that Switzerland basically is prepared to continue payment transactions with Germany. In other words, Switzerland does not wish to create a condition which would mean a break in relations."[25]

Thus Puhl managed to reach an agreement with the Swiss that permitted Germany to continue a wide variety of transactions until the beginning of May, after which new arrangements would have to be negotiated. Puhl noted: "This agreement in fact wipes out the payment blockade against Germany which the Americans and British have made such a strenuous effort to achieve. It leaves the Reichsbank a free hand to make dispositions in detail and does not subject it to approval by the Swiss clearing house." This meant, of course, that the 0.5 percent fee that the clearing house had previously placed on all German business transactions was null and void. This was no small sum for companies like Siemens and I.G. Farben, but ran into the hundreds of thousands of francs. "In that respect," Puhl wrote, "the local German firms may be thankful to the Reichsbank."[26]

22. Ibid., p. 3.
23. Ibid., Puhl to Funk, 30 March 1945, p. 1.
24. Ibid., pp. 2–3.
25. Ibid., p. 4.
26. Ibid., p. 6.

In negotiating a gold policy Puhl encountered an initial resistance that he ascribed to the Swiss fear of Allied wrath, but felt he had gained a victory when they agreed to accept gold for certain German obligations. To effect payment Puhl had arranged for the Swiss National Bank to receive a shipment of gold from the Reichsbank branch in Constance. The Germans agreed in the bargain to supply half the necessary gasoline for the trip that would move six tons of gold into Switzerland. Three tons were scheduled for the Swiss National Bank, one and a half tons for the BIS, and the remainder for the German Legation.[27] Puhl informed Funk that he had received the very best treatment during his Swiss visit: "I might say that the Swiss did not lack in paying me personal attentions. ... Swiss bankers and industrialists again and again called on me despite the fact that the enemy observed everything." He promised the Reichsbank president that he would remain until he could see the gold transfer completed although he was extremely worried because his family was now in a combat zone in Germany.[28] Puhl's final communiqué was dated April 6th from Bern. He wrote Funk that he had secured almost all of the verbal commitment in writing and had absolutely circumvented the Allied payment blockade negotiated by the Currie mission. He boasted that he had persuaded the Swiss National Bank to buy the gold previously mentioned: "I succeeded in concluding a gold transaction involving about three tons, in spite of the fact that this is certainly very unagreeable to our opponents. ... The transfer of the gold took place today. ... [T]he National bank had obligingly sent its Director Schwegler to come along to Constance."[29]

While the Currie agreement with the Swiss carried the interpretation that Germany's payment obligations on a restricted and carefully designated level could be met with gold from a supply presumably already present in Switzerland, it is obvious from Puhl's letters that the Swiss gave him quite a different interpretation. "The fact that ... President Weber [Swiss National Bank] repeatedly and strongly advised me to continue in my endeavors made a forceful impression," Puhl wrote. "He pointed out that under the given present day conditions an agreement between the National bank and the Reichsbank would be of far reaching importance beyond the present day."[30]

Although Puhl was not able to remain in Switzerland to finalize the

27. Ibid., pp. 7–9.
28. Ibid., pp. 10–11.
29. Ibid., Puhl to Funk, 6 April 1945, pp. 2–3.
30. Ibid., p. 5. As Puhl prepared to depart, he also expressed gratitude to the Swiss government for providing him with transportation in their own courier automobile, although by this time his family was already in Allied-captured territory, ibid., p. 9.

gold transaction with the BIS as he had intended, it was quickly concluded once he had returned to Berlin, and on April 12th he instructed the Constance branch that a ton and a half had been sold to the BIS in Basel. The instructions were to place it in a separate deposit labeled with the name of the new owner: "As soon as circumstances permit, this gold should be forwarded to Switzerland after consulting the owners."[31] The entire business in Switzerland had been conducted with the utmost discretion, but Puhl's presence there had not gone unnoticed. Puhl had barely departed when the American Legation at Bern wired Washington that "since the gold is in or close to an active theater of military operations, it is subject to military seizure. It is . . . in all probability, looted gold. It is strongly urged that the military authorities take immediate steps to locate and seize this shipment of gold."[32] Actually, the information that the Americans had was that a shipment of gold had been sent to the small town of Lörrach on the Swiss border just north of Basel, and was awaiting transport into Switzerland. Lörrach was still in German hands, however, so the American military could do little about it for the moment.

In the meantime, angered by what they obviously regarded as Swiss greed to get one last shipment of gold out of Germany, the United States, Britain, and France lodged a strong protest with the Swiss government. Making no specific reference to Constance or Lörrach, the Swiss replied that transactions with the Germans involved no looted gold. Currie's reaction was that "we . . . regard the Swiss purchase of this gold as obvious subterfuge on the part of the Swiss and clear cut contravention of spirit of undertaking given by the Swiss."[33] By the end of April Lörrach had been occupied, but not by the Americans; French troops had moved into the region first. Immediately an American Counter Intelligence Corps (CIC) agent was dispatched to the town to track down the gold, but the French already knew about the Lörrach story and had disappointing news. They had heard the rumors of gold as soon as they entered town, they said, and when control had been established they began interviewing some of the town citizens and officials, but all denied the existence of any gold store.[34] The surprised CIC agent was also told that he had not been the first American there asking about the gold. Only days earlier an American officer had arrived and inquired about it, but the French authorities could not remember his name.[35] General Devers, whose U.S.

31. Ibid., Puhl to Reichsbanknebenstelle, Constance, 12 April 1945.
32. NA, RG 165, Records of the War Department, General Special Staffs, Clayton to Bissell, 13 April 1945.
33. *F.R.U.S.*, vol. 2, 1945, pp. 878–79.
34. NA, RG 331, SHAEF G–5, 1/13, CIC Agent Friebolin Report, 3 May 1945.

Sixth Army Group was responsible for the assignment, later admitted that he had sent a special representative from his headquarters staff ahead to Lörrach to look into the gold affair, but the officer had reported that there was no gold there. An investigation revealed that neither Reichsbank officials nor Swiss customs authorities knew anything of a gold deposit in Lörrach. No further information was forthcoming, and the U.S. Army concluded that there had never been a gold deposit there.[36]

At about the same time that the Lörrach rumor was being put to rest, another gold incident involving Switzerland was unfolding. It concerned the recent arrangements that the BIS had arranged with Reichsbank vice-president Emil Puhl to store a gold purchase at the bank branch in Constance. On May 2d, Supreme Headquarters, Allied Expeditionary Forces (SHAEF), received a letter from BIS president Thomas McKittrick informing them of this fact: "In order to safeguard the rights of free disposal and ownership of this Bank . . . we desire to draw special attention to the privileges relating to such free disposal over its assets, accorded to the Bank for International Settlements by the terms of Art. X of the Hague Agreement dated 29th January 1930."[37] The BIS insisted that there was no question of looted gold here for the property in question had belonged to the Reichsbank long before the war began. To still any doubts the bank offered to permit an American inspection of the certificates of transaction; however, it was emphasized that bank officers had an absolute responsibility to collect what belonged to the BIS.[38] An American officer made a quick visit to Constance and confirmed the existence of the forty cases of gold. An examination of the relevant correspondence between the BIS and the Reichsbank forced the Americans to admit that title to the gold had passed to the Swiss bank, but it was decided that for the moment no transfer would take place, and the gold would remain in Constance until further notice by American authorities.[39]

McKittrick's letter was interpreted by U.S. Treasury officials as a calculated step by his bank to include themselves in the ultimate settlements surrounding the massive German assets. "We feel," Assistant Secretary Harry Dexter White told Morgenthau, "that [it] is a move to increase the prestige and enhance the importance of the BIS, and to show they are in the picture and that they can not be cut off."[40] Dismissing McKittrick's letters as "for the record," Morgenthau immediately pre-

---

35. Ibid.
36. NA, RG 332, ETO, SGS, 132/2, Devers to SHAEF FWD., G–5, 2 May 1945.
37. NA, RG 260, OMGUS FINAD, BIS to SHAEF G–5, 2 May 1945.
38. Ibid., BIS to American Legation Bern, 2 May 1945.
39. Ibid., Cattier to SHAEF, 14 May 1945.
40. *Morgenthau Diary*, vol. 1, p. 1570.

pared a communiqué to all Bretton Woods participants reasserting the demand for the liquidation of the BIS. In the U.S. Treasury deliberations a staff member outlined the problem: "Bretton Woods Resolution No. 5 calls for the liquidation of the BIS at the earliest possible moment. We do not want to appear to be retracting in the slightest from this resolution. On the other hand, we do not want to precipitate a direct battle with BIS until Bretton Woods legislation is enacted and other countries have adhered to it. McKittrick's letters are part of an obvious effort to stake out a claim for the BIS in the post-war world."[41] It was agreed that all signatories to the Bretton Woods Act should be advised of the American position, and that a strong letter might well provide the initiative for hesitant nations to assume an open stand against the BIS.

The Treasury Department's irritation with the BIS was only part of a general conviction in American government circles that the Swiss had profited extensively from the German looted gold and now, during the closing weeks of the war, refused to cooperate fully on Safehaven. Months after the war had ended in Europe, the United States had still not relaxed controls over Swiss accounts in America. U.S. Secretary of State James Byrnes wrote that "we have found [the] Swiss extremely sensitive to our suggestions if they feel their assets in this country are in any way prejudiced, and probably Allied control of Swiss assets is the most potent weapon we have with which to obtain Swiss compliance on *Safehaven*."[42]

The first move in the burgeoning controversy with Switzerland began in August 1945, when the American government (Britain and France were content to remain in the background) requested the right to exercise ownership or control over German assets in that country. The request was based upon the American assumption that anything and everything belonging to the former German state or its citizens now fell under the control of the Allied occupying powers. Politely, but firmly, the Swiss rejected the U.S. contention, insisting that "actual occupation of German territory by Allied Powers can hardly have any effects beyond German borders. Aside from these illegal considerations [Swiss] Federal Council wishes to point out that on March 8 it reached agreement with American, British and French Govts concerning the question of German Assets in Switzerland." The Swiss did not close the door, however, to entertaining claims from those states that had been the object of German spoilation and encouraged them to submit "lists of assets stolen . . . in order to establish if they are in Switzerland and, if so, to facilitate restitution thereof."[43]

41. Ibid., p. 1571.
42. *F.R.U.S.*, vol. 5, 1945, p. 900. Blocked Swiss funds in the United States amounted to about $1,500,000,000.

During this same period in September, the Allied Control Council in Berlin was in the process of preparing a measure that empowered the council to assume control over all German properties outside of Germany. It was evident in the debate that preceded enactment of the measure that both Britain and France wished to avoid further damages to the already worsening Swiss relationship. However, the measure did become Public Law No. 5 in October and directed that all foreign German assets were to be administered by the council's German External Property Commission.[44] It was not clear just how such control could be extended to German assets in Switzerland if the Swiss refused to admit jurisdiction.

Still confident that the Swiss could be brought around by diplomatic persuasion, the Allies were beginning to feel the power that lay in final victory as the war entered its last stage. This confidence was reflected in the tone of their message to Switzerland, exuding a kind of assurance that implied that things could become much tougher if necessary. Little did they know that their struggle with Switzerland would become a prolonged battle that strengthened the Swiss hand the longer it was fought. In their opening shot the Allies presented Switzerland with a proposal that included the suggestion to establish a special tribunal to hear cases of looted-property claims. While the Swiss replied they had no objection to the idea, they reiterated their stand that they had already negotiated policy with the Currie mission and did not recognize the Allied right to claim control of German assets abroad.[45]

Recognizing that they could not get Swiss compliance with the usual diplomatic efforts, the Americans suggested a Washington meeting where representatives of the Allied Control Council could discuss the issues directly with a Swiss delegation. Optimistically, a meeting date for January 1946 was suggested.[46] However, before 1945 had ended the subject of the Swiss financial relationship to Nazi Germany had become public news primarily as a result of an American congressional investigation. A Senate subcommittee chaired by Senator Harley M. Kilgore had released the charges that Switzerland had accepted large quantities of German looted gold during the war and still served as a haven for hidden German assets. Swiss–U.S. relations had been cooling before but now became downright icy as the Kilgore committee provided the news media with copies of the Puhl letters detailing his last visit to Switzerland.[47] Specifically charging Switzerland with violations of the agreement con-

43. Ibid., p. 903.
44. Ibid., pp. 904ff.
45. Ibid., pp. 909–12.
46. Ibid., pp. 912–13.
47. Rings, *Raubgold*, p. 109.

cluded with Currie, Kilgore said that the Swiss had continued to provide the Germans with foreign exchange for looted gold. Using details from the Puhl correspondence, which Kilgore said had come to his committee from the U.S. War Department, the Senator castigated Swiss behavior.[48]

Switzerland's reaction was swift and angry. Dr. Walter Stucki, under-secretary of foreign affairs, denied all accusations and labeled Kilgore's charges as absolutely groundless. The Swiss Bundesrat called the investigation a move that threatened relations with the United States. No foreign exchange had been made available to the Germans since 6 February 1945, several weeks before the conclusion of the agreement with the Currie mission, and for the courtesy extended Puhl, the Swiss carefully pointed out that there was a history of over one hundred years of established business relations with Germany. As for the Allied Control Council Law No. 5, the Swiss concluded, Switzerland "is not a defeated State, therefore the Bundesrat refuses very decidedly to recognize the rights of ownership or control of the Allies over German property in Switzerland."[49]

Soon after this reply the Swiss completed their census of German assets and announced that it totaled about $250,000,000. Instantly this figure was challenged by U.S. Treasury officials who set the amount at three times that sum. With relations now strained to the breaking point, the Washington meeting had to be postponed. A secret U.S. State Department message reflected the degree of government skepticism on the Swiss announcement:

> It was known to monetary statisticians everywhere that at the start of the war the Germans possessed monetary gold reserves of about $70,000,000 in gold which had been spent by Germany at the latest by 1943 in her war effort. If the Swiss accepted 100 tons of gold offered them by the Germans in 1943 which was worth $123,000,000 how can it be conceded to the Swiss that they acted in good faith? Moreover, how can the Swiss claim they acted in good faith when this gold was acquired at the time they knew that it had been refused for those very reasons by the Swedes?[50]

The Americans wanted these questions on the agenda at Washington, and they wanted the full support of both of their allies when gold was discussed. They were aware that the looted gold question was badly weakened by the Swiss refusal to permit an investigation there, but felt

48. *New York Times*, 15 November 1945, pp. 1ff. Morgenthau reported in his diary that President Truman was very definitely against any government hearings on the subject at that time, *Morgenthau Diary*, vol. 2, p. 1569.

49. *New York Times*, 19 November 1945, p. 2.

50. NA, RG 230, OMGUS AG, 1945–46, copy of State Dept. telegram to American Embassy, London, 1 February 1946, p. 1.

this might change if the Swiss knew that the Allies stood united: "The Swiss are not conscience stricken—name calling can serve no purpose—and knowledge of the sensitivity of Swiss neutrality, sovereign rights, and a good business deal need to be shown the people of Switzerland. . . . The Swiss should be informed in advance that an issue will be made in forthcoming negotiations of the acquisition of looted gold."[51]

In accordance with this strategy, the Swiss were invited to send a delegation to the United States for discussions arising out of Public Law No. 5 and were informed that this was meant to include German assets in Switzerland and looted gold. The Swiss accepted this time, and negotiations opened in Washington on March 18th and finished May 26th. The chief representatives were Randolph Paul, a special assistant to Truman, for the United States; F.W. McCombe for Great Britain; Paul Charqueraud for France; and Walter Stucki for Switzerland.[52] After opening statements by both sides, the discussions quickly settled on the Swiss opposition to Public Law No. 5. "The legal status of the Allied Control Council in Germany [is] no different than the legal status of the Hitler Government of Germany," Stucki stated.[53] A deadlock was soon reached and all agreed that more progress might be made if the problems that divided them were worked on by separate committees. Three committees were created to deal with German assets in Switzerland, Swiss claims against Germany, and the looted gold question.

It was the Allied position—primarily American—that at least $200,000,000 worth of looted gold had passed into Switzerland from Germany during the war. Stucki immediately rejected this figure and strongly defended the Swiss National Bank as innocent in any gold purchases from the Germans. He made it very clear that any restoration of so-called looted gold was a subject that only the Swiss Federal Tribunal could decide. He did not close the door, however, to the possibility that Switzerland might consider favorably a voluntary contribution of some sort to aid in Europe's reconstruction.[54] This was not exactly the breakthrough that the Allies were waiting for and the negotiations continued to be heated. At one point Stucki refused to debate any longer and stormed out of the meeting.[55] The Swiss clung stubbornly to their position that the Allies grossly underestimated Germany's prewar gold reserve, which they

---

51. Ibid., p. 2.
52. Paul, whose experience was in Treasury, was assisted by a large staff, including experts from the State Dept.; McCombe was an economics expert from the British embassy; Charquerand had served as French representative on the Currie mission; and Stucki, chief of Swiss foreign affairs, was assisted, among others, by Professor William Rappard.
53. *F.R.U.S.*, vol. 5, 1946, p. 207.
54. Ibid., pp. 210–11.
55. Rings, *Raubgold*, p. 109.

said was at least $450,000,000. Nor did the Allies acknowledge the fact that Switzerland very often simply transferred a significant amount of gold received to third parties. The Swiss delegation denied having any specific information about looted gold and certainly did not consider gold they had purchased from the Reichsbank as looted gold. They had purchased gold on assurances from Puhl that it had come from Germany's prewar reserves.[56]

As the days of weary negotiation passed, it appeared that there was no middle ground to be found on the gold question. The first break came when Stucki returned to his earlier proposal that the Swiss Parliament just might support a voluntary gold contribution to Europe's reconstruction. This was countered by an Allied suggestion that they might just scale down the amount of looted gold transferred to Switzerland by eliminating the Austrian treasury. The Swiss still refused to accept any liability for the sum that remained, but admitted to purchasing about $88,000,000 of the gold that probably came from Belgium. "But in no event would they concede that they were liable to restore this amount of gold to the Allies."[57] Finally, on May 2d, Stucki put forth a compromise plan: a fifty-fifty split between the Swiss and the Allies on all proceeds from the German assets located in Switzerland and a settlement of the gold question through payment of 250,000,000 Swiss gold francs (about $58.4 million) as the reconstruction contribution. He made it quite clear that this was Switzerland's final proposal.[58]

It required little calculation to see that the offer was not only very favorable to the Swiss but basically ignored the largest portion of the German looted gold. The Allied bargaining position was fast eroding, however, for governments and business were weary of wartime controls and the general public sentiment was peace-oriented. Fully cognizant of these factors and in agreement that further negotiations could, at best, only hope to secure a few more dollars out of the stubborn Swiss, the Allied delegations decided to accept Stucki's offer. On May 26th, for a payment of 250,000,000 Swiss gold francs to the "Allied Gold Pool," all claims against the Swiss government and the Swiss National Bank in connection with gold acquired from Germany during the war were dropped.[59]

56. *F.R.U.S.*, vol. 5, 1946, p. 213.
57. Ibid., p. 216.
58. Ibid.
59. Ibid., pp. 216–18, and see pp. 218–20 for Sec. V, Final Agreement, and United States, *Department of State Bulletin*, 30 June 1946, p. 1101. The Germans who lost assets in Switzerland received the equivalent in their own currency. No reference was made to the fact that the mark was virtually worthless at this time and remained so until the 1948 currency reform.

Although the agreement was immediately approved by the respective governments of the contracting parties, it did not pass without criticism. While the Americans continued to harbor a feeling that the Swiss had escaped too easily, the Swiss reaction was quite the opposite. They were convinced that they had been forced into the agreement by the United States because America would not release their frozen assets. To his credit, "Stucki . . . reminded his critics that Switzerland was dependent on the Allies for supplies of coal and wheat."[60] There was no doubt that the United States had played the leading role in the Washington negotiations, but this was not evident in the official records surrounding the talks there. It only became apparent when it was assumed by America's allies that the United States would administer the $58 million Swiss gold payment and liquidate assets for the Allied gold pool. Wrote one American observer, "Why the United States should assume the onus of undertaking this distasteful business for all the Allies, for benefit of a reparation pool is not known."[61]

While the Swiss payment was referred to as a voluntary contribution to Europe's reconstruction, it really symbolized a partial compensation to Belgium for the lost gold that had been in the care of the Bank of France. In fact, shortly before the Washington meeting had convened, Belgium had sent the Swiss National Bank a list of their lost gold bars, asserting that they had been received by the Swiss bank. The Swiss answer was that after a careful comparison of the Belgian numbers with their own records they found far too many discrepancies to reconcile. It was their judgment that no decision could be arrived at without consulting Reichsbank files and officials like Emil Puhl.[62] At approximately the same time that the Belgians were attempting to establish their claim with Switzerland, the Americans were in possession of relevant Reichsbank records that proved that the Belgian gold had moved from the Reichsbank to Switzerland. Unable to trace the disposal of the gold after its acceptance by the Swiss, the American secret reports were, unfortunately, not introduced into the debate at that point because the highly confidential survey of Reichsbank files in Europe had not yet been completed.[63]

60. Arnold and Veronica Toynbee, eds., *Survey of International Affairs, 1939–1946* (London: Oxford University Press, 1946), pp. 227–28; and the *New York Times*, 14 June 1946, p. 20.

61. Edwin Borchard, "The Treatment of Enemy Property," *Georgetown Law Journal* 34, no. 1 (May 1946): 393, n. 12.

62. Rings, *Raubgold*, pp. 114–17. After liberation in 1944, the Bank of France had offered Belgium a gold replacement from their own reserves, in turn asking Switzerland to return the Belgian gold purchased from Germany, ibid., pp. 104–5.

63. NA, RG 260, OMGUS, AGTS/2/6, S. Rose to J. Bennett, 12 July 1946; and L. Steere to Bennett, 12 July 1946.

During the final weeks of the war in Europe the Allies were all anticipating discovery of the remaining German gold reserves and, depending on the amount of course, knew that the whole gold debate would suddenly liven up. When Germany's gold stores were found by units of the American Third Army in April of 1945, that anticipation became a reality. As one U.S. State Department memorandum dryly phrased it, "The gold question may be accentuated by the discovery of the Reichsbank gold by the Third Army."[64]

Geography favored the Americans for their invading forces encountered the important German treasures first. But all of the Allied armies found riches of one sort or another since the Germans had secreted art objects, paintings, rare books and manuscripts, jewelry, securities, coinage, currencies, and bullion in a wide variety of locations and often in haste during the closing days of the war. Most of the larger museum and library collections and the contents of state banks and depositories, however, had been stored away months before the war ended. Since this had been accomplished according to a plan, it meant that location played an important part. In the case of currencies and gold, German banking officials had started their search for safe hiding places in mid-1944, as it became more and more evident that the Luftwaffe could no longer stop the devastating Allied air raids. After a survey of suitable places had been made, the Reichswirtschaftsministerium authorized the use of various kinds of mines and tunnels for the storing of state wealth. A number of Reichsbank employees had been involved in the planning and several of them would later provide the Americans with the details. One of them, Albert Thoms, would prove an invaluable source of information on the gold.[65]

In the last months of the war some of the Reichsbank gold deposited in several of its branches around Germany for selective use was recalled to Berlin and was scheduled to be stored in a mine in Thuringia. Thoms estimated the total amount in branch banks at about $22 million worth; the amount that was returned to Berlin for mine storage was approximately one third of that.[66] As the frequency of the air raids increased so did the urgency to remove the gold as quickly as possible from the capital. A direct hit on the Reichsbank's main building in early February forced much of the daily work to continue in the cellars and only confirmed the decision to get the gold out of Berlin without delay. The site selected for storage was an abandoned potassium mine, the Kaiseroda Mine, located

64. *F.R.U.S.*, vol. 3, 1945, p. 1200.

65. NA, RG 331, SHAEF G–5, 1/113, Historical Report, 12th Army Group, April 1945, p. 25.

66. NA, RG 260, OMGUS FINAD, Nixon to Bernstein, 6 September 1945.

at Merkers, a village not far from Bad Salzungen in western Thuringia. The mine was part of a vast system of tunnels and excavated chambers that spread underground for miles.

Albert Thoms, who played a major role in the moving operations, told his American interrogators later of the sense of desperation that gripped Reichsbank officials as they prepared to move the gold a week after the big raid that had destroyed the Berlin headquarters building. In their haste to get the first shipment underway, it was decided that only bag numbers, not bag contents, would be examined. Thoms said that even with this simplified approach mistakes were made in the counting and a shortage was later discovered.[67] The initial shipment consisted of twenty-two railcars which left Berlin on February 11th, with Thoms aboard. After arrival at Merkers, it took the German personnel and some foreign workers from the town four days to unload it. The second and smaller shipment, which arrived in mid-March, required two days for unloading. Although Thoms was certain that the shipments had contained gold and silver that came from SS sources as well as Foreign Office gold, he insisted that he had no record of the gold and money there. "The papers were either taken away or destroyed . . . the day the Americans arrived."[68]

In describing those final weeks and days of the war, Thoms told of the search by all kinds of agencies and offices for some place to put their precious records or equipment. As things became more chaotic, transportation was at times simply unavailable even if one could find storage space that was safe from the bombing. When word got around that the Reichsbank had found a large mine for storage, Thoms said, they were approached by other government offices seeking to share the space, and he implied that he personally would have refused to take SS and Foreign Office valuables, but could not do so. He did agree that it was proper for the Reichsbank to help other German banks, such as the Dresdner Bank and Deutsche Bank, with storage.[69]

The Reichsbank had moved large quantities of Reichsmarks and foreign currencies into the Kaiseroda Mine along with Germany's gold reserves, and this created a last-minute problem. Allied bombings of Berlin had damaged the printing presses there, and it became necessary to replenish the national currency from the cache in the mine at Merkers. Thoms and a number of other bank employees then found themselves, during the last few weeks of the war, making repeated trips down into the vault they had erected in the mine for bags of Reichsmarks. In fact, as the American troops were approaching the Merkers area, Thoms and a number of his

67. Ibid., Thoms interrogation, 19 April 1945, p. 2.
68. Ibid., pp. 1–2.
69. Ibid., p. 2.

colleagues were busily removing money that was scheduled for Berlin; however, the proximity of the war persuaded them of the futility of their actions and they decided simply to replace the sacks they had hauled out and make a run for it. While they were in the process of returning the sacks, piling them in front of the vault door, American soldiers passed by the mine entrance but made no attempt to stop them; this happened shortly before noon on April 4th.[70]

The Americans, like their Allies, expected to capture some of the German gold reserve during their advance into the Nazi stronghold, but no one could know in advance just when this might happen. With the Hitler regime in the throes of total disintegration, there was no way for Allied intelligence to secure reliable information. The internal chaos rendered any advance knowledge useless as circumstances forced last-minute changes and decisions that completely reversed previous planning. Fully aware of these conditions, the Allies knew that at any moment in the most unexpected of places they could encounter bits and pieces of Nazi treasure ranging from world-renowned paintings to chests of gold coins. In one instance the Americans did secure some advance information; during the capture of Aachen in November 1944, they discovered documents that pointed to a repository at Siegen, near Marburg. The intelligence proved accurate, for when they later occupied the area in question they found some priceless art works stored in an old iron mine.[71]

No doubt the anticipation that they would very soon uncover significant stores of wealth may have been gratifying for some military leaders but probably very few in the American army could appreciate what really lay in store for them. The Finance Section of SHAEF was composed of men who had made their living in finance and banking and they perhaps understood better than most the historical significance of what it meant to capture a nation's monetary wealth. Their reaction to news of the Merkers find was described in a secret but tongue-in-cheek report this way: "If the Finance Group had dreamed of ever participating in the excitement of hidden treasures, it might have been difficult to extract an admission. But they had it; probably the greatest cache in all history. . . . The Chief of the Group was not to be seen in his office for many days, for he was at Merkers trying to make his way among the generals, newspapermen, financial experts and others who could manage to make excuses for their presence there."[72]

By all indications the Americans did not know what they had at first, for the first troops had passed right by on April 4th just as the

70. Ibid., Statement of Dr. Werner Veick, Merkers, 10 April 1945, p. 105.
71. Ibid., RG 331, SHAEF G–5, 1/13, Historical Report, pp. 28–29.
72. Ibid., pp. 19–20.

Germans were carrying money bags back into the Kaiseroda Mine. Official U.S. Army reports record the capture of Merkers by units of the Ninetieth Division of General George Patton's Third Army and the information that some of the soldiers were told by foreign workers in the area of the gold. It was not until the next day, however, that a worker was actually found who had been in the mine and knew of the placement of the gold there. Without examining the mine, the commander of the Ninetieth Division passed the information on to higher headquarters in a brief message that read: "Merkers mine . . . contains marks, gold, silver, paintings, jewels. There are approximately 500 kilometers of passages in ground."[73]

Two more days would elapse before the Americans entered the mine. Obviously, the foreign workers had not impressed Patton's men with their gold story—not unusual under the circumstances, for U.S. troops were hearing many bizarre tales at that time. On the morning of April 6th two soldiers on guard at the Ninetieth Division command post about three kilometers beyond Merkers stopped some foreign workers for questioning. They happened to be two Frenchwomen seeking a doctor because one of them was pregnant and needed medical attention. This prompted the Americans to drive the women back to Merkers, and as they entered the village one of the women pointed to the Kaiseroda Mine and repeated the gold story. Unlike the earlier versions, the story recounted by the two women had some impressive details. They said that great art treasures from the German National Art Museum in Berlin and huge quantities of the German gold reserve were stored there and they were personally acquainted with some of the civilian German workers from Merkers who had worked four days unloading the first train full of treasure that had arrived. The soldiers believed the two women and alerted their commanding officer, who also found the account reasonable enough to investigate. Rounding up some of the workers the women had mentioned produced eyewitnesses who stated they had carried untold quantities of gold, silver, and jewels into the mine. Final verification came from German mine personnel who, when confronted with the story, quickly admitted it was true. To care for the paintings from Berlin an assistant museum director named Dr. Rave was even living in Merkers, they said.[74]

The Americans had heard enough to convince them they had found something important and a tank battalion was ordered to cover the mine entrances. It was too late to try to descend into the mine shaft that day but arrangements were made to start the electrical generators and check the

73. Ibid., "Report of Developments in Removal of Treasure from Kaiseroda Mine at Merkers, 19 April 1945," p. 1.
74. Ibid., p. 2.

elevator and lights for the next day. The German mine officials were placed under house arrest and told to report to the mine entrance the following day.[75] By the next morning, Saturday the 7th, after discovering that the mine had five entrances instead of two, additional reinforcements were called up. Finally, a senior military government officer of the Ninetieth Division, Lt. Col. Russell, accompanied by several of the German mine officials, Dr. Rave, the art curator, and U.S. Army Corps photographers, made the long descent into the mine. They followed the main tunnel to a vault sealed by a large steel door, in front of which were still piled the bags of Reichsmarks that had been so hastily abandoned. Unable to get the big door open, Russell and his group had to be content with a cursory examination of some art works found in a neighboring passage; they would return the next day.[76] The next day, Sunday, Russell's party entered the mine again, this time with some engineers who knew how to use explosives. At first they tried to dislodge the door by digging under it, but to no avail. A charge of dynamite was set in the adjoining wall and a large hole was blasted, giving entry into the vault. The gold seekers now found themselves in a huge, unventilated room full of bags of gold and baled currency. Suitcases with gold and silver jewelry, church ornaments, and tableware were stacked in the back. There was no longer any doubt; they had found Nazi Germany's carefully hidden treasure.[77]

Even in a world at war, the contents of the Kaiseroda Mine made headlines. The broad outlines of the discovery had appeared in print the very day Russell entered the mine. That is how Colonel Bernard Bernstein first heard the astounding gold story and, as deputy chief of the Finance Section of SHAEF G–5, he was more than interested. Within hours after reading the account of the Merkers find in the Paris edition of the *New York Herald Tribune*, Bernstein became the single most important figure in the affair.[78] One day Bernstein was in Paris reading about the gold, the next day he was virtually in command of the entire operation. His position in SHAEF Finance and his prior experience with the Treasury Department certainly made him an eligible candidate to oversee such an operation, but there was something else. The colonel was the choice of Secretary Henry Morgenthau, who wanted a man of his own political persuasions to control the treasure found in Germany and perhaps influence its ultimate disposition. Morgenthau had not succeeded in imposing his "plan" on the defeated Germans,[79] but he could still influence the

75. Ibid.
76. Ibid., pp. 3–4.
77. NA, RG 260, OMGUS FINAD, "G–4 Functions in ETOUSA Operations Merkers-Herringen-Frankfurt Areas of Germany, 9 April to 22 April 1945," p. 3.
78. NA, RG 331, SHAEF G–5, 1/13, Historical Report, p. 4.

nature of the peace.

One of Morgenthau's critics, Lucius Clay, the American general who would soon command the U.S. occupation of Germany, saw Bernstein's mission as evidence of the secretary's attempt to gain some control of postwar economic policy for that country. "I doubt if Colonel Bernstein is big enough to handle the overall financial problem," was Clay's blunt opinion. "He is very smart and energetic but is somewhat warped in his judgment of the problem as a whole."[80] But Washington's influence prevailed and Bernstein was soon informed that General Eisenhower wanted him to proceed to Merkers as quickly as possible and assume control over the contents of the Kaiseroda Mine:

> Col. Bernstein discussed the matter further with General Lucius Clay and General Crawford [assistant chief of staff, SHAEF G–4]. General Crawford stated that General Eisenhower wanted Col. Bernstein to go . . . to the mine and withdraw the contents. Plans for moving and places where it could be moved were discussed. General Crawford suggested Fort Ehrenbreitstein, which is across the river from Coblenz. At this time it was also agreed that Col. Bernstein was to have some discretion as to where the gold would be placed. . . . General Crawford said Col. Bernstein was to go directly to 3rd Army, get in touch with General Gay, Chief of Staff and receive instructions from him.[81]

After this meeting Bernstein flew on to Frankfurt in Crawford's plane for the meeting with Gay, during which time General Patton joined them. Patton wanted the gold moved as quickly as possible because it was tying up too much manpower and equipment, and he was eager to get the troops back in the line.[82] General Gay provided Bernstein with a letter authorizing the colonel to take control of the mine at Merkers and arrange for the removal of the treasure as soon as he could. Bernstein was given full power to decide on the personnel, including newsmen, who would be allowed into the mine or could view its contents. Patton's men would continue to provide security until the contents were moved elsewhere. Gay's letter extended Bernstein's authority to any further discoveries or captures of a like nature.[83]

The extensive war destruction in Germany did not leave Bernstein with a wide choice of depositories for the Merkers treasure. Besides Crawford's suggestion of the massive old Ehrenbreitstein Fortress, there was the large

---

79. See Jacobsen and Smith, *World War II Policy and Strategy*, pp. 404–8.

80. Jean Edward Smith, ed., *The Papers of General Lucius D. Clay*, vol. 1 (Bloomington, IN: Indiana University Press, 1974), p. 12.

81. NA, RG 331, SHAEF G–5, 1/13, "Report of Developments Kaiseroda Mine," p. 5.

82. NA, RG 260, OMGUS FINAD, "G–4 Functions in ETOUSA etc.," p. 4.

83. Ibid., Gen. Gay, letter of Instruction, 9 April 1945.

Reichsbank building in Frankfurt. After looking at both sites, Bernstein immediately decided that the Frankfurt location was far better. Ehrenbreitstein was already overflowing with art works and a variety of valuable archives that had been stored there since 1942 but, more important for Bernstein, the old fortress with its large sprawling buildings presented a security problem.[84] After arranging for the army engineers to begin work on the Reichsbank building in Frankfurt, Bernstein and his small staff of financial experts set off for Merkers. Provided that he could secure the specialists needed for the job, the colonel promised his superiors that he could start moving the treasure out of the Kaiseroda Mine in three or four days at the latest. Only official army photographers were to be permitted filming privileges during the moving operation.[85] Upon arrival at Merkers, Bernstein allowed himself a quick look at the mine contents before making arrangements to establish a command post for his assigned mission. Within hours some of the people he had requested for his staff began to arrive, and soon there would be a full contingent of experts in currency, including a specialist from the Bank of England named Major J. Fairfax Cholmely.[86]

Before the treasure was moved, General Eisenhower decided to make a brief stop at Merkers and see it for himself. Bernstein immediately began a check of all mine equipment—he had been stranded for several hours in the mine himself by a power failure—insuring that there would be competent personnel on duty. His anxieties were no doubt heightened by the news that Eisenhower would be accompanied by Generals Bradley and Patton.[87] The generals arrived the morning of the 13th and were immediately conducted by Bernstein and General Manton Eddy to the mine. In his war story Patton recorded his impressions of the mine: "It is a tremendous affair, having five hundred and eight kilometers of tunnels. These are from thirty to fifty feet high and about the same width. In addition to paper money and gold bricks there was a great deal of French, American, and British gold currency. . . . General Eisenhower said jokingly that he was very much chagrined not to find a box full of diamonds."[88] A Patton aide, Charles Codman, remembered that the flamboyant general tried a joke of his own as they were descending the sixteen-hundred-foot deep mine shaft in a hoist elevator: "If that clothesline should part promotions in the United States Army would be consider-

84. NA, RG 331, SHAEF G–5, 1/13, "Report," p. 6.
85. Ibid., p. 7.
86. Ibid., p. 8.
87. Ibid.
88. George S. Patton, Jr., *War As I Knew It* (Boston: Houghton Mifflin Co., 1947), pp. 291–92.

ably stimulated." Eisenhower advised him to save his witticisms until they were above ground again.[89]

By this time the treasure had only been in American custody approximately a week, but there were already divided opinions on what should be done with it. Bradley hinted at a simple but obviously unacceptable solution as he and Patton stood gazing at the gold horde: "If these were the old freebooting days when a soldier kept his loot, you'd be the richest man in the world." Patton only grinned.[90] Shortly before Eisenhower's visit to Merkers, he had received a copy of a U.S. State Department memorandum which revealed that some intense thought was being given the gold find, but a "final decision as to the ultimate disposition of the foregoing . . . will require careful study and probably consultation with our Allies."[91] Eisenhower's staff immediately prepared an exploratory paper on the legal and political aspects of the question of disposition. International law recognized that any movable property of an enemy state became the property of the capturing power:

> Under these principles, if the facts are as stated, the [German] bullion, coin, and currency would become the property of the United States. Art objects, even of the State, may constitute a special category to which these principles are not applicable. . . . There are international law precedents that where the forces of another nation have directly contributed to the capture and are under the same commander as the capturing forces, such other nation acquires a joint interest in the property. . . . It is not clear that this principle should not be applied to the capture in question.[92]

It was noted that a number of Combined Chiefs of Staff directives permitted the supreme commander to use any captured resources he needed, although it was not yet evident if the gold could or should be treated as other seized enemy property. It was concluded that while voices were being heard from some quarters that the gold belonged to the United States, there were serious political considerations that would influence any final decision.[93]

Immediately after the generals departed Merkers, Bernstein began the move, supervising all operations personally: "To facilitate rapid removal, jeeps with trailers were lowered into the mine to the 1600 foot level and

89. Charles Codman, *Drive* (Boston: Little, Brown, and Co., 1957), p. 281.
90. Omar N. Bradley, *A Soldier's Story* (New York: Henry Holt Co., 1951), p. 540. For Dwight D. Eisenhower's account of the Merkers visit see *Crusade in Europe* (Garden City, NY: Garden City Books, 1952), p. 449.
91. NA, RG 84, OMGUS POLAD, Marshall to Eisenhower, 10 April 1945.
92. NA, RG 332, ETO, SGS, 123/2, McSherry to C/S, 12 April 1945.
93. Ibid.

used to haul the treasure from the gold vault to the foot of shafts Nos. 2 and 3, whereupon the trailers were disconnected from the jeeps and hoisted to the surface, pulled by hand to loading ramps where the material was manhandled aboard the 10 ton trucks. . . . With this loading procedure the convoy was loaded in 20 hours."[94] Prior to the move all gold bags were tagged, and as each bag was moved to a trailer its number was carefully recorded on a loading sheet. Each load was accompanied to the surface and a waiting truck by the loading officer, who gave the tally slip to the officer supervising the truck transport. As each bag was placed on the truck, its number was again checked with the tally sheet for accuracy. The truck number and names and serial numbers of all personnel handling a specific loading were recorded on a separate listing. When a load was completed, the tally sheet and the personnel listing were returned immediately to the supervising officer in the vault. Before any vehicle departed, a check of the tally sheet and personnel was again made. The gold convoy left under heavy guard at 8 A.M. Sunday morning, April 15th, and arrived in Frankfurt am Main, some eighty-five miles away, at 2 P.M. Bernstein accompanied the convoy, and upon arrival at the Reichsbank building supervised immediate unloading, using the same cautionary procedures as those employed in loading. Using similar security measures, the art works were brought to Frankfurt the next day.[95]

Bernstein's initial report on the amount of gold bullion, currency, and other property discovered at Merkers was based primarily on the information his people found on the Reichsbank tags attached to the gold bags, boxes, and other parcels. There was no attempt to weigh or count the bullion or otherwise examine the rest of the treasure. The number of gold bars, bags of coins, and currencies were merely listed as found and the value estimated in dollar sums; the gold was evaluated at thirty-five dollars per fine ounce. The total for gold, including a few silver bars and coinage, came to $241,113,302.[96]

94. NA, RG 260, OMGUS FINAD, "G–4 Functions in ETOUSA," p. 8.

95. NA, RG 331, SHAEF G–5, 1/13, "Report," pp. 10–11. The art works required forty ten-ton trucks for removal and contained about one-fourth of the collections of the Prussian State Museums; none of the works at Merkers was looted.

96. NA, RG 260, OMGUS FINAD, "Gold Bullion, Currency, and Other Property Discovered by Third Army near Merkers," 20 April 1945, app. A.

CHAPTER 5

The Gold Pot

The Americans were acutely aware that those Allied nations that had lost gold to the Germans were monitoring the Merkers gold story every step of the way and expected momentarily to be invited to help sort things out. They were also soon to hear—unofficially—that the United States was entertaining the idea of possibly using the gold to purchase American wheat to feed Europe's starving millions.[1] If true, this would have proven a great blow to nations like Belgium and France, who had begun planning for the recovery of their lost gold since their 1944 liberation from the Germans. They had carefully reconstructed all of their records on the looted gold in anticipation of the day that it would be found again by Allied soldiers—just as it was at Merkers. And when that happened, those nations were ready to provide the Americans with lists that contained all the ingot markings, exact weights, and box numbers that had identified their treasures when the Germans hauled them away. There was no question in their minds that the gold was theirs and they wanted no mistakes: "Representatives of the French and Belgian Embassies at London, Moscow and Washington, took . . . steps to ascertain that if ever recovered, the metal should not be considered as war-booty," read a Franco-Belgian statement, "but should be restored to its legal owner."[2]

Several days after the Merkers find, both the French and Belgian governments made it clear to the United States that they expected restitution in accordance with the UN declaration of 5 January 1943 and requested clearance for their respective teams of bank experts to proceed to Germany to aid in the task of identification. "Where it is a question of precious metal," wrote the French chief of the military mission for German affairs to SHAEF G–5, "it would be desirable that French

1. NA, RG 260, OMGUS AG, 1945–46, War Department to Clay, 30 June 1945.
2. NA, RG 331, SHAEF G–5, 1/13, "Memorandum Relating to Gold Deposit Entrusted by Banque Nationale de Belgique to the Banque de France Prior to May 13, 1940 and Dispatched to Germany by the Enemy," p. 3.

experts be called upon to recognize the characteristics of any ingots discovered. If it is a question of notes on the Bank of France, these were incontestably a plundered French property, and should be wholly and immediately restored to France."[3] The American reply was diplomatic ("it is easy to appreciate the interest which you take in the valuable captures"), but politely pointed out that conditions were simply too "fluid, evidence so incomplete, and long term policy so obscure, that it would be premature for us to attempt to determine title to anything in Germany or undertake restitution as such. . . . [D]ecisions will be made later by the appropriate governmental authorities."[4]

As for adding French experts to the Americans and British already scheduled to join Bernstein in Frankfurt, Washington first wanted Eisenhower's opinion. This was explored in a flurry of telegrams during May–June, with SHAEF's reaction being generally negative. They objected to any additional participation in the appraisal work until a clear policy for disposal had been worked out. A problem would surely arise if the French were admitted to the Frankfurt circle and the Belgians, Dutch, Danes, etc., were kept out. To bring the French in would be to bring everyone else in, and this would be impossible at the moment.[5] To underscore the situation, the point was made by SHAEF that even Italy was clamoring to partake in the gold identification since the Germans had taken gold from them too. The Americans did not have to be so tactful here, however, and their reply to the Italians was short and to the point: "We feel that the time has not yet come when such a request can be considered. If the position changes we will inform you."[6]

The French demands were fueled when a news story about the American plan to buy wheat with the gold appeared. It implied that the Americans were going to use the gold to feed the Germans and rebuild that country, and French leaders were quoted as complaining of their rude treatment when they tried to find out what was happening with the gold. It was also stated that the French knew much more about the contents of Merkers than the Americans thought, for their troops had captured Emil Puhl, former Reichsbank vice-president, and he told them that the mine contained some of the Belgian gold. Since France had already reimbursed the Belgians for the gold they had had in safekeeping, their wrath at American actions was understandable.[7] By now Bernstein's people had already been hard at work on their respective counting tasks for about two months or

3. Ibid., Koeltz to Grassett, 11 April 1945; Koeltz to Grassett, 14 April 1945.
4. Ibid., Grassett to Koeltz, 22 April 1945.
5. NA, RG 332, ETO, SGS, 123/2, Eisenhower to CCS, 22 May 1945.
6. Ibid., SHAEF to AFHQ for Alexander, 23 June 1945.
7. *New York Herald Tribune*, Paris ed., 27 June 1945.

more and had virtually completed the monetary portions. Therefore, it is not too surprising that the Americans soon had no objections whatsoever to either the French or Belgian experts joining them in Frankfurt, if they so wished.[8]

The complete American dominance of the gold find was questioned by some of the Allies with vested interests in its final disposition, but they never openly challenged that control for obvious reasons. Just what the situation may have been had the Soviet Union shown a strong interest in the gold remains open to speculation. The Soviets were at first interested in any existing German gold as a part of their reparations demand; however, as the evidence mounted that the captured gold was not German in origin, but had been looted from occupied Europe, they preferred the more tangible assets. At the Potsdam Conference during July and August 1945, the matter was discussed at some length, and after U.S. Secretary of State James Byrnes informed Josef Stalin that it appeared fairly certain that the gold that had been recovered by U.S. forces in Germany was looted, the Soviet dictator replied that his country's concern was for German gold only. No gold claim would be made by the Soviet Union in return for a quantity of capital equipment.[9] Byrnes's implication that all of the captured gold could be identified as looted would prove premature, although there is probably no doubt that the American secretary was speaking in good faith at Potsdam.[10]

Bernstein's experts did not attempt an evaluation of the hundreds of crates of paintings and art objects that poured into Frankfurt as this was the province of the American Monuments, Fine Arts, and Archives and the Art Looting Investigation Units. Nor did the financial experts concern themselves for the moment with the large quantity of Reich patent-office records that were of immense value. The captured SS properties did contain some gold and silver bars in addition to many boxes of bracelets, rings, spectacles, cigarette cases, tableware, candlesticks, coins, gold dental crowns, and bridges, but the decision was that the entire lot should be considered as possible war-crime evidence. It was stored separately pending a special investigation to determine its evidential value.[11] Even at this early stage, when the SS loot was estimated to be worth several million dollars, the Americans were pessimistic about determining any

8. NA, RG 332, ETO, SGS, 123/2, Clay to SHAEF, 29 June 1945; and C.L. Adcock to USFET Bel., 5 August 1945.

9. *F.R.U.S.*, vol. 2, 1945, pp. 151ff.

10. When the Americans found millions of Russian rubles and documents on the Red Army among their war booty, the Soviets immediately demanded that it be turned over, but the U.S. authorities decided to make copies first, and the money was held for "investigation."

11. NA, RG 331, SHAEF G–5, 1/13, McSherry letter, 19 April 1945.

ownership and, in fact, it was thought virtually impossible. The idea of establishing some kind of charitable foundation from the proceeds was being considered.[12]

After supervising the Merkers move, Bernstein did not waste any time pursuing all the clues he could find in the Reichsbank records to locate other gold stores. Organizing a search expedition from his immediate staff, the colonel prepared to make a quick visit to a number of Reichsbank branches that appeared to have gold deposits on their books. Anticipating some problems in collecting, Bernstein requested that he be given an infantry regiment and a tank company, but his superiors had other pressing priorities and instead offered a nonmotorized platoon. Considering this more hindrance than help because he would have to provide the troops with transport and billets, Bernstein decided to risk it on his own and set off with his staff in two jeeps. Working from a list that he had developed and from some information given to him by several Reichsbank employees, including Thoms, whom he took along, the colonel left Frankfurt early on the morning of April 19th on a five-day trip looking for more gold.[13] It was now a race against time to forestall as many thefts as possible by seizing all known gold deposits or caches. In some instances this could be done as certain areas became a sort of no-man's-land with the retreat of the Germans, but even after the German surrender chaotic conditions continued to exist. The great temptation that gold and currencies presented meant that Bernstein had to be as watchful for Allied theft as for the retreating Germans. Given the circumstances it was inevitable that some gold and paper money disappeared, thus providing the basis for a continuing stream of postwar adventure stories filled with accounts of the people (and treasures) who presumably somehow slipped through Allied fingers and lived richly ever after.[14]

Admittedly, Bernstein encountered problems in trying to gather in the

12. NA, RG 332, ETO, SGS, 123/2, Adcock to C/S, 12 August 1945. The suggestion appears to have come from John McCloy, later German high commissioner, who noted a similar action after the Boxer Rebellion.

13. NA, RG 331, SHAEF, 1/13, Bernstein to C/S 3rd Army, 14 April 1945; and, Bernstein to McSherry, 23 April 1945.

14. Rumors concerning Germans and Allies who made off with sacks of gold at war's end were rife and mostly without substance; however, enough gold did disappear that a number of stories emerged. One American official insisted that "undiscovered" gold supported a number of Nazis who had escaped to South America, Spain, and Portugal, Martin, *All Honorable Men.* W. Stanley Moss explored such accounts more extensively in his book, *Gold Is Where You Hide It.* In 1960 some interest was aroused when Henriette von Schirach, wife of the leader of the Hitlerjugend, reported in *The Price of Glory* that vast quantities of Reichsbank gold had been hidden in Bavaria before Germany's surrender. The latest effort is the work of two British journalists named Ian Sayer and Douglas Botting who, in their book *Nazi Gold*, provide some interesting views on the Reichsbank gold that was not found at Merkers.

remaining gold that was still on the Reichsbank ledgers. At first it seemed purely a matter of chasing down all the leads he had, but it did not prove that simple. He was told by Reichsbank officials at Weimar, for example, that they had sent fifteen bags of gold to the branch at Naumburg shortly before his arrival, but before he could close in it had been dispatched again in the general direction of Hof in Bavaria.[15] At Apolda the colonel was informed that the gold had indeed been in their vaults, but had been sent back to Berlin two weeks ago. The story was repeated several times over, sometimes with a slight variation that involved the appearance of a Reichsbank director who personally took charge of some bags of gold and quickly departed, presumably to bring the gold to a safer place.[16]

Some of the adventures of Bernstein's reconnaissance gold team had an element of black humor in them. One in particular involved a store of gold that was supposedly in the Reichsbank vaults in the city of Plauen. When the finance group arrived—Bernstein had already returned to Frankfurt—they were told that the bank had as many as sixty bags of gold, but one of the essential keys to the vault was not immediately available. It seems the key in question had been in the possession of one of the responsible cashiers, but an Allied bombing raid the day before had destroyed the apartment house in which he lived and his body was presumed at the bottom of a pile of rubble. The Americans could either dig for the corpse and hope the key was to be found in a pocket, or call up some engineers and blast the vault open. They blasted, but to their disappointment did not find the sixty bags of gold there, only a special coin collection deposited in Heinrich Himmler's name.[17]

Considering their expectations of collecting additional large quantities of gold, Bernstein's people were somewhat disappointed. They had been on the road for two weeks, had covered more than nineteen hundred miles, visited banks, traced down clues, but had actually found a total of only about $3 million worth of Reichsbank gold at Zwickau, Eschwege, and Coburg.[18] Not a small sum to be sure, but not the large one they hoped for either. The German banks yielded so much U.S. currency (at Halle it was over $2,000,000) that the Americans began to suspect some of it was counterfeit. Some of the U.S. and British bills found at Merkers were examined and proven genuine, but as large quantities continued to be found suspicions grew and measures were taken to test all the currency that came into Frankfurt. Almost no counterfeit U.S. currency was

15. NA, RG 260, OMGUS FINAD, app. B, "Report on Reconnaissance to Discover Further German Gold, Foreign Exchange and Loot," 19 April to 23 April 1945, pp. 1b–2b.
16. Ibid., pp. 3b–4b.
17. Ibid., pp. 6b–8b.
18. Ibid., pp. 9b–13b.

discovered.[19]

During the period in which Bernstein and his staff were combing the countryside for gold, other U.S. Army units were finding some in the towns and cities they captured. A SHAEF message at the end of April advised army groups that "many dumps or deposits of gold and silver are now being uncovered in central and southern areas of Germany, some large, some small. Experience shows always worth while inquiring at Reichsbank branches concerning recent movements of gold. . . . [G]old stocks may still be in the process of being moved behind our front lines to safer hiding places."[20] Some of the gold that would eventually find its way to the Reichsbank building in Frankfurt was not captured in Germany, but in Austria. An exceptionally large quantity that fell to the Americans was the gold of the Hungarian National Bank. The personnel and the bank assets had moved into Austria in January 1945 from Budapest. As the American army approached Spital am Pyhrn, bank officers made contact and informed them of their holdings; soon U.S. Army trucks began arriving at Frankfurt with the first loads of some thirty-three short tons of Hungarian gold.

As the summer progressed, reports on the gold counting in Frankfurt began to filter out to the concerned parties. The first was a July memorandum to the State Department reading: "Bernstein could not give . . . exact and final figures at this moment, but total German gold captured and held in the American zone is something over $300,000,000. All of it came from the Reichsbank gold reserve. . . . In addition to the above amount, the Hungarian gold reserve of about $33,000,000 was discovered separately."[21]

A few weeks later Colonel Bernstein wrote General Clay that "experts from the U.S. Treasury and the Bank of England have just completed the job of weighing and appraising the value of the bars [and] gold coin. . . . The total value of all gold found in Germany at the rate of $35 per fine ounce is $262,213,000." About half ($131,837,000) was in the form of gold bars, the remainder in coin. The figure for the Hungarian gold was $32,175,000. The colonel noted that the gold found at Merkers represented 91 percent of the total German gold recovered.[22] Rare gold coinage and other miscellaneous items (some silver, platinum, etc.) were

19. NA, RG 332, ETO, SGS, 123/2, McSherry to SHAEF, 23 April, and Jenkins to 12th Army Group, 8 April 1945.

20. NA, RG 331, SHAEF G–5, 1/13, SHAEF Forward to 21st Army Group, 30 April 1945.

21. NA, RG 84, OMGUS POLAD, Heath to Murphy, 29 July 1945.

22. NA, RG 165, Records of War Department, General and Special Staffs CAD 386.3, Bernstein to Clay, 19 August 1945. Hereafter War Dept. Gen. CAD 386.3. The amount of silver recovered was valued at $270,469 and was almost entirely in bars.

not included in the overall dollar value given Clay, but Bernstein assured the general that his Frankfurt experts were able to determine just exactly what had been in the Reichsbank in Berlin: "You may be interested to know that for all of the gold found in Merkers mine and several other shipments, we have been able to reconstruct the exact position in which each bar was originally stored in the Reichsbank . . . before it was moved away, and now have the gold so arranged that any particular bar can be quickly located as a routine operation."[23] When conveying this information to the State Department, Clay revealed that he had given permission for French, Belgian, and Czech bank experts to visit the Reichsbank building in Frankfurt and observe the inventory process. They were not allowed to receive statistical materials, however, nor to take any notes away with them. The general agreed that any public information on the gold operation should come from Washington.[24]

The final—and revised—report came on September 6th and numbered over thirty pages. Entitled "Report on Recovery of Reichsbank Precious Metals," it presented an extremely detailed analysis of the inventory conducted by Bernstein and the Finance Section of SHAEF. Among the numerous details was the fact that the Merkers find was the most important gold discovery made by the Americans and came to a grand total of $238,490,000 worth of gold. The amount of gold recovered by the Americans elsewhere in Germany totaled $14,010,000, making for an overall sum of $252,500,000 captured. By a close examination of records in their possession and a reconstruction of missing files with the help of former German bank officials, the Finance Section was able to determine the exact closing balance of Reichsbank gold in the Berlin Precious Metals Department. The figure was $255,960,000 and, according to Bernstein, the Americans had succeeded in recovering an astounding 98.6 percent of it.[25]

Considering that none of the Allied powers had made specific plans to capture the gold of Germany, nor could they have controlled events sufficiently to have implemented a plan, it remains nothing short of astonishing that almost the entire German gold supply fell into American hands. The Finance Section report noted that there were "unaccounted for, some three and a half million dollars worth, made up as follows: 50 bars never heard of after evacuation from Weimar; 40 bars left in Berlin at the time of the shipment to Merkers; 2 bars lost somewhere in the chain of evacuation from Erfurt to Allgau [a German operation]; and, 147 bags of

23. Ibid.
24. Ibid., Clay to War Dept., 22 August 1945.
25. NA, RG 332, ETO, SGS, 123/2, Nixon to Bernstein, "Report on Recovery of Reichsbank Precious Metals," 6 September 1945.

coin originally at Magdeburg."[26] Even allowing for error or a degree of Army cover-up, the quantities of Reichsbank gold bars and coinage that escaped American confiscation were minimal and the sizable thefts that occurred more often involved currencies.[27]

The question now was just exactly what was to be done with this huge quantity of captured gold that had come exclusively into American hands. Obviously, there were several options available to the United States, but the most logical pointed in the direction of some form of reparation or restitution. There was little controversy among the Allies during the war about the question of German reparations and restitution, two words that seemed to mean much the same thing. There were, however, wide differences of opinion on the quantity and quality of what should be demanded of the Germans. John Maynard Keynes, the distinguished British economist, began pondering the subject even before the U.S. entry into the war. He recalled that "in the Treaty of Versailles a distinction was made between what we called restitution and reparations, restitution being the return in kind of the same or similar articles which had been stolen or requisitioned. Reparations were stated in terms . . . partly deliveries in kind . . . and partly payments in cash."[28] Later, Keynes admitted that a broader interpretation of restitution by some of the Allies could include everything their economy had lost during the German occupation. He speculated on the possible problems that would arise if such latitude were permitted and strongly favored a narrow interpretation, warning that the gold settlement would prove the most difficult to resolve.[29]

While some policy basis for the restoration of looted property was established in principle in the London declaration of January 1943, exact restitution procedures had to await a later date. As the war entered its final year the Allies had to confront the real possibility that Nazi leaders might try to prepare the way for their own escape or future by attempting to hide assets abroad. This realization was closely linked to the question of restitution for gold which would have to figure prominently in any such process. This was recognized at the time of the Bretton Woods Monetary Conference and in fact was noted in resolution VI.[30] By January of 1945, still several months before Patton's soldiers would stumble upon the gold cache at Merkers, British and French European Advisory Commission members were recommending advising the establishment of some kind of

26. Ibid., pp. 1–2.
27. See n. 14 above.
28. Donald Moggridge, ed., *The Collected Writings of John Maynard Keynes: Activities, 1941–1946*, vol. 26 (London: Macmillan, 1980), p. 330.
29. Ibid., p. 393.
30. *F.R.U.S.*, vol. 2, 1944, pp. 216–20.

Map 5.1   The American Gold Find, April–June 1945

(1) April 1945: Units of Patton's American Third Army find German looted gold in Kaiseroda Mine at Merkers, Germany, on April 6th; $238,490,000 worth of gold bars, coins. More than $14 million more in gold found in Reichsbank branches.

(2) All gold found in Germany and Austria by American Forces was sent to the former Reichsbank building in Frankfurt a.M., and placed in the custody of the U.S. Army Foreign Exchange Depository (FED). The total sum soon reached well over $300 million in gold.

(3) $4,743,809 in Austrian gold found by Americans near Salzburg.

(4) Hungarian gold, about $35 million, seized by American forces at Spital am Pyhrn.

(5) American forces captured some $25 million in Italian gold in tunnels of La Fortezza. Gold stored in Rome rather than in Frankfurt by American authorities and not included in the "gold pot."

separate restitution body. Great Britain was in the lead on the proposal, which included the view that all looted gold should come under the definition of identifiable or identical objects marked for replacement in a restitution program. The Americans were not opposed, but regarded January as a somewhat premature time to begin drafting such specific restitution policy.[31]

Naturally the entire debate was of the utmost importance to those nations formerly under German occupation, who were now waiting eagerly for news of what the advancing Allies would find in Germany. When the Merkers discovery became known they understandably wished to be included in order to take part in the counting, if not at Merkers, then in Frankfurt. They also felt that they had some right to be involved in the development of any Allied restitution policy. The Belgian and French national banks had already assumed as much soon after liberation and were preparing their claims to the Reichsbank gold as security against any Allied war-booty assertion. Thus, within hours of the news that the Americans had found the German gold in the mine near Merkers, the respective bank officials from Belgium and France were requesting involvement. Since France had already reimbursed the Belgian National Bank after liberation by providing them with a gold replacement, the French were most eager to gain access to the gold and establish some identification rights, as this letter to American authorities explained:

> As it is a case of spoilation, restitution of this gold should . . . be made to its rightful owner. Following the discovery by the 3rd American Army of an important stock of gold in Germany, the Bank of France has asked the National Bank of Belgium . . . to put in the field in agreement with you a mission able to determine the characteristics of the gold that has been recovered, and to confirm if amongst this stock there is bullion belonging to the National Bank of Belgium. The Bank of France and the French government being principally interested in this restitution . . . would be obliged if you would accord every facility to the mission in question and eventually to the French experts who may be attached.[32]

Although committed to restitution in principle, the United States did give some thought to the "war booty" legalities. The question arose during discussions by the American delegation with President Truman during the Potsdam Conference. It was agreed that the United States was bound by various international declarations to restore identifiable gold taken by the Germans, and most of the gold fell into this category. On the

31. Ibid.
32. NA, RG 331, SHAEF G–5, 1/13, Koeltz Letter, 11 April 1945.

other hand, it was argued, all gold captured was "war booty," but to insist on this would be construed as breaking America's commitments, and "might tend further to undermine the 'gold standard'—certainly contrary to our own interests in view of our already large gold stocks."[33] There was some reluctance, however, to abandon completely any claim rights, for the Americans saw it as a bargaining point that "will turn upon how far other nations yield to our views on reasonable definitions of both 'restitution,' 'war booty' and an accounting therefore. It also promises a lever to use in connection with the French who probably will assert the largest claim for 'restitution' of gold in our possession."[34] This discussion prompted a closer look at the wording of the United Nations declaration on looted property of January 1943, which clearly committed the United States to the return of looted gold. However, according to article LIII of the Hague Regulation of 1907, "if material is actually in use by the enemy forces or is helping its operations," it is liable to confiscation. Therefore the American conclusion was that "the gold in question, whether or not we recognize that title was in the German state, was clearly being used in behalf of the German state. Accordingly, from a strictly legal point of view, apart from the policy considerations involved, the gold may be treated as war booty."[35]

Such reasoning remained confined to the discussions of the American delegation at Potsdam and did not surface seriously when gold was debated later with the other Allies, although it hovered in the background. Rumor had it at one point that the Americans were considering diverting the captured German gold for the reconstruction of that nation. Note was taken of the fact that "none of the Big Three [U.S., U.S.S.R., U.K.] have implicitly or explicitly renounced a voice in the disposition of the gold," and the Americans and British had actually started talking about the "gold-pot theory." This was a recognition of the principle that nations whose gold was looted by Germany were entitled to restitution, but not to so-called identifiable gold. The sentiment was that they should proceed based on a maritime law that applied to a common disaster whereby "if A and B both ship cargo on a particular vessel and during a storm or fire A's cargo is jettisoned to save the ship, B's cargo, when it arrives safely in port, must bear a proportionate share of the loss suffered by A. The analogy has proved quite convenient in the presentation of the 'gold pot' principle."[36]

As Stalin had indicated earlier during the German reparations discus-

33. *F.R.U.S.*, vol. 2, 1945, p. 844.
34. Ibid.
35. Ibid., pp. 919–20.
36. Ibid., pp. 937–38.

sions at Potsdam, the Soviet Union did not intend to make any gold claims against the Western Allies' find, but the generalissimo's statement was not followed by any discussion and this left questions in some people's minds. Did he mean there would be no claims against such states as Austria and Hungary, for example? What of the other states that fell into the Soviet sphere but had gold recovered in the West? These were not answerable immediately.[37]

The more pressing concern for the United States was the development of some sort of compatible plan for disposing of the gold held in Frankfurt. Almost immediately after the American occupation of their zone in Germany, a field agency of the U.S. Army's Finance Section established the Foreign Exchange Depository (FED) in the former Reichsbank building in Frankfurt. It was designated as the central depository for all gold and other valuables found by the American army in the invasion (as well as what was recovered after the shooting stopped), which included the 159 tons of gold from the mine at Merkers. The pressures from America's allies, especially France, increased during those first postwar months, fueled by a statement reputed to have been made by Lt. Gen. Lucius Clay, then deputy military governor of the American zone of occupation. He was reported to favor the use of the gold to purchase imported supplies for Germany, thus giving some substance to the earlier rumor that the United States was preparing to claim the gold as war booty. However, the French were quickly assured that this did not reflect policy of the American government and that an official statement on the disposal of the gold was pending.[38]

Meanwhile, the U.S. representative on the Allied Commission of Reparations, Edwin Pauley, informed President Truman that "two possibilities will shortly become the subject of active discussion: (a) Restitution of any identifiable gold to the specific countries from which it was removed; (b) Regarding the gold . . . as a common pot, and distributing it equitably among those liberated countries which lost gold." Either (a) or (b) was agreeable to Pauley, but he recommended temporary retention of the gold or a sizable portion of it as insurance against any of the liberated nations reneging on existing or soon-to-be-incurred debts to the United States.[39]

The French were not to be put off, however, and continued to press their case for the restitution of the Belgian gold, which they assumed was in its identifiable state. They desired that Washington direct General Eisenhower to introduce the subject of gold found in Germany (all zones) for discussion in the Allied Control Council. The French were convinced

37. Ibid., pp. 566 and 937.
38. *F.R.U.S.*, vol. 3, 1945, p. 1239.
39. Ibid., p. 1240.

that not all of the Belgian gold had been recovered by the Americans, but suspected that a portion had fallen into Russian hands with the capture of Berlin.[40] Unconvinced of the French right to exert any influence over the disposition of gold captured by Patton's forces or any other American army units, U.S. Secretary of State Byrnes also rejected Pauley's suggestion to hold the gold for unsatisfied debts. Byrnes felt that there should be no conditions attached to returning the gold, but he very definitely favored the gold-pot policy and distributing the gold on a pro rata basis in accordance with losses. The secretary was still uncertain of whether the Russians had really excluded themselves from the disposition of all gold found in the West.[41] After gaining the assent of the president, Byrnes informed Pauley that the United States had no legal or moral basis upon which to lay claim to or attach gold belonging to other countries and, in fact, had so pledged itself in various wartime declarations and resolutions: "The position of the United States therefore, which you would express in your dealings with your colleagues on the Allied commission of reparations, is that gold captured by US Forces, as well as gold captured by other Allied forces, should in principle be restored to the countries from which it was looted without reservation, condition, or encumbrance." The American secretary did acknowledge the necessity to modify any commitment to the restitution of identifiable objects and advocated support of "pooling all gold found in Germany and Austria by Allied troops (British, American, French and Soviet) into a common pot. This gold would then be divided among countries which can establish the fact of German looting of gold from their jurisdiction, other than USSR, in proportion to their established losses."[42]

Since much more than monetary gold had been captured, agreement among the Allies on some aspects of the gold-pot policy, such as just what was to be included, had not yet been reached. The question of unminted gold, gold objects, other precious metals, monetary silver, and so on, had not been dealt with, although there was some agreement among the British, French, and Russians that all printed currencies and securities should be returned to their country of origin. Another undecided factor was whether German satellites such as Austria and Italy, who would be potential gold-pot claimants, should be treated equally with the liberated nations. Finally, the matter of how looted gold sold by Germany could be recovered and, if so, whether it should be added to the gold pot, still remained to be resolved in the wake of the Potsdam Conference.[43]

40. Ibid., pp. 1249–51.
41. Ibid., pp. 1250–51.
42. NA, RG 260, OMGUS FINAD, Byrnes to Pauley, 19 August 1945.
43. See Chapter 4.

In subsequent discussions the French, mostly through their Reparations commission representative Jacques Rueff, were reluctant to accept any proposal which did not reimburse them fully. In addition, they desired an agreement on the distribution of captured gold stored in the American zone that excluded the Soviets. What appeared to be the obvious was given in reply by the American chargé in Paris: "I . . . explained that when he [Rueff] used the 'or equivalent' that meant to me restitution in kind and that was not looked upon by my Govt with favor . . . when it was applied to gold as all the countries could not expect to secure more than the total amount captured."[44]

The French were not alone in expressing an intense interest in U.S. plans for the captured gold. The British were equally anxious to arrive at a policy, for continued delay simply meant that a final restitution plan was also held up. It was this impatience that probably prompted their suggestion in September 1945 that a special body be created to facilitate matters. Receiving both American and French support, it was proposed that an Inter-Allied Reparation Agency (IARA) be established to deal with the broad range of functions that the reparations responsibilities required as designated in the Potsdam Protocol. The IARA, to be headquartered in Brussels, would represent all claimants for reparations and restitution to the Allied Control Council, although neither the Soviet Union nor Poland were members of the agency. It was further stipulated that when agreement on an issue could not be reached in the control council, individual Western-zone commanders should accept the IARA recommendations.[45]

While these affairs were being debated during that fall of 1945, the bulk of the captured gold remained under the control of the American military, specifically, under the control of Colonel Bernard Bernstein, now director of the Finance Section of OMGUS, in Frankfurt. Although both France and Britain had finally accepted the gold-pot policy that America wanted, they complained that they were not getting all the relevant information on the gold stored in Frankfurt, such as assayers' reports, exact counting figures, and data on possible identification. It was in this connection that comments on Bernstein's behavior surfaced; one British report characterized him as "most discourteous" to their representative, while a French complaint said that their representative had simply been told that the information he had asked for had already been forwarded to the U.S. Treasury Department in Washington.[46]

This was indicative, no doubt, of the political influence exerted by

44. *F.R.U.S.*, vol. 3, 1945, p. 1262.
45. NA, RG 43, WW II Conf. Files, Waley to Dunn, September 1945; Reinstein to Rueff, 1 ct. 1945; and provisional note of Executive Committee, IARA, 11 October 1945, pp. 1–6.
46. *F.R.U.S.*, vol. 3, 1945, pp. 1366 and 1370.

Morgenthau and the Treasury Department earlier, for Bernstein was the secretary's handpicked candidate. When Morgenthau and his staff had discussed the question of who would be selected as the top man in German finance the previous April, it was firmly agreed that "Bernstein must not have a man above him who would disagree with him and frustrate him."[47] But what had been at one time an asset for Bernstein in securing him this important position soon turned into a liability as national policy shifted from harsh economic treatment of Germany to harsh reality. While General Clay denied being the party responsible for removing Bernstein from his job, he did admit that Potsdam chartered a more lenient course for Germany, and he was in full agreement.[48]

Events were now finally moving toward an international settlement on procedure in reparations and restitution which generally endorsed the British-proposed IARA. To this end a Paris Conference on Reparations was convened from 9 November to 21 December 1945, with representatives from eighteen nations present,[49] all claimants in one way or another of reparations from Germany. A lengthy and complex series of signed recommendations included the establishment of the Inter-Allied Reparation Agency; in addition, there was general adherence to the gold-pot policy, with distribution based upon proportionate shares as related to a proven amount of monetary gold looted by the Germans. A beginning date marking the point for establishing claims was set as 12 March 1938, the date of the Austrian *Anschluß* by Germany. All gold claims, with verifying data, had to be submitted to the governments of the three Western occupying powers for processing and distribution.[50] The door was left ajar for the consideration of those claims that would probably come from nations not represented at the Paris conference. Each of these cases entailed complications and unique circumstances that had precluded their participation at Paris; one of these was Hungary.

As the American forces neared Spital am Pyhrn, the Austrian town where the personnel from the Hungarian National Bank had brought their gold for safekeeping, it was decided to ask the Americans for protection. The Americans were told of the treasure as well as other important valuables carefully hidden in the cellar of an old monastery and watched over by a Hungarian Royal Police unit.[51] The gold horde and other state

---

47. *Morgenthau Diary*, vol. 1, p. 48.
48. Smith, ed., *Clay Papers*, vol. 1, pp. 70–71.
49. Albania, U.S., Australia, Belgium, Canada, Denmark, Egypt, France, U.K., Greece, India, Luxembourg, Norway, New Zealand, Netherlands, Czechoslovakia, South Africa, and Yugoslavia.
50. *Department of State Bulletin*, "Reparations from Germany," 27 January 1946 (Washington, D.C.: U.S.G.P.O., 1946), pp. 114–24.
51. NA, RG 260, OMGUS FINAD, "History of Hungarian Gold," August 1946, p. 1.

valuables had been moved into Austria a few months earlier by Hungarian officials fearful of capture by the rapidly advancing Red Army. Since Hungary under the Szalasy regime was a German ally at the time, it was logical to take such action, but just as predictably the National Provisional Government that quickly replaced it called the act one of thievery. A June note to U.S. authorities phrased it thus: "Hungarian Govt does *not* doubt that United States Army is properly safeguarding above mentioned valuables which represent Hungarian property and that in its generosity to Democratic Hungary these valuables will be returned to Hungary by United States Govt."[52]

This brief message does not really convey the tremendous significance that the Hungarians attached to the "valuables" now in U.S. possession because included was that most precious of historic national symbols for Hungary, the crown of Saint Stephen. Possibly the most renowned of Europe's royal crowns, presumably it was presented to Stephen I, king of the Magyars, at his coronation in the year 1000 by Pope Sylvester II, in gratitude for having established Christianity in his kingdom. The crown had been among the gold and other national treasures that had been moved westward, some to be deposited in the Spital monastery, some near Salzburg.[53]

The Hungarian situation presented the Americans with a problem they were not eager to confront at that moment. Although in possession of the treasure, they were well aware that the new Hungarian government had every legal right to it. Unlike the other gold stored in Frankfurt, it was completely identifiable and had not been looted by the Germans. The fact that it had been turned over to the Americans by representatives of a regime that had been a Hitler ally carried the clear implication that it should be used in some manner for postwar reconstruction in the liberated nations. The problem was that the new Hungarian regime had the Soviets' blessing and desperately needed the gold to get started. Before the Paris Conference on Reparations in November and December 1945, Western Allied sentiment had momentarily leaned toward the placing of all Hungarian gold into the gold pot while reserving some for any later Hungarian claims, but only after a peace settlement with that nation. At the Paris conference, however, the decision was made to exempt the Hungarian gold from the gold pot. It is not clear if this agreement reflected the changing political climate of the preceding seven months. In

52. NA, RG 332, ETO, SGS, 123/2, AGWAR to SHAEF (Gen. Key), 19 August 1945, p. 2.

53. Some scholars doubt that the crown captured by the Americans was actually the one placed on Saint Stephen's head in 1000, but rather was another crown made in 1270, after the first one disappeared. See Chapter 8.

referring to just how the gold came into American possession, conference language no longer characterized it as having been "captured" or "seized," but instead as having been "delivered."[54]

It was important to the United States to avoid any gold discussions that would open the debate on exactly what the position of the Soviet Union was. During the course of the Paris conference, U.S. representatives were cautioned by their State Department to assume that the Russian gold renunciation at Potsdam covered all gold found by Allied forces in Germany. The Americans were anxious to settle the Hungarian gold question quickly and quietly by simply excluding it from the gold pot. "Upon examination of the question," Acting Secretary Acheson wrote, "whether Soviet renunciation in fact covers gold found in Austria, Dept feels that Soviets are in position to advance strong arguments re their continued interest in Hungarian gold. . . . Dept feels it advisable therefore to avoid discussion at Paris whether Potsdam covers gold found in Austria." Acheson successfully recommended that there be no reference in any conference text to gold found in Austria on the grounds that, since Hungarian gold was not included in the gold pot, no mention was necessary.[55] This should have ended the controversy, but it did not. After the Paris decision, the U.S. made no immediate move to effect transfer of the Hungarian gold and as the months dragged by the Hungarian complaints grew louder and more strident. Their monetary system was on the verge of collapse and inflation rampant while they berated the Americans for their slowness, finally turning to the Soviet Union for help. The Russians responded by requesting, through the Council of Foreign Ministers, an immediate return of the gold.[56]

Shortly after the Soviet request the American ambassador to Hungary reported an interesting conversation with Premier Ferenc Nagy, who was later to be accused of conspiracy by the Communists and removed from office. The ambassador wrote that in late May 1946 Nagy had informed him that the complete bankruptcy of his government was inevitable if currency stabilization was not promptly achieved. The premier expressed

54. NA, RG 160, OMGUS FINAD, "History of Hungarian Gold." Actually, Allied forces had "seized" a train carrying some Hungarian gold and other valuables, the so-called "Budapest loot train," as the news media dubbed it. The train contained some items that had been taken from Hungarian Jews, and some of the valuables were removed by German guards and never recovered. Bernard Bernstein, who subsequently became a legal adviser to the American Jewish Conference, pressed the claim of Hungarian Jews (and Romanians) to what was then called heirless property since it could not be identified. It was recommended that the Hungarian government transfer all rights over the property to the United Nations to be used for Jewish relief and rehabilitation in Hungary.

55. Ibid.

56. NA, RG 260, OMGUS AG, 1945, Heath to Clay, 14 May 1946.

regret over what he termed American ignorance and indifference to the desperate situation that the Hungarians now faced and urged the utmost speed in making practical arrangements for his people to enter the American zone of occupation to prepare the gold for transport. Nagy admitted being caught between the Americans, who pointed to the Russian pressures for reparations on Hungary as the cause of that nation's inflation, and the Russians' view that the return of the gold would bring stabilization and the ability to pay. He told the U.S. ambassador that his strategy was to get the gold first from the Americans and then try to persuade the Russians to reduce their reparations demands. "My comment," wrote the American ambassador, "to which he readily agreed, was that he was perhaps pressing us first because of confidence in customary American benevolence."[57] To insure action on his plea for speed, Nagy led a special economics delegation to Washington, where he successfully presented his case, and on June 14th he secured a promise that steps would be taken instantly to start the gold transfer. Meanwhile, permission was granted for Hungarian finance and banking experts to travel to Frankfurt to examine the bar lists, and within days preparations for transporting the gold to Budapest had been completed with the FED.

The long-awaited transfer actually began with teams of Americans and Hungarians stacking some ninety piles of gold bars, recording each number, and exchanging countersigned receipts. After three days of this tedious undertaking, they had packaged 2,669 gold bars and forty-nine bags of gold coins and were ready to depart. In the early morning hours on August 3d, guarded by thirty-three American military policemen, the gold was loaded aboard a fleet of trucks and driven through the deserted streets of Frankfurt to the central train station. There it was placed in a waiting train, the cars of which carried a warning in five languages: "U.S. Army supplies. Persons attempting to pilfer this car will be shot without warning!"[58] The train, one that Hitler had built as a present for Mussolini, departed with the Hungarian gold on its six-hundred-mile journey to Budapest. The high-ranking American and Hungarian passengers were joined briefly by a Russian delegation as the train passed through the Soviet-occupied portion of Austria. Decorated with huge American and Hungarian flags, the train finally arrived in Budapest amidst the cheering of thousands of people, Nagy among them.[59] One U.S. newsman reporting the scene wrote: "In diplomatic circles the return of the gold was viewed as a strong American political bid to 'keep a window open to the west' in Russian-occupied Hungary, and as

57. Ibid., Murphy to Clay, 3 June 1946.
58. Ibid., OMGUS FINAD, "History of Hungarian Gold," August 1946, pp. 2–3.
59. Ibid., p. 304.

a challenge to the Soviet regime in its efforts to obtain cooperation in the American State Department program to rehabilitate the one-time German satellite."[60] The gold delivery was regarded by the Allies as direct restitution, since the entire amount in question was returned and it did not represent a proportional share in the gold pot. The return of the Hungarian royal crown was not included, however, and this was to place a shadow over U.S.–Hungarian relations for years to come.

During the unfolding of the negotiations on Hungarian gold, the Allies also focused some attention to Romania. As a nation that had lost territory and independence to both the Russians and the Germans in the war years, Romania had at one time received gold from the German Reichsbank. When the Americans began their interrogations of Reichsbank employees at Merkers in April 1945, it was discovered that Belgian gold had been used by the Germans to pay for Romanian oil. One former Reichsbank official set the amount shipped direct to the Romanian National Bank at over $53 million worth.[61] The Allies had known for some time that the Romanians were acquiring gold from Germany in exchange for their oil, but were unaware that it was some of the gold that had come from Belgium. France was the first of the Allies to request the Romanian government to leave the acquired gold unaltered until it could be thoroughly examined, but was soon joined by the Americans and the British. The three Allies asked for a look at the records detailing wartime gold transactions conducted by the Romanian National Bank. In a relatively prompt reply, the Romanians acquiesced and in March 1946, provided a careful breakdown of all wartime gold activity involving their national bank. The interrogated Reichsbank official had given a fairly accurate report, for between September 1939 and August 1944 the records showed that the gold coming from Germany amounted to $65.5 million, $11.7 million of which had not come direct to Bucharest but had been deposited to a Romanian account in Switzerland (Union des Banques Suisses). The $53 million balance still remained in Bucharest in its original form as marked gold bars received from the Reichsbank.[62]

As noted earlier, Colonel Bernstein had established that the Belgian gold had been resmelted and given new numbers at the Prussian State Mint. In 1946 a secret American State Department report on Romania stated:

60. Ibid., AP Correspondent Hal Boyle, 6 August 1946.
61. Ibid., OMGUS FINAD, Thoms's Statement, 12 April 1945, p. 2.; and Jahnke Report, "Special Gold Transaction, 1938," pp. 2–3.
62. NA, RG 43, WW II Conf. Files, Fletcher to Reinstein, "Rumanian Gold," 12 November 1946, pp. 1–2.

> On the basis of careful studies made in the Department and by the U.S. Treasury, it can be assumed that on the average 74% of all gold that the Germans sold to foreign central banks was looted. We already possess documentary evidence that from the gold held in Rumania 33.8 million dollars-worth was Belgian looted and from the gold deposited in Switzerland 2.8 million dollars-worth was Belgian looted.[63]

Matters were further complicated by the fact that, while the Allies had the problem under study, the Romanians were busily negotiating a loan from Switzerland that would provide them with 75 to 100 million francs' credit, using the gold that was deposited there as collateral. The Swiss bankers had asked the Romanians to secure Allied Control Council approval; however, the Americans refused their consent pending the conclusion of a satisfactory agreement on the "tainted gold" question in general.[64]

Some gold also unexpectedly turned up in the former German embassy in Madrid, Spain, in May 1945. Estimated at one ton, with a value of $1,250,000, the gold became part of the gold pot on the basis of an American decision that it belonged with the other gold in Frankfurt. It consisted entirely of gold coins, mostly British gold sovereigns, and after some unnecessarily complicated negotiations it was flown by an American plane to Frankfurt in 1946.[65]

In an action to sweep up any gold, silver, or jewels that had been missed after the initial occupation began, the American and British military authorities ordered a series of raids in their respective zones. Planned on the basis of lists of gold rings, dental fillings, watches, and other jewelry items found in the files of the Reichsstelle für Edelmetalle, it was assumed that most of these valuables were still in Germany (the French and Russians did not participate). Dubbed "Operation Sparkler," the roundup netted millions of dollars worth of miscellaneous valuables. Since the gold found was primarily nonmonetary, it was not scheduled for the gold pot although it was eventually subject to claim.[66]

By the summer of 1946, it was evident that additional machinery was now needed to implement the provisions of the Paris Agreement on Reparations that had been signed at the beginning of the year. Specifically, a supervisory body was needed to develop and oversee the restitution of gold to claimant nations. Even long before the Paris Conference

---

63. Ibid., p. 3

64. Ibid., U.S. Delegation to Council of For. Min., New York, 3 December 1946.

65. NA, RG 260, OMGUS AG, Correspondence, Dodge to Office of Political Affairs, December 1945.

66. *New York Times*, 12 September 1946, p. 8, and 14 September 1946, p. 2. From an estimated $150 million in value recovered, about $40 million worth of gold and gold items were included.

on Reparations in November and December 1945, the prevailing sentiment among the three Western Allies, France, Great Britain, and the
United States, had always been that they, and they alone, should constitute the deciding factor in the disposition of the gold captured in Germany
and Austria. Therefore, the next important step in the Second World War
gold saga would be dominated by the Allied creation of an agency known
as the Tripartite Commission for the Restitution of Monetary Gold.

CHAPTER 6

The Politics of Allied Cooperation

It is probably safe to speculate that, as the Allies began their plans for the restitution of monetary gold in 1946, not a single official connected with the process dreamed that the books would still be open more than thirty-five years later. Of course, many claims were quickly resolved by the Tripartite Commission for the Restitution of Monetary Gold, but some were not, and this was to prolong the life of that body created in 1946 for an indefinite period. It meant that the problem of Nazi looted gold, a subject that would soon fade from the minds of most people to be relegated to seldom-recalled memories of that unpleasant wartime, would continue to haunt the fringes of the diplomatic world. It would become a matter rarely referred to publicly by the major powers and mentioned in only the briefest of press announcements.

Before the Paris Conference on Reparations ended, the United States expressed an interest in establishing a gold distribution system speedily, urging that it be done as soon as agreement could be reached in Paris. American Secretary of State Byrnes advised that the "allocation of shares in the pot is for determination by U.S., Brit and French Govts. . . . Determination of shares will require presentation of claims by Govts of countries from which Germans looted gold together with proof of such looting. Nature of invitation to submit such claims and method of processing claims . . . [to be] worked out with Brit and French."[1]

The Paris conference recommended that all monetary gold found in Germany (including coins), to which restitution claims could apply, be considered looted gold to be pooled for distribution to those nations permitted to participate in the gold pot. It was obvious that claimants would not receive full restitution, but that all settled claims would liquidate further demands against Germany for looted gold.[2] The over-

1. *F.R.U.S.*, vol. 3, 1945, pp. 1403–4.
2. Ibid., pp. 1405–6.

whelming portion of gold marked for distribution consisted of monetary gold looted by Germany and recovered by U.S. forces in the huge cache hidden in the Merkers mine in April 1945. An additional amount came from miscellaneous sources plus the sum agreed to by Switzerland under the Washington accord of May 1946, which represented the stolen monetary gold sold by Germany to the Swiss. Gold looted from the victims of the concentration camps and recovered in Germany was placed under the administration of the Intergovernmental Committee on Refugees for use in rehabilitating and resettling victims.

In simultaneous statements on 27 September 1946 in the U.S. *Department of State Bulletin*, the *London Gazette*, and the *Journal Officiel de la République Française*, the three Allied governments announced the establishment of a Tripartite Commission for the Restitution of Monetary Gold in accordance with part III of the Paris Agreement on Reparations. In a joint communiqué to all concerned nations ("Letter to IARA Countries on Gold") the Allies noted that the Tripartite Commission was not connected in any way with the IARA, although both bodies were headquartered in Brussels. IARA nations were assured that the commission would be guided by the applicable UN wartime declarations on gold and that the following definition of "monetary gold" had been adopted: "All gold which, at the time of its looting or wrongful removal, was carried as a part of the claimant's monetary reserve, either in the accounts of the claimant government itself or in the accounts of the claimant country's central bank or other monetary authority at home or abroad."[3]

The Tripartite Commission, in its quasi-independence, was empowered to speak for its respective governments on matters related to their assigned task under the Paris Agreement on Reparations; however, it did not devise policy for sharing in the German gold pot. The official languages for commission work were English and French, and all documentation was issued in those languages. The stated functions of the commission were to: (1) request and receive monetary gold claims that were supported by verifiable data; (2) examine said claims and determine their validity to share in the gold pot; (3) announce eventually the total value of the gold pool available for restitution; (4) declare the amount available from the gold pot to each eligible recipient after all claims were received and evaluated; and (5) carry out any additional instructions on gold distribution agreed upon by the three governments that established the commission. All expenses incurred by the commission in the performance of its duties were charged to the monetary gold pool.[4]

3. NA, RG 43, WW II Conf. Files, "Letter to IARA Countries on Gold," 4 December 1946, pp. 1–2.
4. *Department of State Bulletin*, 29 September 1946.

The first Allied delegates, called commissioners, were Jacques Rueff for France, Desmond Morton for the U.K., and Russell Dorr for the United States. Decisions had to be unanimous. The commissioners were instructed to deal only with authorized representatives of the claimant governments and were not permitted to enter into or accept any communication from individuals attempting to make gold claims. Claimant governments were cautioned to prepare their supporting documentation with the utmost care and give special attention to the completeness of all materials submitted. For example, thorough bank records pertaining to all gold transfers considered looted or wrongfully removed by Germany during the war were absolutely essential to support claims and determine the ultimate shares. All documents submitted had to be in six copies with both English and French translations. A concluding note in the commission literature distributed to prospective claimants read: "It will be understood that the Commission, in view of the very large sums involved, and of its responsibility for determining the relative shares of the claimant Governments, will feel obliged to scrutinize with the greatest care all information received."[5] Ronald Wingate, who served for a time in Brussels as an assistant to British commissioner Desmond Morton and later was to replace Morton, recalled that the claims were far in excess of the amount of gold available for distribution. This resulted in "plenty of cut and thrust in debate, which was in English and French, and a great deal of diplomacy and bargaining behind the scenes between the various powers."[6] As the commissioners' work progressed, however, it was evident that records that came into their hands as substantiating documentation permitted them to establish precisely the movements of gold that had occurred between one bank and another during the war.

It did not take long before ten nations—Albania, Austria, Belgium, Czechoslovakia, Greece, Italy, Luxembourg, the Netherlands, Poland, and Yugoslavia—filed claims with the commission for shares in the Nazi looted gold. The first problem the commission encountered was that some of the claims were fully verifiable on the basis of the data submitted, while others were not. In some cases data were insufficient, questions surfaced on certain purported facts, and this usually required additional time before any judgment could be rendered. Concerned about the delay in placing the gold back into circulation, the commission agreed that undisputed claims would be paid as quickly as possible while deliberation on others would continue. Additionally, the commission could not determine the claims made by those nations not represented at the Paris conference

5. NA, RG 43, WW II Conf. Files, "IARA Letter," 4 December 1946, p. 2.
6. Ronald Wingate, *Not in the Limelight* (London: Hutchinson and Co., 1959), p. 226.

until the exact nature of their participation had been decided.[7]

Unlike Hungary and Romania, which had come under Soviet influence immediately at the war's end, states such as Austria and Italy presented the Allies with quite different problems when it came to the matter of gold distribution. While there was a certain confusion about whether they should also be permitted to share in the gold pot along with those nations entitled to restitution, there was acknowledgment that they did occupy a special position. This was based primarily upon the Allied intent to offer early peace treaties to Austria, a country that had somehow come to be regarded more as a captive than an ally of Germany, and Italy, a nation that had surrendered to the Allies in 1943.

Prior to the Paris Conference on Reparations in November 1945, Britain had proposed that Italy should be entitled to make claims against Germany for restitution of identifiable property. This was in reference to the gold from the Bank of Italy that had been secreted in the La Fortezza stronghold in 1943.[8] A portion of it had been moved into Germany, and some had been shipped to Switzerland (to the Swiss National Bank and the BIS) as the Allies neared. In May 1945 units of the U.S. Fifth Army, under a combined Anglo-American command, occupied the region and found the gold that still remained stored in the Fortezza tunnels. Officials of the Bank of Italy had stayed with the gold and assisted American and British officers in their inspection. The decision was to return the gold to the bank vaults in Rome, where it was to remain under the custody of the Allied Financial Agency until such time as the Combined Chiefs of Staff issued orders for its disposal.[9] For the Allies there was no question but that the gold belonged to Italy, although the French thought it should go into the gold pot with the Italian share being determined after a peace treaty had been signed. France also insisted that since Vichy had been forced to provide Italy with certain credits that involved the exchange of gold in 1941, the Italians now owed them some fifteen tons of gold.[10] Ultimately, it was decided that Italy would share in the gold pot, but was obliged to effect gold restitution to France (fifteen tons), Yugoslavia (ten tons), and Albania (three tons), nations from which Italy had taken gold during the war. The gold that had been returned to the Bank of Italy in Rome was not destined for the gold pot, only that portion that had earlier gone to Germany. Presumably, the gold that had been sent to Switzerland would also be placed in the gold pot, if and when it was recovered.

7. United States, Department of State, *Germany, 1947–1949: The Story in Documents* (Washington, D.C.: U.S.G.P.O., 1950), p. 429.

8. See Chapter 1.

9. NA, RG 43, WW II Conf. Files, "Gold at La Fortezza, Italy," p. 3.

10. *F.R.U.S.*, vol. 3, 1945, pp. 1375–80.

Just as in the cases of Hungary and Italy, the Allies recognized the special circumstances that applied to Austria on the gold question. They had in fact set the starting date of the German gold looting with the beginning of the Austrian *Anschluß* in March 1938, as noted. While there had been some skepticism in the first period that the German absorption of the Austrian gold could be defined as "looting," this view changed as the war progressed. Although Austria was not regarded as a nation that had been occupied and looted as other nations had, the Allied opinion was that the Austrians had very definitely been victims of German expansion and deserved some consideration. The gold stock of the Austrian National Bank—over 100 million in dollar value—was transferred by the Germans into the Reichsbank, leaving only a small amount, almost entirely in gold coins, in Vienna.[11] By the time of the Paris Conference on Reparations in 1945, the Allies had decided that Austria should share in the gold pot. Since it was agreed at Potsdam that Austria did not have to pay reparations and should have economic independence, the U.S. position was that they should have immediate participation rights in the gold-pot distribution, but this was not generally supported. In the summer of 1946, in a letter to the U.S. Treasury Department, Austria formally reported its gold loss to Germany as $102,000,000 and indicated that both France and Great Britain were in agreement that Austria participate in the disposition of gold found in Germany.[12]

While the Tripartite Commission had the responsibility for implementing Allied decisions in regard to the German looted gold as established in the Paris agreement, policy for those nations not represented at the Paris conference was set by the economic delegations of the United States, France, and Great Britain to the Council of Foreign Ministers. Each delegation was composed of financial and banking experts led by Sir David Waley for England, Mr. Jacques Reinstein for the United States, and M. François Valery for France. The secret talks conducted by these delegations were marked by considerable disagreement on a number of basic issues, which made progress slow and difficult since decisions had to be unanimous. Debate very often ended in strong differences of opinion and no formal action was taken on the problem at hand. Many of the disagreements revolved around the American determination to move quickly in gathering data and making decisions on who was to share in the German gold pot and under what conditions. The United States preferred the approach of giving the benefit of doubt to potential claimant nations such as Austria, Italy, and Poland, and passing the details on to the

11. NA, RG 43, WW II Conf. Files, "Gold for Italy and Austria," 3 December 1946.
12. *F.R.U.S.*, vol. 3, 1945, pp. 1366–67; and NA, RG 43, WW II Conf. Files, USFA, Vienna to War Dept., 15 October 1946, p. 1.

Tripartite Commission for ultimate settlement. While Great Britain usually favored the American lead, although not always, the real contest was between France and the United States. The French position, in contrast to that of the Americans, was to spend more time on each unresolved issue, take each item under thorough consideration while gathering additional data, and most important, clarify exactly the degree of French involvement. This often resulted in prolonged and frustrating discussions with no holds barred, the Americans pushing for a decision and the French refusing to agree until more instructions had arrived or more information had been collected. One example of these thorny issues was the Salzburg gold affair.

At war's end American forces had taken possession of nearly $5 million in gold near Salzburg, Austria; it was what remained in the Austrian National Bank after Germany's departure in 1945, but it was gold that had been in the bank from 1938 and before. Since this was the case, the American inclination was to release the gold back to the Austrian National Bank at some appropriate time on the assumption that it was not looted gold and therefore not subject to the gold pot.[13] Before taking any action in that direction, however, the American occupation authorities in Austria requested the Austrian National Bank to submit an ownership claim with supporting evidence that the Salzburg gold was in fact Austrian by virtue of having been there before the German annexation. Declarations from several Austrian bank officials pointed out that the gold consisted primarily of gold coins that had been in the bank's possession before the *Anschluß*.[14] The Austrian officials submitted declarations detailing the gold coins and a small amount of gold bullion that remained in the bank in April 1945. The Finance Section of U.S. forces in Austria then recommended that the gold, valued at $4,743,809, be released to the Austrians:

> The gold should be physically turned over, in Salzburg, to representatives of the Austrian National Bank, after a statement will have been signed by the Austrian Government to the effect that it will honor all claims to any part of the gold by any person who, in the opinion of the Government of the United States, establishes his rightful ownership. . . . Preparations should be made for an official ceremony, appropriate on the occasion for the return of a part of Austria's original gold holdings.[15]

13. NA, RG 43, WW II Conf. Files, "Return of Gold," 22 November 1946, pp. 1–2.
14. See Chapter 1.
15. NA, RG 43, WW II Conf. Files, "Return of Gold," file, H.Q., U.S. Forces in Austria, USACA Section, Finance Div., 22 November 1946, p. 2.

It was established that German forces had brought about $98,000 worth of gold into Austria, and this amount was deducted from the gold sum returned to the Austrian National Bank in December 1946. Therefore the Salzburg gold was no longer in U.S. possession when the economic representatives to the Council of Foreign Ministers began their discussions in London in late January 1947. After the French representative, Calvet, complained that the United States was creating a situation that would cause many legal complications, Reinstein suggested that since the gold transfer had already occurred France lodge its objection with the Tripartite Commission.[16]

In a lengthy series of intensive discussions in London in January 1947, the search for a set of mutually acceptable protocols setting forth the exact terms for Austrian, Italian, and Polish participation in the German gold pot continued. It began with an examination of previous drafts for Austria and Italy, which already outlined the fact that both nations had been conceded share rights in the gold pot although different particulars applied. In both instances shares were to be reserved by the Tripartite Commission until its work had finished and/or peace treaties had been concluded. Neither Austria nor Italy were to share in the gold recovered from Switzerland. Presumably, since Austria did not have to pay reparations and no outstanding claims were pending, their share, yet to be determined by the commission, would be unencumbered. In this initial draft, drawn in late 1946, Austria was described as "the first country to fall victim to Hitlerite aggression," language that was to be omitted from subsequent drafts.[17] While Italy was admitted to claimant's status in the early draft protocol, with payment tied to the signing of a peace treaty, outstanding liabilities in the form of a French claim for fifteen tons of gold, a Yugoslav claim for ten tons of gold, and an Albanian claim for three tons of gold still existed.[18] In previous talks among the three Western Allies, France had taken the strongest stand against either Austria or Italy sharing in the gold recovered through the Swiss negotiations, threatening to refuse any settlement that allowed for claims by former enemy states. This argument was to prevail despite some American reservations that such action might legally close the door for these nations in any future claims against Switzerland.[19]

It was the American suggestion that Poland be placed on the same

16. Ibid., "Restitution of Monetary Gold," London meeting, 4 February 1947, p. 2.
17. Ibid., "Secret Draft Protocol regarding Austrian Participation in the German Gold Pool," 20 December 1946, p. 1.
18. Ibid., "Secret Draft Protocol regarding Italian Participation in the German Gold Pool," 20 December 1946, pp. 1–2.
19. NA, RG 43, WW II Conf. Files, Rubin to Reinstein, 6 January 1947, pp. 1–2.

general basis as Austria and Italy at this time, and this met with British support. It raised the question of the former Free City of Danzig, whose gold had been taken over by the Nazis in 1939; now the city was under Polish administration. The Anglo-American solution was simply to postpone any decision but recognize that Danzig might be a future claimant.[20] France was absolutely opposed, however, and did not feel that Poland should be given entitlement to the gold pool shares, including those of Danzig, under any circumstances. To even send that nation a gold questionnaire, France maintained, "would tend to encourage [the] Polish Government to believe that it might have some valid claim."[21]

From the very beginning of the discussions France had objected to the sending of gold questionnaires to any of these three nations, contending that since the final draft of the protocols had not even been agreed upon, it only raised false hopes to send a questionnaire.[22] The American view was that dispatching a questionnaire did not signal a commitment, and any misunderstanding could be avoided by a simple note of explanation. Additionally, Reinstein thought that helpful information could be gained by the submission of questionnaires, especially in the case of Poland:

> In the opinion of the American Government, such information is necessary for the proper execution of the Paris Agreement, regardless of whether the three governments are eventually admitted to participation in the gold pool. We have encountered considerable difficulty in obtaining the agreement of the French to our views despite the fact that we have been willing to make clear in draft invitations that they are without prejudice to the ultimate disposition of the gold.[23]

In an observation on the months of discussion that he had participated in already in New York, Paris, and now London, Reinstein pointed out that they (the Americans, British, and French) had come very close at times to tentative agreements on Austria, Italy, and Poland, "but on each occasion, agreement has been upset, usually by the French." He was particularly concerned that the continuous delays would probably prevent the placement in the pending peace treaty, scheduled to be signed 10 February 1947, of the specific terms to be applied to Italy.[24]

20. Ibid., "Secret Draft regarding Participation in the German Gold Pool," 8 January 1947, p. 2. This was obviously an attempt to defer any consideration of Danzig beyond a general statement pending a final peace treaty with Germany, which appeared a distant prospect at that moment.
21. Ibid., Caffery to American Embassy London, 17 January 1947, p. 1.
22. Ibid., American Embassy to French Foreign Minister, 11 January 1947.
23. Ibid., Reinstein to Murphy, 20 January 1947, p. 1.
24. Ibid., p. 2.

While the U.S. position urged all possible haste in an attempt to meet the Italian treaty deadline, France continued to voice numerous objections. During meetings that began in the British Treasury offices on January 30th and continued until February 10th, the French representative continually maintained that while he was anxious that Italy meet the claim that his country had made (fifteen tons of gold), he felt that the language in the draft treaty did not sufficiently clarify that claim. Reinstein, eager to insure the dispatch of a questionnaire to Italy, assured his French colleague that this problem could be discussed but that the immediate business at hand was to agree on the sending of a gold questionnaire to Italy. Waley raised the rather delicate question "that the Trustee Powers would be placed in a difficult position if Italian participation in the pool was made conditional on satisfying the claims of one country which happened to be a trustee whilst other claimants had to wait for later consideration of their claims."[25] Calvet was not to be put off, however, replying that Italy had never denied France's claim and had tacitly acknowledged it in both the Paris agreement and the Italian peace-treaty draft. He proposed that either Italy's participation in the gold pool be conditioned on the formal recognition of the French claim or that a share of Italy's gold from the pool be earmarked for France. Reinstein disagreed; still returning to the subject of sending the Italians a gold questionnaire regardless of any resolution on the claim at the moment, he pointed out that France's gold-claim documentation, submitted the previous year, was still incomplete, and furthermore, the United States was not prepared to support the introduction of any new conditions at this time.[26]

M. Valery, from the French delegation, stated that Italy had specifically requested the French government to support their participation in the gold pot for their gold need was so urgent that it was critical that they receive this aid as soon as possible. This did not mean that Italy had accepted the French claim, however, Waley countered; although the Italians had issued no official denial, it was known that they had not reached an agreement with France either. Therefore, the British representative continued, it would have to be assumed that neither his government nor the United States could accept a still-unresolved outcome as the basis for determining Italy's participation in the gold pool. Repeating his earlier statement, Waley concluded: "The British position can only be one of wishing the French success but as trustees for this gold the U.K. would not permit another trustee to take advantage of its position." He was sure

25. Ibid., "Secret Minutes Tripartite Meeting on Gold," London, 30 January 1947, p. 1.
26. Ibid., p. 2.

that the U.S. representative concurred. (Mr. Reinstein concurred.)[27]

Both Waley and Reinstein continued to focus their efforts on securing a consensus to send the gold questionnaire as the first step, pointing out to their French counterpart that Italian participation would be dependent upon that government's reserving a sufficient amount of gold to satisfy any intended claims. Both men were emphatic in their opposition to deciding the merits of the French claim as part of their responsibility; that was the work of a judicial tribunal. "It just so happens," Reinstein said, "by a set of fortuitous circumstances, that the Italian gold in Germany is clearly marked and can be easily identified. Since we have promised Italy restitution, the Italian position is thereby made stronger. France as one of the trustees must realize that it would be unethical to settle her case out of court."[28] As Valery insisted that his country's claim must be put in reserve before any Italian treaty was signed, both Waley and Reinstein agreed that if France tried to force Italy into such a commitment, they would inform the Italian government of their opposition to it. In a plea for unity, Waley said there was nothing that would prevent some of the Italian gold from being reserved for later settlements, but that it was not a question they could resolve now. This prompted one of the delegate members to ask just how much the French claim against Italy was, but no one seemed to have exact figures available. It was estimated that the French claim amounted to about $14 million and the claim against Italy and Yugoslavia to about $9 million. Since the Italian gold loss was some $78 million, if each gold claimant received a 40 percent return from the gold pot this meant that Italy would get approximately $30 million back, more than enough to satisfy the claims. On this somewhat comforting note, the French finally agreed to make unanimous the vote for the sending of a gold questionnaire to Italy.[29]

Actually, there was another claim against Italy from Albania, but when the economic representatives in London explored it, there was general agreement that very little seemed to be known about it beyond the submission of the claim by the National Bank of Albania. There was some doubt about whether the claim should be recognized for the Albanian bank had been headquartered in Rome, and there was a possibility that Italy might have some basis for laying claim to the gold. Unable to insert its claim into the Italian peace treaty, Albania would then have to make a claim against the German gold pool, and if Italy did the same, it would mean that two nations would claim the same gold. It was agreed that more could be learned by sending the Albanians a gold questionnaire to

27. Ibid.
28. Ibid., p. 3.
29. Ibid.

see what their documentation looked like. There was no opposition to sending a questionnaire to Yugoslavia either, although it was understood that the only claim that nation could have against the German gold pot involved the gold that had originally been looted by Italy.[30]

Although Reinstein had already informed the assembled delegations that the United States had returned the Salzburg gold to the Austrians, both Waley and Valery raised the issue again at this meeting. While neither objected to the sending of a gold questionnaire to Austria, they did chide Reinstein for permitting the gold transfer before there had been adequate discussion by the other two Allies. The French representative wanted to know just how the Americans were so sure that the gold found near Salzburg was actually pre-*Anschluß* gold for he had it upon the authority of French financial experts currently in Vienna that such identification was impossible. Reinstein explained that he too had had some reservations about returning the Salzburg gold but had been absent when the decisions were made; he promised to secure all the facts.[31]

The discussions on Poland proved somewhat more complicated for France was adamant that Poland not share in the gold pool, insisting that any question of returning gold to that nation was a matter for reparation, not restitution, and this made it a question for the Soviet Union, not the Western Allies. Britain's Waley disputed this interpretation, saying that Poland was definitely entitled to restitution insofar as monetary gold was concerned, but Valery refused to agree to the sending of a gold question-naire, indicating that he would ask for additional instructions from his government. Since the French could not be moved, for the moment it was agreed that there was no point in discussing the Danzig gold because it was tied to the Polish situation and a resolution of the frontier question.[32]

Blocked in the discussions from inserting their Italian claim into the treaty, France tried in the meantime to resolve it by direct negotiations with Italy. France proposed that Italy compensate them by the payment of 16 billion lire, but the Italians rejected this since they valued the gold the French sought (fifteen tons) at only 7 billion lire.[33] As the negotiations dragged on, making the French reluctant to agree to a gold questionnaire until some resolution was reached, Reinstein became increasingly im-patient because the Italian peace-treaty signing was coming closer and closer, and both he and Waley wanted the gold-pool participation terms concluded in that treaty. Reinstein had already written a draft protocol for

30. Ibid., pp. 4–5.
31. Ibid., p. 6.
32. Ibid., p. 5.
33. NA, RG 43, WW II Conf. Files, U.S. State Dept. to American Embassy London, 30 January 1947.

Italy stipulating that the Italian government would be required to leave on deposit with the Allied governments 24,017 kilograms of fine gold from its gold-pool share received, a sum judged to be equal to the French and Yugoslav claims.[34] When Reinstein's draft was discussed among the London delegates, Valery revealed that he had received some new information from his government that should be considered: "In November 1941, and outside the terms of the [French–Italian] armistice, the Italians required the French to provide a quantity of money which was used to purchase gold from the Bank of France. Three deliveries were made to the Bank of Italy in the early part of 1942, for which the French have receipts." Since this was done under duress and was therefore not legally valid, France regarded it as the basis for their present claim. It was the French desire that specific reference to their claim against Italy for 14,422 kilograms of gold be stated in the protocol. On this basis the British and American representatives ultimately agreed.[35]

Moving to another of France's concerns, Calvet, one of the French delegates, reminded his American colleagues of the earlier inquiry about the details on the Salzburg gold that had been turned over to Austria. Reinstein repeated most of his previous statement, emphasizing the U.S. conviction that the gold did belong to the Austrian National Bank; nevertheless, he had no objection to the matter being reviewed by the Tripartite Commission, although in his position it was a case of gold that was Austrian, had remained in Austria, and did not fall under the provisions of the Paris agreement. Calvet disagreed on this point for he believed that the U.S. decision had been made before all of the facts were known. For example, he asked the assembled delegates, what had been the relationship of the Austrian National Bank to the Reichsbank in the period between the *Anschluß* and the outbreak of war? If Austria was a part of Greater Germany, then shouldn't all gold found there be considered looted gold? Reinstein replied that these matters had all been discussed at Paris, a clause in the Paris act specifically exempted Austria, and besides, he noted, the United States had already delivered the gold to Austria.[36] While this should have ended the debate, it did not:

Calvet was rather insistent on continuing the Austrian discussion and stated that if an agreement was reached to let Austria keep the gold without deducting it from her share of the gold pool, it was a recognition of the continuity of the Austrian Government and therefore it followed that all external debt commit-

34. Ibid., "Secret Protocol with Italy," 31 January 1947, pp. 1–2.
35. Ibid., "Secret Minutes of Meeting in Sir D. Waley's Office," 4 February 1947, pp. 1–2.
36. Ibid., pp. 3–4.

125

ments of the Austrian Government should be met. He mentioned specifically the French and U.K. service of the Austria loan during the *Anschluss*. Reinstein . . . failed to see the connection with the question of gold. Calvet repeated his story several times, Reinstein pointed out that the British draft on Austria . . . provides that Austrian debts falling due after the *Anschluss* became a debt of the German Government; he also stated that after the *Anschluss* the U.S. sent Germany a note saying we held Germany responsible for the Austrian debt. In view of this, it would be very difficult to say now that we hold Austria responsible.[37]

In what could only have been a tone of exasperation Reinstein asked if there was agreement that Austria share in the German gold pool, commenting on the importance that the United States attached to the early distribution of the Salzburg gold. While both Waley and Calvet expressed support of the Austrian participation in the gold pool, they also had reservations on the Salzburg gold.[38]

One of the topics for discussion centered around those nations that had traded with Germany during the war and had accepted looted gold in the process. This generally, although not always, concerned the neutral nations of Europe. At the time of the London talks, the negotiations with Switzerland had already been concluded and final approval of a settlement with Sweden was pending.[39]

Romania, with a convoluted history of foreign relations not dissimilar from its Balkan neighbors during the war, sided for a time with Germany, broke relations later, and concluded an armistice with the Allies in September 1944. Before the war ended Romania had installed a Communist government, but this did not alter the fact that a significant sum of looted gold had already been acquired from Germany earlier. The gold came under Allied scrutiny when the Romanian government found itself in desperate straits after the war and decided to use the gold to secure a loan from Switzerland. In January 1947 there was some preliminary

37. Ibid., p. 5.

38. Ibid., pp. 5–6. Somewhat later, in a confidential communique on the subject, Reinstein expressed his doubts on the wisdom of returning the Salzburg gold. He based his reservations on the fact that when he finally had the opportunity to examine the claim of the Austrian National Bank, there had been no submission of evidence or statement that referred to the original ownership of the gold in question. He wrote that "the fact of the matter is that the decision to return the gold was primarily a political one," although he did feel that the gold did not belong in the gold pot, ibid., Reinstein to McGuire, 26 January 1948.

39. An Allied–Swedish accord on the subject of German assets in Sweden had been drafted in July 1947. On the specific question of looted gold Sweden agreed to restitution, and the negotiations were quickly reduced to the technical matter of identifying the gold that had been transferred from Germany during the war. All available records were provided and proved that Sweden had accepted 7,155 kilograms of fine gold and was now prepared to restitute that amount. *Department of State Bulletin*, 27 July 1947, p. 160.

discussion amongst the U.S., British, and French governments to the effect that the Allied Control Council had not authorized any gold pledges by Romania, and Switzerland had been informed of this. As the economic representatives of the Council of Foreign Ministers prepared to deal with the gold problem in London, it was agreed that there should be coordinated action in approving an investigation of the Romanian National Bank and securing possible recovery of the looted gold. The Romanian gold acquisition was not news to the London delegates for almost a year before their respective governments had informed the Romanian Foreign Ministry that they were aware that the Romanian National Bank had received quantities of looted gold from Germany. Referring to the strong possibility that the gold was looted, or "tainted" as some preferred, the Allied governments had requested Romanian cooperation in a full investigation of the transactions of the Romanian National Bank for the period in question. The Romanian response was to provide a record of the bank's gold dealings, indicating that it had received $65.5 million worth of gold from Germany, but no additional information was offered and no mention made of an "investigation."[40]

In the fall of 1946 it became known in banking circles that the Romanian government intended to use the gold reserve of their national bank as collateral for certain commercial transactions with Switzerland. This prompted an inquiry by the United States, through its Allied Control Council representative, asking if any measures should be taken to prevent this action. The motion did not receive Soviet support, and there the matter rested until the economic experts began their deliberations in London at the end of January 1947.[41] When the subject came up for discussion, Reinstein suggested that since it had been reported that the Romanian government wished to use the gold as collateral for a loan perhaps there should be some kind of public statement to the effect that the gold was certainly looted. He revealed that a warning to the Netherlands and Belgium had already prevented the Romanians from using it for a purchase or loan there. The British and French representatives agreed that an investigation by Allied banking experts into the accounts of the Romanian National Bank was called for and promised the cooperation of their governments.[42]

While the London meetings were in session Romanian Foreign Minister Tatarescu informed the U.S. State Department that his country intended to return all tainted gold which, he said, described only six of the sixty

40. NA, RG 43, WW II Conf. Files, U.S. State Dept. to American Embassy London, 21 January 1947, p. 1.
41. Ibid., p. 2.
42. Ibid., Tripartite Meeting on Gold, 4 February 1947, p. 3.

tons of gold that had been acquired from Germany; the other fifty-four tons had been acquired in the course of legitimate commercial dealings. The foreign minister stated that his government had seventy tons of gold in Bucharest for potential grain purchases, and while denying the rumor that it would probably be sent to Russia, he did admit that some of it might go in that direction.[43] Since Tatarescu was obviously testing the waters for a loan—the Swiss-American Banking Group had already requested U.S. State Department permission to grant a $50 million loan to Romania with the gold as security—the American State Department set the following conditions to be met: (1) Romania must recognize and adhere to the principal Allied gold declarations; (2) full data on all gold transactions must be provided as requested; (3) all gold labeled as looted by Allied investigators must be returned; and (4) permission had to be requested to make the aforementioned restitution.[44]

The vulnerability of Romania's position made acceptance of these conditions likely for the Allies, but at a subsequent London meeting Valery reported that he had confidential information indicating that conditions had become so perilous in Bucharest that he doubted the efficacy of the Allied position. The country was being pushed from both sides and he feared that the gold was already "slipping out the back door." He was of the opinion that a strong message should be sent to the Romanians making them aware that the Allies were monitoring the situation very closely. Neither Waley nor Reinstein thought that any communication was necessary because Romania had been trying for the past nine months to use their gold to get a loan and had not yet found a source, so they advised no action.[45] This proved a mistake, for shortly after this meeting the news was received that the Romanian government had submitted a request to U.S. authorities to send a special train carrying fifty tons of gold through the American zone of occupation in Austria on its way to Switzerland. About all that could be done, short of denying the transit request, was to advise both the Romanians and the Swiss that they were dealing in gold regarded as tainted, but the fact was that Valery had been right for the gold was getting out the back door.[46]

A secret U.S. State Department memorandum on the situation revealed that Cold War apprehensions over the Communist influence in Romania outweighed concerns over the tainted gold. Opposition sources within Romania reported that although the country was in desperate need of food

43. Ibid., American Embassy Bucharest to American Embassy London, 4 February 1947, pp. 1–2.
44. Ibid., U.S. State Dept. to American Embassy London, 4 February 1947, pp. 1–3.
45. Ibid., Tripartite Meeting on Gold, 4 February 1947, p. 3.
46. Ibid., U.S. State Dept. to American Embassy London, 19 February 1947, 2 pp.

relief, with even starvation conditions in some areas, to permit them access to relief by using the gold would only strengthen the Communist hand. The opposition believed, according to the memorandum, that not only would Romanian Communist party membership be a prerequisite to securing any food, but that much of it would be diverted to feed the 400,000 Soviet occupation troops. The Romanian source also reported the movement of eight train carloads of gold from the Romanian National Bank to Switzerland as collateral for a loan from the Chase National Bank for the purchase of food.[47] All of this meant, of course, a circumvention of the Allied Control Council and a failure by the London experts to have initiated any policy or provided any recommendations soon enough to be effective in the Romanian situation.

The problem that Portugal presented was quite different since that nation had been included in Safehaven negotiations in 1946, when it had been determined by Allied gold investigations that the Portuguese held 962 bars of resmelted Belgian gold valued at $13,271,600. There were continued efforts during that year to ascertain just how much gold the Bank of Portugal had purchased from Germany during the war and how it was disposed of, but without the full cooperation of the Portuguese and the Swiss National Bank, which had handled the transactions, this had to remain educated guesswork. It was known from the seized German Reichsbank records that a quantity of gold purchased by the Bank of Portugal from the Reichsbank depot in the Swiss National Bank was dated 1942 and did not consist of resmelted Belgian gold. On the basis of a French investigation made in 1946, it was established that the bulk of the gold that had been resmelted by the Prussian mint in 1942 had consisted of gold from the Netherlands; therefore it was assumed that this had been the gold transferred by the Swiss to the Bank of Portugal that year.[48] In the London talks France was most critical at the lack of progress in coming to terms with the Portuguese government on a settlement and criticized the United States for not pressing the Allied case far more vigorously. It appeared that the U.S. negotiator on the case had been withdrawn from Lisbon, but then it was discovered that France had withdrawn their man from Lisbon too. Only the Netherlands was persistent in pursuing their interests there, hopeful that the Portuguese would acknowledge that some Dutch gold had found its way into the Bank of Portugal in 1942.[49]

Despite the criticism of the French representative in the London talks,

47. Ibid., U.S. Embassy Bern to Washington, 8 March 1947, 2 pp.

48. NA, RG 260, OMGUS AG 1945–6, Secret brief, "Gold Looted by Germany and Sold to the Bank of Portugal," 10 October 1946, 4 pp.

49. NA, RG 43, WW II Conf. Files, Tripartite Meeting on Gold, 2 February 1947, p. 3.

there was ongoing Safehaven discussion with Portugal. It centered primarily on attempting to persuade the Portuguese to acknowledge a restitution payment in a formal accord that was being negotiated relative to blocked assets.[50] It was the U.S. view that Portugal was dragging its feet hoping to get a more favorable settlement on the assets accord because of the Allied desire to secure a resolution to the gold issue. However, the United States maintained that the gold question was a part of the assets debate and that the accord should not be signed until that was agreed upon and included in it. The United States also wished the discussions to be moved from Lisbon to Washington, feeling that more concessions might be obtained in a different environment.[51] While Britain and France supported the Washington move, it was thought that the United States should not push the issue of linking the gold to the assets accord too far. France made the suggestion that the Allied negotiators agree to initial the assets accord in Lisbon and at the same time extend an invitation to Portugal to continue the discussions on the gold issue in Washington.[52]

Meanwhile, the London meetings ended on February 10th with the agreement that Waley, Reinstein, and Calvet would make the following recommendations to their respective governments: (1) the Tripartite Commission should send gold questionnaires to all member nations of the IARA immediately; (2) gold questionnaires should also be dispatched immediately to the governments of Austria, Italy, and Poland with accompanying statements indicating that the receipt of the questionnaire did not insure inclusion in the gold-pot claims; (3) Italy should be permitted participation on the basis set forth in the protocol to be signed in Paris; and the Italian government should be given the gold captured by American forces at Fortezza; (4) Poland should be allowed to participate in the gold pool like the other Paris signatories; (5) notification to all governments concerned and the information in points 3 and 4 should be given publicity; (6) no questionnaire should be sent to Danzig by the Tripartite Commission pending final settlement of Danzig's political status, although this implies no prejudice to the final gold disposition; if no status decision is made before work of the Tripartite Commission has finished, provision should be made for the Danzig gold; (7) Austria should be allowed gold participation on the same basis as other Paris

50. Just why the French representative in London had raised the objection about the United States not pursuing Portugal with sufficient vigor is somewhat puzzling. The distribution of some of the correspondence of the U.S. State Dept. showed copies to Reinstein and Colvill, of the British delegation. Since there was no French delegate on the distribution, it has to be assumed that the London representative was not informed.

51. NA, RG 43 WW II Conf. Files, Marshall to Bernstein, 5 February 1947.

52. Ibid., Marshall to American Embassy London, 10 February 1947.

signatories, effective when the Austrian protocol is signed; this could be earlier than the signing of an Austrian peace treaty, but the subject will be discussed by representatives of the three governments at the coming Council of Foreign Ministers' meeting in Moscow; France reserves the right to raise the question of the Salzburg gold disposition with the Tripartite Commission; (8) there should be continued consultation with respect to the recovery of looted gold from Romania;[53] (9) early distribution of gold should take place in instances where there is no complication in deciding claims; and, (10) methods of receiving and holding gold from their countries (gold that was being restituted, as in the case of Switzerland) should be quickly decided.[54]

Thus, by February 1947 all the problems connected with looted gold had been explored by the Allies, much basic policy had been thrashed out, and some machinery had been set into motion to begin restitution. It is important to note, however, that decisions were already being influenced by Cold War considerations and not always by the factual merits of a case.

53. Throughout the almost two weeks of London discussions there were repeated references to the problem of the gold in Romania's possession, which had probably been looted by the Germans.

54. NA, RG 43, WW II Conf. Files, memorandum: Conversations with Respect to the Paris Agreement, London, 7 February 1947, 6 pp.

CHAPTER 7

Making Restitution

History has decided that the terrible struggle waged by the Allies against Hitler and Mussolini in the Second World War was justified. During the course of those tumultuous years the Allies proclaimed the principles they hoped would form the basis for a better world. Above all was the determination that justice would play a larger role in international relations. A small but not insignificant manifestation of their intent was seen in the various gold declarations that damned the despoilers and looters and those who assisted them, and promised justice, that is, restitution, when victory was achieved. The declarations were clear, forthright and fair, and valid expressions of the goals expounded by Allied leadership.

By 1947 such a profound shift in the former wartime alliance of the United States, Great Britain, and the Soviet Union had occurred that the two Western Allies and their anti-Hitler partner had become enemies. War had become cold war, and the language of the well-intentioned war proclamations had already become sadly dated. The Western Allies' aims were now entirely different and earlier commitments had to be reappraised and reinterpreted to fit the new political reality. Certain facts remained unalterable, of course. Poland, Albania, Czechoslovakia, and Yugoslavia had been plundered by the German occupiers while Italy and Austria had generally been aligned with Germany during those same years, but the new reality dictated a new logic. New alliances had forged new partnerships and the power to make the decisions on the restitution of hundreds of millions of dollars of gold was far too powerful to ignore as a political and economic weapon.

To understand fully the history of gold restitution after 1946, these factors must be kept firmly in mind. As the discussions and conferences of the three Western Allies focused on the details of restitution of looted gold, wrestling with the wording of protocols, setting requirements for considering gold claims, and debating the pros and cons of each case submitted by one of the ten claimant nations, it was impossible to separate Cold War policy from gold distribution. Rarely, if ever, does any of the relevant documentation—always official and usually secret—permit, in its recording of letters, meetings, conferences, and lengthy telegrams, any expression to surface that specifically points out the connection with Western Allied national policies calculated to damage the Soviet Union or the Western Allies' reluctance to treat Poland, Albania, Czechoslovakia, and Yugoslavia on the same basis as Belgium, France, Luxembourg, and the Netherlands. This, despite the fact that they were all victims of Nazi exploitation. The Allied decision to accept and ultimately to respond to the claimants is illustrative of their intent to interpret wartime declarations in support of postwar policies. An examination of the development of gold protocols for Austria, Italy, and Poland reveals the predominant influence wielded by the United States in its determination to shape Cold War policy in spite of the occasional necessity to mollify its French and British partners.

As noted, in early 1947 the economic representatives to the Council of Foreign Ministers' meeting in London began a search for general agreement on a set of protocols for Austria, Italy, and Poland that would continue for several months despite the fact that the final documents would ultimately constitute only a few paragraphs of relatively uncomplicated content. In the case of Italy, it was quickly decided that the Italians should receive a proportional share of the gold distribution on the same terms as the Paris signatories although a deposit was to be left with the Allies to cover the French and Yugoslavian claims. The protocol was intended to coincide with the anticipated Italian peace treaty scheduled for signing on February 10th. In the subsequent drafts the substance of the protocol remained much the same with some slight language modification, usually requested by the French representative, that required the Italians to pay their claims before using any of the gold themselves. Italy's proportionate share of the gold was based upon the amount of monetary gold looted by the Germans from that nation after the date of 3 September 1943 and removed to Germany. At French insistence the exact amounts of the pending claims, by France for 14,422 kilograms of gold and by Yugoslavia for 9,595 kilograms of gold, were inserted.[1]

When it appeared that a satisfactory draft had been completed, Reinstein notified his government that Italy would probably be given a copy in London along with the assurance that the Fortezza gold would be returned soon. The British demurred, however, suggesting instead that

1. NA, RG 43, WW II Conf. Files, Secret Protocol Draft, 7 February 1943, 2 pp.; and Secret Protocol Draft, 8 February 1943.

the Fortezza gold be used as a possible inducement to get the Italians to ratify the peace treaty quickly. At this, the French and American representatives agreed to change the protocol to read that it would come into force when the Italian peace treaty was signed. It was proposed that the Fortezza gold be turned over at the ratification of the treaty by the Italian government. The U.S. State Department balked at these changes, however, and instructed Reinstein that he was not to approve an alteration of the protocol as proposed by the British: "Dept desires draft protocol be given Italians immediately and strongly opposes its use by Brit for bilateral bargaining purposes."[2]

Responding to the U.S. position, Sir David Waley noted that Great Britain was willing to accept the Italian protocol as it was if a separate written statement was presented to the Italian ambassador in London to the effect that the Fortezza gold return would await the signing of a peace treaty. The United States agreed, and before March was over it appeared as if a draft of the Italian protocol satisfactory to all parties had finally been produced. Ironically, when it came time to approve the draft the Americans could not find a suitable copy and had to rely on their British colleagues to supply one. The only change was in the date that Italy was permitted to use for the beginning of German gold looting, and for a reason not revealed in the debates, the representative had selected the same date as that applied to Austria, 12 March 1938.[3] In spite of the haste and pressures to get a finished protocol, usually applied by Reinstein, the actual signing was months away.

The same procedures were used to produce an Austrian protocol and, in fact, the wording in most of the draft documents was almost identical although there was no specific date set for the Austrian signing. Since the Allied representatives expected to continue their discussion at the next scheduled Council of Foreign Ministers' conference in Moscow in March, it was decided that the time for an Austrian signing could be reviewed there. It was anticipated that there would be objections from some of the IARA nations to including Austria in the gold pool, but the United States wanted to give the Austrians notification at the same time that Italy and Poland were informed.[4] There was a possibility that all of the protocols under discussion could be completed during the Moscow session and later presented in a single formal meeting in London with the respective

2. Ibid., Reinstein to Washington, 11 February 1947; and U.S. State Dept. to American Embassy London, 26 February 1947.

3. Ibid., Gallman to Reinstein, 8 March 1947; Acheson to U.S. Delegation, London, 14 March 1947; and Douglas to U.S. State Dept., 22 March 1947.

4. Ibid., Gallman to Washington, 11 February 1947; and Marshall to American Embassy London, 26 February 1947.

ambassadors from Austria, Italy, and Poland. At this stage of discussions the Polish protocol appeared to present no problems other than the Danzig question so the focus in Moscow was upon finishing the Austrian protocol. The Salzburg gold still presented somewhat of a problem, but this was quickly resolved by passing the responsibility on to the Tripartite Commission for the Restitution of Monetary Gold, which was to have the authority for executing the protocols. The commission would decide if the Salzburg gold should be considered a part of Austria's gold share or not.[5] Just as with the Italian protocol, however, any actual signing was still months away.

An intriguing feature of these negotiations, perhaps like many involving international relations, was that many of the participants were interested in a speedy process and much of the day-to-day debate left the impression that a solution was just a matter of skimming over a few unimportant details, but this was deceiving. Any gains were canceled out by a glacial period of indecision whereby all action had to await home government approval or further instructions. In this instance the long delays worked to the benefit of Italy and Austria and to the detriment of Poland and the other Soviet satellites. This also meant that the early assumption that formulating a protocol for Poland would present no problem soon had to be revised.

The first drafts of a Polish protocol had contained no reservations on Poland's right to share equally in a proportional gold distribution with the Paris signatory nations, and the beginning claim date for German looting of monetary gold was the same as Austria's.[6] Except for the question of Danzig, there was very little debate about granting Poland this right and preparing a protocol draft during the London discussions in January and February 1947. In March the first hint that matters were not going to flow ahead so smoothly came with the news that Poland and the Soviet Union had complete arrangements for the Poles to receive $28,855,000 in gold. This raised speculation about what the Russians expected in return, as well as the observation that Poland had not yet returned the gold questionnaire to the Tripartite Commission.[7]

One of the questions that arose during the London talks was whether or not Austria and Italy would be entitled to share in the gold that had been paid by Switzerland under the terms of the Washington agreement in 1946. If so, it was then assumed that they would also share in all of the

5. Ibid., American Embassy London to Washington, 14 April 1947.

6. Ibid., Draft Protocol for Poland, 7 February 1947.

7. U.S. Dept. of State, Decimal File 800.515/3–1147, Acheson to American Embassy Warsaw, 3 April 1947. It was thought that the Russians may have received a share of Polish industry in the Silesian Basin.

gold that would be returned by the so-called third nations, those wartime neutrals who had accepted German looted gold. Earlier discussion had arrived at the consensus that Austria and Italy should definitely not share in the Swiss payment, as noted in a 1946 U.S. State Department memorandum: "The three Delegations will, if the subject should come up, take the position that the claims of Italy, Austria or other possible claimants not signatory to the Paris Reparation Agreement cannot be affected by these negotiations."[8] The subject was reviewed briefly at the Moscow Council of Foreign Ministers conference, at which time both the British and American representatives appeared ready to change earlier positions, but the French insisted that they had not had a change of heart and would not agree to permitting the Italians and the Austrians to share in third-nation gold payments. They were on firm ground since there was a written agreement in connection with the Swiss negotiations, which had not been modified nor superceded. This prompted Reinstein to comment: "I share . . . [the] view that there is no hope in getting the French to reconsider their position. . . . The French have never given up their rights under that agreement [although] they were fairly close to doing so."[9]

Meanwhile, the American secretary of state, George Marshall, was making it clear that the United States desired an early distribution of the gold pool and, in order to expedite that division, wanted uncontroversial claims settled as soon as possible. For other claims, he advised simply setting aside adequate quantities of gold to meet later obligations.[10] Soon thereafter the Tripartite Commission requested that all concerned nations return their gold questionnaires by the end of April so they could begin to calculate shares. It was expected that each claimant nation would receive about 40 percent of its claim and all decisions would be final. The questionnaire made clear that monetary gold was specifically defined as a nation's monetary reserve, wherever deposited, that had been looted and wrongfully removed by the Germans. This fact had to be documented to the satisfaction of the Tripartite Commission and was spelled out in a series of questions. For example, the fineness of the gold, gold taken from citizens by German decree, gold removed from state banks, ownership of all gold looted, form and weight of all gold lost, the exact monetary character (coins, bars, etc.), and the exact factual circumstances surrounding the lootings had to be provided. The point that all claims had to accept the definition established by the commission was stressed.[11]

8. NA, RG 43, WW II Conf. Files, U.S. State Dept. memorandum, 21 May 1946.

9. Ibid., Douglas to U.S. Secretary of State, 28 May 1947; and Reinstein note, 21 July 1947.

10. Ibid., Marshall to American Embassy London, 27 February 1947.

11. Although the Allies had found huge sums of foreign currencies in Germany, it did not

The gold available to the Tripartite Commission for distribution soon amounted to approximately $330 million worth, $260 million of which was on deposit in Frankfurt while $70 million was in the process of being returned from third nations. At the London meetings of the Council of Foreign Ministers' experts the question of handling the gold was brought up. There had already been some previous discussion between the Bank of France and the Bank of England about it which indicated that the French had some reservations about the condition of the gold as maintained in the FED in Frankfurt. The thought was that it would all have to be revalued again and possibly resmelted, but not at the FED. They also wanted to undertake a formal tripartite verification first to insure before any removal that there was proof of the looted character of the gold because this would be lost once the gold was resmelted. These suggestions were not rejected outright by the United States, which saw the verification as a process that would occur anyway when distribution started; but as for any resmelting, that was for the Brussels Tripartite Commission to struggle with.[12] In Washington in 1946 a tentative agreement on the handling of the gold received from Switzerland had been reached with both Great Britain and France to the effect that an account would be created with the Federal Reserve Bank in New York in the name of the Tripartite Commission. All costs and fees were to be borne by the gold pot. Since the Swiss had handed over the gold in New York, this appeared a logical arrangement and therefore the policy was adopted that in each third-nation gold transaction the gold would be held at the nearest convenient banking center; exceptions could be made if deemed necessary.[13]

While the various Allied bodies responsible for restitution policy talked Europe suffered. Understandably, guidelines had to be developed carefully and each case contained its complexities, but by 1947 it was time to begin returning some of the gold to the claimants. In September of that year U.S. Undersecretary of State Robert Lovett announced plans to release at least one half of the gold on hand (about $330 million) for distribution in October. It was indicated that the gold commission was fully in accord with the need for urgency and the American representative, Russell Dorr, had already been given the date of the 15th as the starting time. Lovett revealed that while current negotiations with third nations would undoubtedly yield additional gold for the pot, the claims that had been submitted to date totaled almost $800 million, which of course went well

---

come under the jurisdiction of the Tripartite Commission to distribute it.

12. NA, RG 43, WW II Conf. Files, U.S. Delegation, Council of Foreign Ministers, meeting summary, 10 February 1947, p. 3; and Colville to Waley, 26 February 1947.

13. Ibid., Colville to Waley, 26 February 1947; and Douglas to U.S. Secretary of State, 20 March 1947.

beyond the size of the gold pool.[14] Not affected by Lovett's announcement, but certainly in line with its meaning, was the news that an Anglo-U.S.–Italian agreement had been signed in London (October 10th), returning almost all of the monetary gold which was in Italy in 1945. Its return was not part of the work of the Tripartite Commission in Brussels.[15]

In a secret summary prepared for the U.S. secretary of state that same month, gold-commission member Russell Dorr reviewed their work on the eve of starting the first gold distribution: approval had been given to include the Netherlands in the first distribution; after lengthy argument it was agreed that the Salzburg gold would not be considered a part of the gold pool, but no decision had been reached as to whether it would be deducted from Austria's gold-pool share as both Great Britain and France wanted; it appeared that Albania had a valid claim, although more information was needed before a final decision could be made because there were discrepancies between the Italian and Albanian figures for just how much gold was involved; it was decided that the Polish claim would not be included for consideration in the first gold distribution, but a hearing would be granted the Polish ambassador to argue his case; and, finally, it was anticipated that gold on the Yugoslavian account would be paid to Italy rather than held by the Allies, which would probably bring strong criticism from the Yugoslavs.[16]

On 17 October 1947, the first monetary gold distribution was announced through a Tripartite Commission news release from their Brussels office. It was a lengthy memorandum outlining the commission's duties, responsibilities, and intent in making the preliminary distribution of 128,468 kilograms of fine gold. Belgium was to receive 90,649 kilograms (over $100,000,000); Luxembourg 1,929 kilograms (about $500,000); and the Netherlands 35,890 kilograms (about $45,000,000). It was noted that the gold share to Belgium would be delivered to France since that nation had already returned a like sum to the National Bank of Belgium. The same applied to the gold allocation for Luxembourg. The total value of the gold France was to receive was $104,150,250.[17]

The Tripartite Commission release pointed out the fact that by the terms of the Paris Agreement on Reparations (part III), shares of the gold pool were to be set aside for countries not represented at the conference pending later decisions on their eligibility. The commission had now

14. *New York Times*, 25 September 1947, pp. 1 and 3.
15. *Keesing's Contemporary Archives*, 11–18 October 1947, p. 8872.
16. NA, RG 43, WW II Conf. Files, Brussels to U.S. Secretary of State, 5 October 1947, 3 pp.
17. Ibid., U.S. State Dept. press release, 17 October 1947, 2 pp.

determined that a portion of the claims submitted by Austria and Italy were valid under these terms, and therefore 26,187 kilograms of gold were to be set aside for Austria and 3,085 kilograms for Italy. Negotiations were in progress, and it was anticipated that those two nations would soon be given their gold shares. Similar negotiations were also underway with Poland.[18] The press release stated that the additional claims from Albania, Czechoslovakia, Greece, and Yugoslavia were being carefully examined along with the supporting evidence that had been submitted, but further clarification was needed. The gold commission was, however, reserving a sufficient quantity of gold to cover in equal proportion all pending claims.[19]

It was revealed that there were ongoing discussions for the recovery of additional monetary gold looted by Germany and sold to other nations during the war. Reference was made to Sweden and the success achieved with that nation in an agreement providing for total return of all gold in question. It was hoped that the Swedish example would prove a model for settlements with other nations that had been involved in similar gold transactions with Nazi Germany. In summary, the Tripartite Commission explicitly described its responsibilities in the distribution of the monetary-gold pool that had been created as a result of the Paris agreement, making the point that gold looted from concentration-camp victims was not included.[20]

The FED in Frankfurt, which was the custodian for the gold pool, among other assets, was authorized by the commission to transfer to those accredited representatives of each designated government specific sums of gold. The FED then readied payment in the form of gold bars and gold coins which they deemed acceptable by banks dealing in the settlement of international balances. The commission provided instructions on the distribution of gold bars bearing assays of certain IARA countries and those that were distinctly of German origin, resmelted or not.[21] All gold inventoried in the U.S Army Frankfurt depository was recorded in the so-called Howard Report (Howard was an employee of the U.S. Treasury Department), which provided a careful account of the entire contents. For each compartment in the vaults there was a corresponding folder which contained a separate work sheet for every pile of gold bars or bag of gold coins. The work sheet for the gold bars indicated the bar numbers, gross

18. Ibid., p. 1.

19. Ibid., p. 2.

20. Ibid. Gold and other valuables taken from concentration-camp victims were placed in the custody of the Inter-Governmental Committee on Refugees to be used for the rehabilitation and resettlement of nonrepatriable victims of Nazi Germany.

21. NA, RG 260, OMGUS FINAD, Monetary Gold—First Distribution, 28 October 1947, pp. 1–2.

and fine weights, and other details. The work sheet for the gold coins carried the bag number, the type of coin and its rough and fine weight in ounces, and the bag's total weight in kilograms. In a master-locater file there was a chart for each compartment giving the exact location of each pile and bag, with an identifying coordinate for the work sheets.[22] According to the Howard Report, approximately 68 percent of the gold bars held in the FED had assay markings from the Prussian State Mint. The Tripartite Commission decided that the distribution of gold delivered to the respective Belgian, Dutch, and Luxembourg representatives contain 68 percent in Prussian-mint bars and 32 in bars non-German in origin, described as "good delivery bars." The commission accepted the Howard Report as accurate and did not order a recalculation before the start of distribution.[23]

The FED was responsible for all security in the gold transfers until delivery was acknowledged by the foreign representative with a completion receipt. This meant security personnel had to be supplied for every stage of the transaction in routing, handling, weighing, recording, and sealing. A security officer was stationed at every compartment with a Howard Report folder to record every operation pertaining to the compartment contents. Another security officer accompanied every loaded cart to the weighing station, where it was turned over to the weighing officer. That officer was responsible for a team of two recorders, two handlers, a weigher, and a sealer.[24]

The actual physical transfer involving the movement of the gold from the FED in Frankfurt began on November 19th, when some eighty-eight tons of gold worth $85,300,000 were loaded aboard a freight train for transport to the Bank of France. Beyond the information that the train was under heavy guard and consisted of eighteen cars, American authorities refused to elaborate on the details of the shipment. Several days later a further distribution was made to the Netherlands government when more than 29,300 fine kilograms of gold valued at about $33,000,000 were transferred. An accompanying news release stated: "It is believed that this return to the Netherlands of a substantial portion of its monetary gold reserves should assist her in overcoming present financial difficulties."[25]

During the same period that the first gold distributions were being made, the three Western Allies cleared the final hurdle toward the redistribution of gold to Austria and Italy by signing the long-awaited

22. Ibid., pp. 2 and 7.
23. Ibid., pp. 7 and 8.
24. Ibid., pp. 3–4.
25. Ibid., Monetary Gold—First and Second Distribution, OMGUS, Public Information Office, 21 November 1947.

protocols. The Austrian protocol was signed in November and the Italian protocol in December. The protocol for Austria, a brief four paragraphs, contained no changes from the earlier drafts and placed that nation on an equal footing with the signatories of the 1946 Paris agreement. The only requirement, which had already emerged in the drafts, stipulated that the burden of proof was upon Austria to "establish that a definite amount of monetary gold belonging to it was looted by Germany, or, at any time after 12th March 1938, was wrongfully removed into German territory."[26] The wording of the first three paragraphs of the Italian protocol was identical to that of the Austrian one except for a difference in the beginning date for the establishment of proof of German gold looting, which was set at 3 September 1943. In the final paragraph Italy promised to leave on deposit with the Allies a sufficient sum of gold to cover the French and Yugoslavian gold claims (14,422 and 8,857 kilograms, respectively).[27]

As these events transpired and no provision was forthcoming that included Poland in the gold distribution, the Polish government lodged a strong protest in Washington. After conveying his government's sentiments, Polish ambassador Josef Winiewicz informed the Americans that there was no basis for going ahead with a gold distribution program when claims such as Poland's were still under consideration. He especially called attention to the continued Allied indecision in defining monetary gold and maintained that the Paris agreement intended that appropriate gold shares for those nations not represented at the conference be calculated and held in reserve prior to any gold distribution. He protested that gold was already being distributed to three countries (the Netherlands, Luxembourg, and Belgium), and sums had specifically been set aside for two others (Italy and Austria). In all of this activity, Winiewicz noted, absolutely no provision was being made for the other legitimate gold claimants. The real concern, the ambassador wrote, was that there would not be enough gold left to satisfy their claim for 134,000 kilograms. He reminded the U.S. government of the devastation to Poland's economy as a result of German aggression and stated that to have "been omitted in the first distribution program cannot but create an impression of political discrimination, especially in view of the circumstance that large amounts of gold to be now distributed have been removed from Poland. The Polish government requests: a) That the implementation of the distribution program be postponed; b) That this program be revised in such a manner that . . . distribution take place after the shares of all countries concerned have been established."[28] The American reply was terse and to the point:

26. *Germany, 1947–1949: The Story in Documents*, p. 430.
27. NA, RG 43 WW II Conf. Files, Winiewicz to Lovett, 23 October 1947.
28. Ibid., Lovett to Winiewicz, 1 December 1947.

Poland's "observation could now only be dealt with by the Tripartite Commission for Monetary Gold in Brussels, for that body was now empowered to adjudicate all matters pertaining to the restitution of monetary gold. Further contact would have to be initiated through the proper Polish representative in Brussels."[29]

Despite the U.S. rebuttal Poland was not to be so easily put off. Since the Polish gold protocol was still under consideration and it was expected that it would soon be signed, it became the vehicle for further Polish efforts to apply some pressure on the gold-distribution program. In early January 1948 the Polish Foreign Office proposed that Poland be admitted to the gold pool on the same basis as other nations and be permitted to present their case to the Tripartite Commission. The three Western governments were skeptical, however, fearing that once Poland was granted this status they would attempt to halt all gold distributions until their demands were met. Obviously the Polish intent was that their proposal should be incorporated into the gold protocol, but the Allies balked at this, insisting that the protocol could not be altered in this manner. Instead, it was agreed that a statement could be added to the effect that Poland would be granted "equal and no lesser rights than those which are enjoyed by any other Government participating in the distribution of gold," with all prior decisions of the Tripartite Commission to be accepted as final.[30]

Winiewicz had raised the question of gold definitions used by the commission and, although for working purposes monetary and nonmonetary gold had been defined much earlier by the Western Allies, the subject continued to surface as disputes arose over claims. Some of the difficulty was simply inherent in handling and processing such vast quantities of gold from a wide variety of sources. For example, as the Americans began preparations at the end of 1947 to move the remaining gold out of the FED in Frankfurt, there were alloy and irregular bars, scrap gold, sweepings, etc., which were not classified as monetary gold by these definitions, although the Tripartite Commission had the authority to define them as such. Gold presumed looted from victims of Nazi persecution, which constituted much of the gold claimed by Poland, had been defined as nonmonetary gold, and this was strongly disputed by the Polish government.[31]

As Poland pressed its case to alter the gold-distribution program, an OMGUS memorandum to Washington sought additional clarification on

29. Ibid., Lovett to Winiewicz, 1 December 1947.

30. Ibid., Polish Gold Claim telegram, London to Washington, No. 50, 6 January 1948; Johnson and Bartlett, 30 March 1948, and Bartlett to U.S. Secretary of State, 2 April 1948.

31. NA, RG 260, OMGUS FINAD, Lovett to Dorr, 31 December 1947.

some of the problems arising out of the argument brought by Poland on the definitions in use. It was noted that the FED was in possession of gold, both coins and bullion, that had been surrendered to the Germans in occupied nations, and was absolutely identifiable as to former individual owners. The FED also had some minted gold looted by the Germans from individuals, which had not been held by any government's central bank or any other recognized monetary authority, and thus did not strictly count as part of a nation's monetary reserve. Neither of these situations, the memorandum pointed out, were covered by the current monetary and nonmonetary gold definitions. Part of the problem resulted from the fact that a country could only file a claim for gold held at the time of looting or wrongful removal when the gold was a portion of its monetary reserve held in a government central bank. OMGUS suggested that the gold they had described, though technically excluded from existing restitution directives, be returned to its original owners anyway as soon as proper ownership was officially established. The memorandum called attention to the fact that, contrary to announced policy, gold coin that had come from concentration camps and had less numismatic than monetary value was earmarked for the gold pot.[32]

In an attempt to adjust the gold definitions to fit the situation, OMGUS suggested adding two new categories to the already existing ones. Gold that had been surrendered to the Germans by individuals in occupied nations according to a law promulgated by Germany or that had been taken from individuals but was still in its original identifiable form should be called "restitutable gold" and returned to its rightful owners or heirs. Then there was so-called "German gold," which was held by OMGUS and was neither monetary nor nonmonetary under the current definitions; this should be placed in the gold pot with the stipulation that it be used for the German economy as deemed necessary by the Allied governing authorities.[33]

By April 1948, six claims were referred to in official but confidential correspondence by the various Allied agencies dealing with the gold question as "USSR Satellite Countries." These were Czechoslovakia, Albania, Greece, Poland, Danzig, and Yugoslavia. None of the claims had been paid to date.

Czechoslovakia claimed 45 tons of gold; of this amount the Tripartite Commission recognized 13.3 tons without argument and was prepared to transfer it upon proper request. Another 12.7 tons had been judged tentatively allowable as constituting the amount that had been held in the

32. Ibid., OMGUS to C/S, U.S. Army, Washington, 2 February 1948, p. 1.
33. Ibid., pp. 2–3.

Bank of England and sold to the German Reichsbank. Finally, 14.5 tons were regarded as possibly valid, but no decision had yet been made on the claim.[34]

Poland's claim was for 138.7 tons of gold, none of which was recognized or tentatively allowed by the commission because it was regarded as nonmonetary gold that had come from concentration camps. In fact, 132 tons had been specifically classed as concentration-camp gold in origin by the commission, and all supporting evidence for the claim was lacking. Only 6.3 tons of gold was considered as possibly valid, but no final decision had yet been made on that claim. This sum represented the amount the commission acknowledged to have been collected by German-controlled monetary institutions in Poland from private citizens during the period of occupation.[35]

The Yugoslavs had a total claim of 11.7 tons of gold, but as with Poland, the Tripartite Commission had not recognized it, tentatively allowing only 0.5 tons, which was proved to be cases of gold looted by the Germans during the war. A small additional amount of 0.1 tons, which had been collected from private Yugoslav citizens by the Yugoslav Central Bank, was considered as possibly valid. Over 90 tons of gold, most of it set aside from Italy's share in accordance with the peace treaty for that nation and some extracted from mines (the Bor mines), was disallowed.[36]

The Albanian claim of 2.6 tons of gold represented that gold which had been on deposit in Rome and was taken by the retreating Germans, along with the Italian gold. The commission recognized this claim for 2.4 tons, with the additional 0.2 regarded as possibly valid, but no decision was made and no gold had been transferred.[37]

Danzig, still an unresolved issue for the Western Allies, had a 4.7-ton gold claim (presumably submitted by Polish authorities), 3.8 of which the commission accepted without dispute because it was the published amount of the holdings of the Bank of Danzig in 1939. A claim of 0.9 tons was considered as possibly valid, making the total claim 4.7 tons. Of course, the commission had absolutely no intention of paying over this claim to Poland "pending decision on the ultimate fate of Danzig."[38]

The Greek claim for 12.7 tons of gold—all judged as possibly valid by the commission—was included with those of the other Russian satellite states in the correspondence, but this may not have been intentional. Greece fell into the category of the other states only in so far as it was on

34. NA, RG 43, WW II Conf. Files, Reinstein memorandum, 19 April 1948, p. 1.
35. Ibid.
36. Ibid., pp. 1–2. Gold mined after 8 May 1945 was not subject to the Final Act of Paris.
37. Ibid.
38. Ibid.

the list of unresolved claims and therefore may have been placed there for that reason. A note beside the Greek entry read: "Looted from private persons directly, not collected through Central Bank; no evidence submitted; only 0.1 was looted from Bank of Greece."[39]

That same month, however, Jacques Reinstein prepared a secret summary entitled "Restitution of Gold to the Soviet Satellite Countries," and did not include Greece on the list. His commentary added a few relevant notes to the situation. For instance, on the Czech claim involving 14.5 tons of gold deemed possibly valid by the Tripartite Commission because it had been transferred to Germany as a result of the Munich Agreement, Reinstein wrote: "The British and French suggest that action on this claim be stalled without taking a final decision."[40] On Poland, Reinstein was of the opinion that "the greater part, and perhaps the whole of the Polish claim would not be allowed by the Gold Commission in any event. It is rather unlikely that Poland would agree to sign a protocol adhering to the gold pool under these circumstances, but a decision is needed as to whether we should sign in the event Poland accepts the protocol in the form offered to her."[41]

Reinstein by no means anticipated the prolonged delay of years that did eventually develop, for he calculated that $143,000,000 in gold had already been distributed from the available $340,000,000, "mostly to Western European countries. Additional claims are now being reviewed and acted on and transfers will be made in the near future, including some to Soviet satellite countries." It was his recommendation that claims from those satellite states which were clear obligations under the Paris Agreement on Reparations should be allowed and payment made. "This involves a total of $16,000,000 in the case of Czechoslovakia, and small amounts in the case of Albania and Yugoslavia." He concluded, "If the Poles are willing to sign the protocol in the form offered to them . . . we should sign it. In the event they do not sign, an amount of gold sufficient to cover any possible valid Polish claim should be set aside until the final liquidation of the pool. If the Poles have not signed the protocol by that time, this amount should be distributed to other claimants."[42]

As the Tripartite Commission deliberations continued, it was decided that the remaining gold stored with the FED in Frankfurt, amounting to approximately 110 tons, should be moved out of Germany. A February 1948 cable from Colonel William Brey, chief of the FED, reported to the commission that all gold covered by the Howard Report was being

39. Ibid.
40. Ibid., Reinstein, "Restitution of Gold to the Soviet Satellite Countries," p. 2.
41. Ibid.
42. Ibid., pp. 2–3.

145

prepared for shipment and requested that all shipping instruction be coordinated with an FED listing to be submitted: "We feel that specific instructions . . . should be received. This position is urged with respect to gold packed and awaiting shipment at FED."[43] OMGUS officials released a news bulletin announcing the gold move to the United States and Great Britain from the German depository, emphasizing that there were "no ulterior purposes" to be drawn from the decision. It was projected to be an operation lasting several weeks since the gold was transported by air in commercial aircraft (Pan American). The mode of transportation was described merely as a matter of convenience and expense, for dozens of trips were necessary to move the sixty tons of gold destined for the Bank of England and the remaining fifty for deposit in the United States. The reader was assured, however, that all phases of the move were carefully monitored by the Department of the Army.[44]

The gold was still at the disposal of the Tripartite Commission for continued distribution as the FED began the careful and detailed process of transfer. OMGUS called attention to the fact that the Howard Report was an "inventory performed by foremost US mint experts" and was regarded as extremely accurate; therefore any discrepancies would now become the concern of the commission: "OMGUS had no responsibility for accuracy of weights listed in Howard inventory and in event Bank of England finds discrepancy OMGUS not responsible therefore and any less shall be for act of Tripartite Commission."[45] OMGUS suggested that the commission provide a receipt for each shipment on the basis of an OMGUS certification that said shipment contained the items listed in the Howard inventory: "In consideration of the delivery of such sealed boxes . . . the Tripartite Commission for the Restitution of Monetary Gold herewith releases OMGUS from any responsibility for such differences in the contents of the sealed bags from the description of the contents contained in the Howard Inventory."[46]

This did not end the relationship between the FED and the Tripartite Commission, however. Although the FED was no longer the custodian for the monetary gold, it did possess files with valuable and extensive data bearing on the origin, ownership, markings, and other particulars pertaining to the gold. FED personnel had also compiled much of their data into studies and reports that provided important perspectives and summaries on many aspects of the looted gold story. In adjudicating gold claims, the commission had and would continue to have many occasions

43. NA, RG 260, OMGUS FINAD, Brey cable, 9 February 1948, p. 1.
44. *New York Times*, 8 February 1948, p. 26.
45. NA, RG 260, OMGUS FINAD, Dept. of Army to OMGUS, 10 April 1948, p. 1.
46. Ibid., p. 2.

to refer such claims for comparison to the FED records and the copies of Reichsbank records that they continued to hold.[47]

According to FED records, there had only been one direct restitution of monetary gold to Hungary; the rest of the gold was disposed of pursuant to instructions from the Tripartite Commission as follows: France had received 74.6 tons of gold ($85,290,000); the Netherlands, 29 tons of gold ($33,065,000); and the Bank of England, 127.1 tons of gold ($145,312,000). The grand total: 258.9 tons of gold valued at $295,821,000, calculated at $35 per troy ounce, were dispensed while the FED was still acting custodian.[48] The delivery of gold to Hungary was characterized as a direct restitution since it did not represent a proportional share in the gold pot but constituted the entire amount of the Hungarian gold recovered intact. An FED report stated that the gold that went to the Bank of England on commission instructions was the remainder of the monetary gold in the Frankfurt depository and was marked for adjudication of the remaining claims.[49] No reference was made to the 1948 OMGUS news release to the effect that approximately half of the Frankfurt gold held by the FED had been sent to the United States.

When establishing the Tripartite Commission in 1946, it had been the Allies' intent that its life would definitely be a limited one and the work of deciding on claims received and distributing the gold would be of relatively short duration. Actually, a significant amount of the work did go rather quickly, but it was becoming evident by 1948 that certain decisions relating to the final distribution of the gold might well stall indefinitely. Even the complexities of the Polish problem did not suggest that there would still be a portion of undistributed gold as well as a Tripartite Commission some forty years later!

Between May 1948 and the signing of a gold protocol with Poland in July 1949, a number of basic questions on German looted gold and the Cold War emerged even though this was not the express intent of the Allied negotiators at the time. Poland had submitted a claim for about 140,000 kilograms ($155,000,000) to the commission, but the commission had disallowed 130,382 kilograms as not covered by the definition of monetary gold and considered as valid only 7,259 kilograms of gold ($8,000,000). The Polish claim included 4,000 kilograms in the name of Danzig, aimed at the commission's allowance of 3,821 kilograms for the city, and was based on Danzig's published gold reserve in August 1939. The commission ruled that no allocation would be made to Poland until that nation was formally admitted to the gold pool by signing the "Lon-

47. Ibid., "Disposition of Monetary Gold by FED," 28 February 1950, 2 pp.
48. Ibid., p. 1.
49. Ibid.

don Protocol," which meant full acceptance of the Paris agreement.[50]

Confronted with the Tripartite Commission's decision, Poland sought to circumvent its authority by going directly to the British Foreign Office and the French and American embassies in London; these were the sources from which the protocol offer had first come in October of the previous year. Despite the fact that the commission was empowered to represent these nations and even had some independent quasi-judicial authority to make decisions on the gold claims, Poland requested that an arbitration clause be inserted in the protocol. This was meant to replace the statement that made the commission decisions final. The request was denied because the commission continued to insist that the Polish claim was essentially made for gold taken by the Germans from privately owned banking institutions and individuals and thus was not monetary gold. The three Western governments stood behind their commission and refused all comment on the Polish claim. The stand on Danzig gold remained unchanged.[51]

American commissioner Dorr told U.S. secretary of state Marshall that it "might be possible [to] allow one claim for around 1600 kgs . . . approximately one percent of [the] claims filed by Poland," but to admit any more would "likely result in controversy and possible litigation. Polish admission would increase any embarrassment now existing due [to] participation [of] Iron Curtain countries."[52] In Dorr's opinion the problem could be avoided by simply refusing Poland's participation entirely on the grounds that "she suffered no loss of gold reserves and Nazi looting [was] confined to individuals." Since the commission's deliberations concluded that Poland's claim did not qualify for restitution according to the established guidelines, Dorr advised Marshall that "under [the] Paris agreement the Allied powers have full authority to decide on admission or nonadmission of nonsignatories to the gold pot, [and] Poland could prefer no claim before [an] arbitral tribunal or [the] International Court. If, however, Poland [was] admitted to share, then she would be in a position to litigate [the] propriety of Commission's decision."[53] Dorr had always been against the admission of Poland's claim and had assumed from the beginning that it was the commission's role to settle the issue without involving their respective governments in extended diplomatic negotiations directly with Poland. Earlier, when acting as the commission's primary strategist on the Polish problem, Dorr had suggested that instead of taking up the question of the validity of the

50. NA, RG 43, WW II Conf. Files, Fletcher to Reinstein, 5 May 1948.
51. Ibid., Reinstein to Thorp, 6 May 1948.
52. Ibid., Dorr to Marshall, 12 May 1948.
53. Ibid.

claim they should just solicit additional information. He reasoned that in doing so the commission would receive "much valuable ammunition when it comes to answering their contentions on the merits. For example, it is likely that they will be forced to admit that they do not know exactly how much or what quality of gold was looted. . . . Even more important," Dorr wrote, "if we can get them tied down to a statement of how much monetary gold is involved we shall minimize the possibility of any attempt to include inadmissible items after we have rejected their contentions in regard to nonmonetary gold."[54]

While not rejecting Dorr's argument, Secretary Marshall pointed out the fact that the Polish claim had already been submitted to the commission before the three Western governments had offered to sign the protocol. Furthermore, the commission had not yet acted upon the Polish claim. He instructed the American embassy in London to "explore with Brit and France desirability three govts asking Commission whether Poles have made prima facie case less of 'a definite amount of monetary gold.' If Commission reply negative, as Door's tel indicates likely, this might be used as basis for terminating negotiations if Polish Govt pursues matter or if present [protocol] text not promptly accepted."[55]

The Polish government definitely did pursue the matter. A June meeting in Washington with French, British, and Polish representatives tried to resolve the problem, but little progress was made because Poland persisted in its determination to have the right to present its case formally before the Tripartite Commission before it would sign the protocol. The minutes of one of the Washington sessions read: "The Polish representative, apparently anxious to be able to report something favorably back to Warsaw, then requested that a letter accompany the Protocol which would assure Poland that it would have full opportunity to present its case. . . . This suggestion could not be agreed to since . . . one of the basic reasons for not including an interpretative letter had been to keep a complicated situation from becoming more so."[56] Following the Washington meeting, a U.S. State Department memorandum summarized policy on Polish participation in the gold pool as follows: Poland was to be admitted to the pool under the same conditions as Italy and Austria and would have to accept the decisions of the Tripartite Commission as final as stated in the protocol. Poland had already been informed that a refusal meant no admittance to the gold pool.[57]

Faced with the Allies' adamant stand, Poland still attempted to wrest

54. Ibid., Dorr to Todd, 17 May 1947.
55. Ibid., Marshall to American Embassy London, 25 May 1948.
56. Ibid., "Polish Gold Talks," 8 June 1948.
57. Ibid., "Polish Participation on Gold Pool," 22 June 1948.

149

some concessions from the situation. Obviously reconciled to the fact that they could not force any change in protocol nor gain a stated right to press their case before the Tripartite Commission, Poland turned to other demands currently pending decision in the arena of U.S.–Polish relations. Suggesting that the Polish signing of the protocol might be hastened, the Polish government reminded the United States that there were current requests for a variety of export licenses as well as some financial assistance. This maneuver turned out to be a two-edged sword, however, as the U.S. responded by asking for payment due on the Polish Lend-Lease account in the sum of 125 million zlotys to be placed at the disposal of the U.S. mission in Poland. The United States was also in a position to block Poland's expansion of civil aviation services, which they wanted to expand into Belgium, Denmark, and the Middle East. The U.S. position was to restrict the Soviet Union and its satellites to their own territory and "to seek cooperation of other non-[Iron] [C]urtain states in carrying out our policy on a 'common front' basis. The State Department is actively engaged in endeavors to carry out the objectives of this policy, which is applicable to Poland as a satellite of the Soviet Union."[58] The only concession made to Poland was oral assurance that they could, through their accredited representative in Brussels, raise any questions they wished with the Tripartite Commission, and would certainly receive "a full and courteous reply."[59] On 6 July 1948 in London the Polish representative signed the long awaited protocol with the United States, Great Britain, and France. It was signed in full accordance with part III of the Paris agreement of January 1946, "which reserved the question of eventual participation in the restitution of monetary gold of countries not represented at the conference which drew up the agreement."[60] No mention was made of the unresolved Danzig issue.

58. *F.R.U.S.*, vol. 5, 1949, p. 510.
59. NA, RG43, WW II Conf. Files, "Participation of Poland in the Distribution of Gold by the Tripartite Commission for the Restitution of Monetary Gold," 26 June 1948, pp. 3–4.
60. *Germany, 1947–1949: The Story in Documents*, p. 432.

CHAPTER 8

Unfinished Business

In less than a year the Tripartite Commission for the Restitution of Monetary Gold had accomplished a great deal and had been extremely effective in carrying out most of its mission of gold restitution. Any neutral observer in 1948 would have concluded that the commission had been a success and with the bulk of its work completed only a bit of unfinished business remained. This bit of business would remain unfinished for many years to come, however. One of the problems confronting the commission in 1948 was recovering the looted gold sums from certain neutral nations that had accepted German gold during the war.

One would assume that with the war over the victorious Allies would have little real difficulty in persuading neutrals to return the gold in question, but it was not to prove so easy for new alliances were being forged as war gave way to cold war. For example, Spain, as one of the delinquent neutrals that stalled on gold repayment, was governed by a leader with an exemplary anti-Communist record. As a secret U.S. State Department memorandum noted: "the primary objective of United States policy toward Spain at this time [1948] is the reintegration of Spain politically, economically and militarily into the western European community of nations."[1] The gold issue could not be ignored, but there could not be any further punitive action either.

Spanish assets in the United States were still blocked and, in fact, had been so since 1941, but after some intensive negotiations it was announced in Washington that the $60 million had been released. This was followed by a statement from the Madrid government that it was expropriating about $80 million worth of German properties in Spain in accord with the Bretton Woods agreement calling for the destruction of German economic war potential. The looted gold that had found its way into Spain would be

1. *F.R.U.S.*, vol. 3, 1948, p. 1041.

turned over to the United States, Great Britain, and France to be added to the gold pot. In so doing, Spain was careful to point out its innocence in having accepted it in the first place.[2] The return of the gold was regarded by the United States as a "satisfactory conclusion of the looted gold negotiations [and] . . . should relieve this situation and facilitate the extension of private American credits since the Spaniards are now able to use gold as collateral."[3]

Portugal, a nation that presented a problem very similar to that of Spain for the Allies, did not prove very amenable to negotiation, however. In February 1948, Portuguese premier Antonio de Oliveira Salazar had concluded an agreement that provided for a continuation of American military aircraft use of landing facilities in the Azores, a fact that made the U.S.–Portuguese relationship a bit different from that with Spain. Salazar made no secret of his outrage that his nation's assets continued to be frozen in America, but he refused to budge on the question of a gold repayment. It was his contention that the $55 million in gold acquired from Germany in wartime had been through legitimate sales of goods, and Portugal was under no obligation to return anything. Considering Salazar's uncompromising stand and the importance of the air rights in the Azores, which the American Joint Chiefs of Staff desired on a long-term lease, the United States decided to release Portugal's assets.[4] This occurred in August 1948 and effectively ended any continued efforts by the Tripartite Commission to apply pressure on Portugal for gold repayment.[5]

An equally unsatisfying finish to the controversy over the fate of the BIS unfolded at approximately the same time. Ironically, it had been the Polish delegation at the wartime Bretton Woods Monetary Conference that had raised the hue and cry against the actions of the BIS, when the measure was introduced to investigate that bank's activities. There was almost unanimous support from the other attending delegations for liquidating the BIS after the war. Subsequent events only strengthened this resolve when a postwar U.S. investigation of the BIS indicated that the reason there had been failure to link BIS activity with extensive "gold-

---

2. *New York Times*, 9 May 1948, p. 20.
3. *F.R.U.S.* vol. 3, 1948, p. 1042.
4. Ibid., pp. 995–1002.
5. A January news release reported the conclusion of a five-day Tripartite Commission meeting in Brussels on the question of the $55 million in gold Portugal had received from Germany in the war. Revealing absolutely nothing about their discussions, the commission issued a statement to the effect that a new approach to the problem was being considered, pointing out that $100 million in gold had already been recovered from Switzerland, Spain, Sweden, and Romania, as well as the BIS, and even Turkey had agreed to negotiate over the $4.5 million in gold they had accepted from Germany during the war, *New York Times*, 11 January 1950, p. 4.

washing" was the refusal of the Swiss National Bank to open its files.[6] The Americans did succeed, however, in compiling enough evidence from Reichsbank records and oral testimony from its staff to confirm their suspicions about the BIS. Another irony in the U.S. investigation of the BIS in late 1945 was the fact that the bank was criticized for having refused to transfer the Baltic gold to the USSR in 1940. The secret U.S. report read: "in July 1940 when the central banks of Lithuania, Estonia, and Latvia . . . ordered delivery of the gold in their BIS accounts to the Russian State Bank whom they declared to have purchased it, the BIS refused to recognize these instructions. This action was based upon legal opinion which concluded that: 'These orders apparently did not result from the free will of the three banks, but have presumably been influenced by the will of the Soviet Russian Government or the political party controlling the latter.'"[7] No mention was made of the fact that the BIS had failed to exercise such insight in its transfer of Czech gold to the German Reichsbank in 1938.

Considering the immediate postwar mood of the victors, it was probably prudent of the BIS to offer full cooperation to the central banks of Europe in tracing looted monetary gold. Complete listing of the gold bars and markings received from Germany during the war was gathered for comparison with the records offered by the central banks. In 1946, after the national banks of both Belgium and France had examined the BIS data, it was concluded that only the Belgian gold that had been turned over by the Vichy government to Germany could be identified as having passed into Switzerland.[8] One American official connected with the investigation expressed some reservation that the BIS should be absolved so easily:

Many questions about the operation of the Bank for International Settlements during the war have never been answered. Mr. McKittrick has not disclosed the arrangements which enabled the Nazis to ship to the Bank for International Settlements large quantities of gold looted from various countries in occupied Europe, worth hundreds of millions of dollars. No accounting has yet been made of it. Dr. Emil Puhl . . . revealed that the last time he went to Switzerland in April 1945 . . . he had succeeded in getting his friends to defer the publication of the bank's financial statements because he wanted to conceal the extent of the Nazi gold transactions.[9]

6. NA, RG 332, ETO, SGS, 123/2, McNarney to Nixon, 25 November 1945, p. 4.
7. Ibid., p. 2.
8. *New York Times*, 19 July 1948, p. 23.
9. Martin, *All Honorable Men*, p. 281. Martin was a lawyer employed in the Economic Warfare Section of the U.S. Dept. of Justice and worked in Germany after the war.

Despite such doubts about the BIS the tide was already turning in 1946, and the many negative opinions of Bretton Woods were rapidly fading. The BIS was far too valuable an institution to dissolve amidst the great devastation of postwar Europe. It was soon evident that the prevailing opinion among Western Europe bankers—including the central banks— was that the BIS definitely served a purpose and should be continued as an institution. It represented a financial source that could complement the efforts of the International Monetary Fund and the International Bank for Reconstruction and Development; it had flexibility and experience, and its geographic location made it an ideal meeting place for Europe's banking community to exchange views and do business.[10] By the end of 1946 the BIS had already begun to resume those functions that had been suspended during the war, and the directorate quickly agreed to open discussions on a settlement of the looted gold question, although the evidence indicated that relatively little of the gold in the form of gold bars could be traced to the BIS.[11] The result was that an agreement was concluded that read: "Representatives of the United States of America, the United Kingdom of Great Britain and Northern Ireland, and France, on the one hand, and the Bank for International Settlements on the other, have conferred in Washington on the subject of gold transferred by Germany to the Bank for International Settlements and have agreed that the Bank for International Settlements shall deliver in London to the three governments upon demand 3,740 kilograms of fine gold."[12] In praise of the settlement, and with a reference to the generosity of the BIS, Maurice Frere, the bank chairman, remarked that it had been absolutely impossible to check any gold origins during the war.[13] In late 1950 the United States formally admitted that the Bretton Woods resolution calling for the liquidation of the BIS back in 1944 had been totally ineffective: "The United States Government has decided that it will no longer urge the implementation of Bretton Woods Resolution V and that unless any other member country desires to pursue the matter further, the United States Government regards the issue as closed."[14]

Perhaps Frere was right and the exact amount of gold that was

10. *Financial Times* (London), 25 November and 27 December 1946, as quoted in Schloss, *The Bank for International Settlements*, p. 121.

11. NA, RG 43, WW II Conf. Files, American Embassy London to Washington, 5 March 1948, Subject: "Arrangements for Monetary Gold of Illegal Issuance Held by BIS."

12. Great Britain, Parliamentary Command Paper 7456, *Treaty Series no. 38 (1948)*, Exchange of Letters between the Governments of the United Kingdom of Great Britain and Northern Ireland, the United States of America, and France and the Bank for International Settlements Constituting an Agreement for the Return to Those Governments of Gold Looted by Germany, 13 May 1948, p. 1.

13. *New York Times*, 19 July 1948, p. 23.

14. Quoted in a letter to Schloss, *The Bank for International Settlements*, p. 121, n. 3.

exchanged or transferred into Switzerland by Germany will never be known, but that it did amount to hundreds of millions of dollars worth is not open to much dispute. The quantity of gold looted by the Germans exceeded $621 million worth and was valued at ten times that sum later, as the price of gold climbed. When the approximately $150 million gold reserve Germany possessed at the beginning of the war is added to this it means that Hitler had at his disposal over $770 million of gold.[15] Since the Allies succeeded in recovering $252 million, this left some $500 million in gold that the Germans directed into their war effort. The vast bulk of this gold, about $378 million, was passed into Switzerland where, in the underground vaults of the Swiss National Bank, it was moved from one depot to another for debit or credit as the needs of the Reichsbank were met. By a stroke of the pen the origin of the gold was immediately wiped away, and the receiving nation's depot maintained the fiction that it was acquiring gold from Switzerland.[16]

While the point has been made that 98.6 percent of Germany's remaining gold in 1945 fell into American hands, it is an additional curiosity that even the gold that was not in Germany, namely that of Austria, Italy, and Hungary, also came into American possession. Without succumbing to any speculation had the Soviets been so fortunate as to have found the gold, the fact remains that the United States found itself in a very fortuitous position on the gold question vis-à-vis its two allies, Great Britain and France. Had the gold fallen to France, or even Great Britain, the subsequent discussions that have been explored in detail here would have followed a far different course.

It is obvious that the most important gold recovery was that made at the Kaiseroda Mine in Merkers. The quick action by American authorities to uncover and confiscate any additional amounts of Reichsbank gold scattered among its branches was a very effective maneuver. Within two weeks after the Merkers' discovery, American military reconnaissance parties had traveled almost two thousand miles and had visited all of the bank branches in central and southern Germany. No clue or rumor was neglected in the search that resulted in the recovery of $14.01 million in gold. This left only about $3.5 million unaccounted for according to the Reichsbank records. Somehow fifty bars of gold had disappeared in the evacuation from Weimar; forty bars of gold sent from Berlin to Merkers by the Reichsbank had never arrived; two gold bars were lost or stolen

15. Funk testified that when he took over control of the Reichsbank in 1938, it contained about 500,000,000 Reichsmarks of gold reserves, much higher than the public estimate of $70,000,000, *I.M.T.*, vol. 13, p. 168. See also NA, RG 260, OMGUS FINAD, "Overall Gold Report," 20 November 1946, p. 2.

16. Rings, *Raubgold*, pp. 68–69.

from the Erfurt branch; and 147 bags of gold coins originally stored at Magdeburg were never found.[17] The books of the Reichsbank showed a closing balance of $255.96 million in gold, $238.49 million of which was found in the mine at Merkers. The bank records also noted some $37.3 million (largely resmelted) that had come from the National Bank of Belgium. Of this amount $20.9 million was found with the Merkers treasure, and later $14 million more was recovered, leaving only $2.4 million missing.[18]

An interesting item carried on the Reichsbank books was a quantity of platinum with a value of $34,000. It had never been listed in any of the published reserve reports but carried the notation that it had been a gift to Adolf Hitler from a South African resident named Hans Merensky. The platinum had come to the Reichsbank through the August Thyssen firm in Berlin and was listed not in Hitler's name, but in the firm's account. It was evacuated along with the Reichsbank gold to Merkers and then to the custody of the FED in Frankfurt.[19]

The huge quantity of gold coinage found with the gold bars in the Kaiseroda Mine presented some difficulties. The bags contained gold coins, and some silver, from many nations. Some of the coins were from museums and private collections and were extremely rare and valuable, thus simplifying the process of identifying them . But the vast bulk of gold coinage proved virtually impossible to identify for it bore no serial numbers. This meant that FED personnel had to rely on matching amounts and types when trying to make comparisons. Sometimes, the Reichsbank records could be used, but since many of the bags did not have numbers that was not always helpful; it was found that the bank had not sorted out some of the coinage by type and it was simply entered in a miscellaneous category.[20] The most accurate approach in establishing a value for the coinage was by weight. Although the Reichsbank had not yet weighed large quantities of the gold coin, the FED decided to use the German formula—face value times mint weight minus an assumed wear of 2 percent. An FED report on the subject read: "It is believed significant that the estimate for German coin, on the basis of [German] wear factor, comes within one hundredth of one percent of the weight shown by the Frankfurt inventory. The inventory weights for other coin do not check so closely with the estimate, but none of the major types (amounting to a million grams or more) shows a difference of more than one and one half

17. NA, RG 332, ETO, SGS, 123/2, "Report on Recovery of Reichsbank Precious Metals," 6 September 1945, pp. 1–2.

18. Ibid.

19. Ibid., pt. 1, "Schedule A," A1.

20. Ibid., p. 3.

percent of the book estimate and the difference for total coin wear is only four tenths of one percent."[21] Almost half of the gold recovered at Merkers was in coin form, over $124 million worth. According to Reichsbank records this represented 98.3 percent of the total amount that the bank possessed; approximately $2 million in gold coins remained unaccounted for and was either lost during the move to Merkers, or from Merkers to Frankfurt, or a combination of both.[22]

The Allied Tripartite Commission for the Restitution of Monetary Gold had about $330 million in gold when they began their distribution program in October 1947. With claims of over $800 million, the commission succeeded in quickly disbursing some $295 million (258.9 tons of gold) by mid-1948. Working with the remaining balance of approximately $35 million in gold, it appeared that the Allied restitution program would soon be completed. The deepening of the Cold War was to prevent this and Gold Commission activity on the claims of states like Albania, Czechoslovakia, and Poland slowed to a virtual halt. In the meantime, the market value of gold was to start its climb, and what had looked like a rather modest amount in 1946 began to assume significant proportions.

An example of this was the Danzig gold. Despite the Tripartite Commission's strong negative stand about returning this gold to Poland in the immediate postwar era, the issue was finally settled by doing so in 1976! A brief news item informed the world in August 1976 that "West Returns Danzig Gold. Two tons of fine monetary gold quietly slipped into Poland in recent weeks to close one of World War II's oldest chapters. Worth perhaps $10 million, the gold had been held in the vaults of the Bank of England and the Federal Reserve Bank of New York since the end of the War. It had belonged to the free City of Danzig, a political entity which existed between the two world wars."[23] The decision by the Tripartite Commission to return the Danzig gold to Poland reflected the much changed relations between nations, especially the United States and Poland. Although Poland's boundaries had not changed since the war ended, the return of the gold was a confirmation of the existence of its western border. Maintaining its usual reticence, the Tripartite Commission would neither confirm nor deny that the return of the Danzig gold signaled an end to that question. It was not entirely a Polish victory, however, for there had been many claimants holding bonds issued by the former Free City of Danzig, now called Gdansk. While the commission refused to divulge any hint of their deliberations, no doubt Poland had agreed to settle these debts. It was understood that the gold was used as

21. Ibid.
22. Ibid., pt. 2, "Schedule K," K1.
23. *Los Angeles Times*, 26 August 1976, 3, p. 1.

bait to resolve prewar debts that the Communists refused to pay.[24]

In the case of Czechoslovakia it had appeared at first that the gold issue there would be solved before the Danzig situation, but complications developed. In 1974, United States and Czechoslovak negotiators had reached an agreement that produced an accord on the gold issue, but it had to be approved by both governments before becoming effective. It provided for the return of 18.4 metric tons of fine gold, which had an estimated value by this time of about $80 million, to Czechoslovakia. In return the Czechs promised to settle a number of outstanding debts to the United States.[25] The proposed accord did not secure U.S. congressional approval, however. Instead the matter became the subject of debate for several more years and the price of gold continued to rise. By late 1978 the gold in question was worth a very impressive $118 million. And Czechoslovakia was offering to pay forty-six cents on the dollar to settle their claims, six cents higher than the settlements that had already been made by Poland and Hungary. As the negotiations remained locked, Moscow's *New Times* referred to the gold as "arrested gold" that America had been holding since it had come into American "custody" after having been stolen from the Czechs by the Nazis almost forty years ago.[26] As factions within the U.S. Congress continued to block any settlement, the 18.4 tons of Czech gold climbed to the staggering value of $162.5 million. Some U.S. congressmen were urging that the gold be sold to satisfy the demands of the American claimants. Actually, Czechoslovakia had originally been entitled to 24 tons of gold by the calculations of the Tripartite Commission in 1946 and had received 5.6 tons on account before the Communist coup in 1948. After that President Truman had ordered a freezing of the portion that was in the United States, about 8 tons, and Great Britain froze the other 10 tons. By the date an agreement was finally reached in December of 1981, the gold was worth $230 million!

The 1981 settlement was the result of talks opened by the Reagan administration, and unlike the earlier negotiations there was congressional support for a resolution this time. French and British approval had already been granted so the Tripartite Commission moved to complete the arrangements.[27] Under the terms of settlement, in return for the gold, Czechoslovakia agreed to pay $81.5 million to U.S. citizens for their claims plus interest. An additional $8 million went to the United States for

24. Ibid., p. 15.
25. Claims by U.S. citizens amounted to $72.6 million and by the U.S. government, $7 million. In the past the United States had accepted forty cents on the dollar in such settlements.
26. Gherman Ustinov, "Arrested Gold," *New Times* (Moscow), no. 8 (F 1979): 28–30.
27. See "Public Laws 97–127–Dec. 29, 1981," *United States Statutes at Large, 1981* (Washington D.C.: U.S.G.P.O., 1982), pp. 1675–80.

the cost of equipment never paid for some years earlier and some U.S. bank assets that had been confiscated.[28]

In some ways the fate of Albania's gold was just as muddled as the Czech case, although it did not take as many years to resolve. From the very outset the Albanians had little chance of receiving any restitution for the gold that had belonged to the Bank of Albania. The bank had been established in 1925, and its gold was later looted by the Germans during the war along with the Italian gold. As noted, the Tripartite Commission had not awarded Italy the gold after the war although that nation had a claim to it, contending that the Albanian bank had been created with Italian capital. In 1953, disgruntled and frustrated in its attempts to recover some gold compensation, Italy initiated proceedings in the International Court of Justice to try to enforce its claim for the gold, now worth about $2.8 million. Earlier the commission had ruled that the gold did indeed belong to Albania, but that it should be paid to Great Britain for debt. Britain's claim for the gold had resulted from an action by Albania in 1946, when that nation had mined the Corfu Channel, causing the sinking of some British ships and the death of British seamen. The International Court of Justice had ruled on the case too and in 1949 had agreed that the debt was definitely owed by Albania, but made no ruling on whether it should be paid from the gold or not. At the time of the dispute over the Albanian gold, it still rested in the vaults of the Bank of England awaiting final disposition by the commission.[29] It was Italy's argument that their claim preceded that of the British, a logic that the International Court of Justice supported; however, the court stated that it lacked jurisdiction to rule in the case because Albania was an essential party to the proceedings but refused to participate. Italy was granted appeal rights, but they were useless unless Albania agreed to become involved.[30]

The fact that the commission had decided the claim in Britain's favor appears to be a departure from its assigned task of restitution. The commission's responsibility was basically the disbursement of gold to those nations whose banks had been looted by Germany in the war. Its entire function was rooted in wartime occurrences and the settlement of claims stemming from that time between the years 1938 and 1945. Deciding to rule in Britain's behalf on an issue totally unrelated to wartime events or the loss of gold (by Great Britain) would seem to be an intrusion of Tripartite Commission authority into an area more suitably dealt with by the International Court.

While the focus of attention here has been upon the restitution of mone-

28. *Congressional Quarterly Weekly Report*, 2 January 1982.
29. *New York Times*, 23 May 1953, p. 10.
30. Ibid., 16 June 1954, p. 7.

tary gold by the Tripartite Commission, some mention of Hungary's crown of Saint Stephen is relevant to the gold story since it was captured by American forces along with the Hungarian gold and became the responsibility of the commission. Just why this historic relic, regarded with such national reverence by the Hungarians, was included in the work to be done by the commission is not exactly clear. It is more puzzling due to the fact that the commission was not directly involved in the return of Hungary's gold because it was not regarded as looted gold and, being fully identifiable, was soon returned. Thus, it was never part of the gold pot that the commission administered. Actually, the crown was not the only important relic which came into American possession with the gold; the mummified hand of Saint Stephen was also among the items turned over to the Americans, but this was returned with the gold in 1946. The crown was eventually sent to the United States, where it was placed in Fort Knox, to remain for the next thirty years. The crown has been described as "the world's ugliest crown, a jumble . . . of enamel plates, precious stones and pendala hung or fastened to a golden circlet and arches. Greek art is mixed with Roman, Byzantine with Latin."[31]

It is possible that the way in which the Americans acquired the crown has some bearing upon the fact that it was not returned as promptly as the gold and the mummified hand. When the U.S. Seventh Army captured the Hungarian treasure in Austria, an elaborate chest, said to contain the crown, was among the items. No keys were found and since the chest was obviously a historic relic of value there was some reluctance to open it until the keys were located. Meanwhile, the chest was moved to FED custody in Frankfurt. Approximately two months later, when the chest was opened, it was found to be empty. Immediately, an intelligence unit of the Seventh Army launched an investigation and quickly determined that a member of the Hungarian Royal Police had hidden the crown in Austria. It was then recovered from its hiding place (the Hungarian policeman had buried it in an oil drum) and brought to Frankfurt.[32] Since these events occurred several months after the Hungarian gold had been received perhaps, some administrative decision had separated the crown from the gold and it was then dispatched to the United States. The problem with such speculation is that it must assume both ignorance and indifference on the part of the U.S. Army personnel in regard to the enormous importance of the crown to the Hungarian people; a not-impossible situation, however.

After the advent of the Cold War a number of anti-Communist organi-

31. *Los Angeles Times*, 5 November 1974, p. 1.
32. Ibid., p. 15.

zations in the United States, some of which included Hungarians who had fled their homeland, strongly opposed the return of the crown to a nation still under Communist rule. Over the intervening years several resolutions to that same effect were introduced in the American Congress. As time passed, however, sentiment for returning the crown to Hungary began to surface, and as one news editorial expressed it in 1977: "It is time that the United States return to the Hungarian people a national relic that is as historically and symbolically important to them as the Liberty Bell is to Americans—St. Stephen's Crown."[33] Finally, in 1978, after thirty-two years in American custody, the crown of Saint Stephen was sent back to Hungary. Amidst considerable pomp the crown arrived in Budapest on January 6th aboard a U.S. Army Air Force jet. To the accompaniment of a military band a large metal crate containing the crown was carefully lowered into a waiting Hungarian van. Included with the crown was a silver orb, a gold-plated scepter, a sword, and a coronation robe, all sacred relics of the Hungarian nation. The following day, at a public ceremony attended by a number of American and Hungarian officials, the crown was formally accepted in the name of the Hungarian people.[34]

While some of these events have been peripheral to the story of looted gold and its ultimate disposition, they are not without interest. The same may be said for the adventurous accounts that dwell upon the gold that somehow evaded both the Reichsbank and the Allied victors in the chaos of war's ending and disappeared into a trail of interesting but mostly unsubstantiated rumor.

Perhaps from a historical standpoint the fact that the Tripartite Commission for the Restitution of Monetary Gold is still a functioning Allied body places it in a curious position in relation to the overall gold story that basically unfolded between 1938 and 1949. The continued existence of the commission, with its policy of jealously guarding its activity in recent years in restituting gold to Poland, Czechoslovakia, or Albania, certainly must classify it as a surviving remnant of the early Cold War period.

A history of the Tripartite Commission after 1949, utilizing its still-classified materials, would probably provide insight into the clandestine dealings of nations, but at this point, considering the small amount of gold remaining, it can only be regarded as a footnote to the gold story.[35]

33. Ibid., 20 July 1977, p. 26.

34. Ibid., 6 January 1978, p. 17. For a number of years previously the crown had become a pawn in the bitter feud over Hungarian Cardinal Jozef Mindszenty's opposition to the Communist regime. The cardinal took refuge in the U.S. embassy in Budapest for fifteen years as the struggle continued. Only after his death in 1975 did relations improve enough that the crown could be returned. János Kádár, Hungary's Communist chief in 1978, did not take part in the ceremonies when the crown was handed over.

35. The author attempted every legitimate means to obtain access to the Tripartite

Commission files after 1949, now forty years old, but to no avail. Direct correspondence and discussion with the U.S. State Department and the American representative to the Brussels commission failed to budge the classification of the commission records.

The efforts were rebuffed with the explanation that its work was still in progress and involved French and British government participation. Despite a Freedom of Information request and the support of a U.S. congressman, all access was denied. A suggestion by the author to a U.S. State Department legal representative that the files in question remain restricted because the gold has been used and still is being used for the Cold War trade-off was described as "nonsense."

162

Data on Looted Gold

1. Summary[1]

Gold looted by Nazi Germany, 1938–45:

from Austria	$ 102,689,215
from Czechoslovakia	44,000,000
from the Bank of Danzig (Polish claim)	4,100,000
from the Netherlands	163,000,000
(the Dutch claimed $200,000,000)	
from Luxembourg (via Vichy France)	4,857,823
from Belgium (via Vichy France)	223,200,000
from Italy	80,000,000

Gold recovered by the U.S. Army, 1945 (in Germany):

from Kaiseroda Mine, Merkers, Thuringia	$ 238,490,000
from Reichsbank branches	14,010,000
from other sources	9,713,000

Gold shipped from Nazi Germany to Switzerland (Swiss National Bank), 1940–45:

$ 378,000,000

---

1. A dollar value (pre-1939 U.S. dollar) is used in calculating all gold sums. The price of gold was $35 per troy ounce. The figures for totals are often supplied in round numbers reflecting the best estimates provided either by Reichsbank records or Allied finance materials.

2. Miscellaneous Gold Data

Nazi Germany transferred $53,800,000 in gold to Romania for oil. The gold was Belgian gold. An additional $11,700,000 was deposited in the Romanian account in Switzerland.

The SHAEF Finance Section concluded from documentation that was available in 1945 that the closing balance of the Reichsbank's gold account at war's end was $255,960,000 and that the United States had recovered 98.6 percent of it. An estimated $4,300,000 was seized by the Russians from Reichsbank sources in Berlin. SHAEF also estimated that about $3,500,000 in gold remained unaccounted for (92 gold bars and 147 bags of coinage).

By SHAEF calculations in 1945, the total of all gold found in Germany amounted to $262,213,000 (one-half in gold bars and one-half in coins).

Nazi Germany began predating resmelted looted gold bars in February 1943, placing pre-1939 dates on them.

After the war the Western Allies (France, England, and the United States) established a "gold pool" into which recovered looted gold was placed for restitution purposes. In return for dropping all postwar claims on gold received from wartime Nazi Germany, Switzerland agreed to contribute $58,400,000.

Bibliography

1. Primary Unpublished Sources

Great Britain
  Public Record Office, London
  Premier, 4/19/1
Federal Republic of Germany
  Bundesarchiv, Koblenz
    NL   141
    NS   6
    R   2
    R   8X
    R   28
  Institut für Zeitgeschichte, Munich
    MA   125/14
    MA   190/2–5
    MA   326
    MA   677/2–4
United States
  National Archives, Washington, D.C.
    RG   43
    RG   84
    RG   165
    RG   218
    RG   260
    RG   331
    RG   332
    T–   501
  State Department, Washington, D.C.
  Decimal File 800.515/3–1147

2. Primary Published Sources

Acheson, Dean, *Present at the Creation*, New York: W.W. Norton and Co., 1969

Beyen, Johan W., *Money in a Maelstrom*, New York: Macmillan Co., 1949

Bradley, Omar N., *A Soldier's Story*, New York: Henry Holt Co., 1951

Bretton Woods Agreement Act: Hearings on Banking and Currency, Vol. 1, H.R., 79th Cong., 1st sess., 7–23 March 1945, Washington, D.C.: U.S.G.P.O., 1945

Churchill, Winston S., *Their Finest Hour*, Boston: Houghton Mifflin Co., 1949

——, *Triumph and Tragedy*, Boston: Houghton Mifflin Co., 1953

Ciechanowski, Jan, *Defeat in Victory*, New York: Doubleday and Co., 1947

Eisenhower, Dwight D., *Crusade in Europe*, Garden City, NY: Garden City Books, 1952

The Federal Republic of Germany, London: H.M.S.O., 1955

Germany, *Akten zur deutschen auswärtigen Politik, 1918–1945*, 8 vols., series E, 1941–1945. Göttingen: Vandenhoeck and Ruprecht, 1979

——, *Documents on German Foreign Policy, 1918–1945*, Series D, 1937–1945, Vols. 11–13, Washington D.C.: U.S.G.P.O., 1960, 1962, 1964

Great Britain, *Parliamentary Debates*, House of Commons, Vol. 345, pt. B, 1939

——, *Parliamentary Debates*, House of Commons, Vol. 348, pt. B, 1939

——, *Parliamentary Debates*, House of Commons, Vol. 114, no. 84, 1939

——, *Treaty Series no. 38 (1948). Exchange of Letters between the Governments of the United Kingdom of Great Britain and Northern Ireland, the United States of America, and France and the Bank for International Settlements.* London: H.M.S.O., 1948

Hull, Cordell, *The Memoirs of Cordell Hull*, New York: Macmillan Co., 1948

Jacobsen, Hans-Adolf, and Arthur L. Smith, Jr., *World War II Policy and Strategy: Selected Documents with Commentary*, Santa Barbara, CA, and Oxford, England: ABC Clio, 1979

Keesing's Contemporary Archives, 11–18 October 1947

Martin, James S., *All Honorable Men*, Boston: Little, Brown, and Co., 1950

Moggridge, Donald, ed., *The Collected Writings of John Maynard Keynes: Activities, 1941–1946*. Vol. 26. London: Macmillan, 1980

Morgenthau Diary, 2 vols., Washington, D.C.: U.S.G.P.O., 1967

Nazi Conspiracy and Aggression, 14 vols., Washington, D.C.: U.S.G.P.O., 1946

Patton, George S., Jr., *War As I Knew It*, Boston: Houghton Mifflin Co., 1947

Proceedings and Documents of the United Nations Monetary and Financial Conference, Bretton Woods, New Hampshire, July 1–22, 1944, Washington, D.C.: U.S.G.P.O., 1948

Raczynski, Edward, *In Allied London*, London: Weidenfeld and Nicolson, 1962

Schirach, Henriette von, *The Price of Glory*, Translated by Willi Frischauer. London: Frederick Muller, 1960

Toynbee, Arnold, and Veronica Toynbee, eds., *Survey of International Affairs, 1939–1946*. London: Oxford University Press, 1956

Trial of the Major War Criminals before the International Military Tribunal, 42 vols., Nuremberg, 1947

United States, *Department of State Bulletin*, Washington, D.C.: U.S.G.P.O., 9 July

1943; 27 January 1946; 30 June 1946; 28 September 1946; 27 July 1947; 24 August 1947; 14 December 1947; 4 January 1948

——, Department of State, *Germany, 1947–1949: The Story in Documents*, Washington, D.C.: U.S.G.P.O., 1950

——, Department of State, *Treaties and Other International Acts*, Series no. 1655, or 61 Stat. (pt. 3), 3157, Washington, D.C.: U.S.G.P.O.

——, *Elimination of German Resources for War: Hearings before a Sub-Committee of the Committee on Military Affairs*. U.S. Senate: Part 2, 25 June 1945; and Part 5, 2 July 1945. Washington, D.C.: U.S.G.P.O., 1945

——, *Foreign Relations of the United States*, Washington, D.C.: U.S.G.P.O.

——, *United States Statutes at Large, 1981*, "Public Laws 97–127–Dec. 29, 1981," Washington, D.C.: U.S.G.P.O., 1982

Wingate, Ronald, *Not in the Limelight*, London: Hutchinson and Co., 1959

3. Secondary Sources

Aubion, Roger, *The Bank for International Settlements, 1930–1955*, Princeton, NJ: Princeton University, Essays in International Finance, 1955

Blum, John Morton, *From the Morgenthau Diaries*, Vol. 2, Boston: Houghton Mifflin Co., 1965

Boelcke, Willi A., *Die deutsche Wirtschaft, 1939–1945, Interna des Reichswirtschaftsministerium*, Düsseldorf: Droste Verlag, 1983

——, "Zur internationalen Goldpolitik des NS-Staates—Ein Beitrag zur deutschen Währungs- und Außenwirtschaftspolitik, 1933–1945," in *Hitler, Deutschland, und die Mächte*, edited by Manfred Funke. Düsseldorf: Droste Verlag, 1977

Borchard, Edwin, "The 'Treatment of Enemy Property," *Georgetown Law Journal*, 34, no. 1 (May 1946): 389–406

Codman, Charles, *Drive*, Boston: Little, Brown, and Co., 1957

Domke, Martin, *The Control of Alien Property*, New York: Central Books, 1947

——, *Trading with the Enemy in World War II*, New York: Central Book Co., 1943

Dormael, Armand van, *Bretton Woods: Birth of a Monetary System*, New York: Holmes and Meier Publishers, 1978

Einzig, Paul, *In the Centre of Things*, London: Hutchinson, 1960

——, *World Finance, 1939–1940*, London: Kegan Paul, Trench, Trubner, 1940

Ellis, Howard S., *Exchange Control in Central Europe*, Westport, CT: Greenwood Press, 1971

Enzensberger, Hans Magnus, *OMGUS: Ermittlungen gegen die Deutsche Bank*, Noerdlingen: Greno Verlagsgesellschaft, 1985

Federau, Fritz, *Der Zweite Weltkrieg: Seine Finanzierung in Deutschland*, Tübingen: Rainer Wunderlich Verlag, 1962

Forstmeier, Friedrich, and Hans-Erich Volkmann, eds., *Kriegswirtschaft und Rüstung, 1939–1945*, Düsseldorf: Droste Verlag, 1977

Gordon, David L., and Royden Dangerfield, *The Hidden Weapon: The Story of Economic Warfare*, New York: Da Capo Press, 1976

Gunston, C.A. and C.M. Corner, *Deutsch–Englisches Glossarium, finanzieller und wirtschaftlicher Fachausdrücke*, 4th ed. Frankfurt a.M.: Fritz Knapp Verlag, 1962

Hawtrey, Ralph G., *Bretton Woods, For Better or Worse*, London: Longmans, Green Co., 1946

Higham, Charles, *Trading with the Enemy*, New York: Delacorte Press, 1983

Homberger, Heinrich, *Schweizerische Handelspolitik im Zweiten Weltkrieg*, Erlenbach-Zurich: Eugen Rentsch Verlag, 1970

Langer, William, *Our Vichy Gamble*, New York: Alfred A. Knopf, 1947

Lemkin, Raphael, *Axis Rule in Occupied Europe*, New York: Howard Fertig, 1973

Mastny, Vojtech, *The Czechs under Nazi Rule: The Failure of National Resistance, 1939–1942*, New York: Columbia University Press, 1971

Medlicott, William N., *The Economic Blockade*, Vol. 2, London: H.M.S.O., 1959

Milward, Alan S., *War, Economy, and Society, 1939–1945*, Berkeley and Los Angeles: University of California Press, 1977

Moss, Stanley, *Gold Is Where You Hide It: What Happened to the Reichsbank Treasures?* London: Andre Deutsch, 1956

"Recognition of German Occupation of Czechoslovakia," *Australian Law Journal* 17 (18 February 1944): 329–30

Reville, Thomas, *The Spoil of Europe: The Nazi Technique in Political and Economic Conquest*, New York: W.W. Norton and Co., 1941

Rings, Werner, *Raubgold aus Deutschland: Die "Golddrehscheibe" Schweiz im Zweiten Weltkrieg*, Zurich: Artemis Verlag, 1985

Sayer, Ian, and Douglas Botting, *Nazi Gold*, New York: Congdon and Weed, 1984

Schloss, Henry H., *The Bank for International Settlements*, Amsterdam: North Holland Publishing Co., 1958

Schneeberger, Ernst, "Property and War, In Particular the Swiss–American–German Conditions," *Georgetown Law Journal* 34 (March 1946): 265–87

Scott, James Brown, *The Hague Peace Conferences of 1899 and 1907*, 2 vols., New York: Garland Publishers, 1972

Smith, Jean Edward, ed. *The Papers of General Lucius D. Clay.* 2 vols. Bloomington, IN: Indiana University Press, 1974

Thomsen, Erich, *Deutsche Besatzungspolitik in Dänemark, 1940–1945*, Düsseldorf: Bertelsmann, 1971

Trefousse, Hans L., *Germany and American Neutrality, 1939–1941*, New York: Bookman Associates, 1951

Ustinov, Gherman, "Arrested Gold," *New Times* (Moscow), no. 8 (F 1979): 28–30

Vicker, Ray, *Those Swiss Money Men*, New York: Charles Scribner's Sons, 1973

Volger, Robert Urs, *Die Wirtschaftshandlungen zwischen der Schweiz und Deutschland, 1940 und 1941*, Zurich: Schweizerische National Bank, 1983

Ziemke, Earl, *The U.S. Army in the Occupation of Germany, 1944–1946*, Washington, D.C.: Center of Military History, U.S. Army, 1975

Zimmermann, Horst, *Die Schweiz und Grossdeutschland*, Munich: Wilhelm Fink Verlag, 1980

4. Newspapers

Los Angeles Times
New York Herald Tribune, Paris edition
New York Times

Index

171